SCOTLAND

HOME OF GOLF

2001-2002

pastime publications ltd

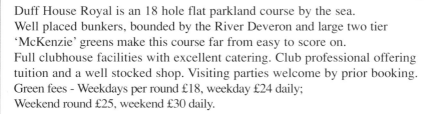

Contents

This edition published by Pastime Publications Ltd,
5/9 Rennie's Isle, Edinburgh EH6 6QA
Tel/Fax: 0131 553 4444

2001 © Pastime Publications Ltd

First published by the Scottish Tourist Board 1970

Designed by Robbie Porteous. Project managed by MPPS.

Printed and bound in Scotland

UK and Worldwide distribution

Introduction

WELCOME to the oldest guide to Scottish Golf courses – published every year since 1970. As we promised last year, we continue to improve our Guide in every way we can think of and our improvements have obviously been welcomed by our readers, as can be seen by some of the comments we have reproduced on the back cover.

This year we have continued our theme of featured courses and hidden gems with another 71 new entries. They are not paid-for advertisements; they are our own selection based on our collective knowledge of all the courses in Scotland. Obviously, some people might question our choice but the intention is to introduce you, the reader, to the many and varied courses Scotland has to offer.

The Gazetteer section has been updated again and several courses have been added including Kingsbarns, which opened its doors in its new 18-hole format for the first time last year.

The Open moves to England this year so we chose the Ailsa course at Turnberry for Donald Ford to play a round on with the pro Guy Redford. In spite of one of the wettest and windiest days of the year, we managed all 18 holes!

Before we let you go, we have another new development to bring to your attention – our own search and find database driven website. So you can visit us at **www.scotland-for-golf.com**

Lastly, can we ask you to mention *Scotland Home of Golf* as the source from which you gathered the information you needed to plan your golf trip.

Thank you.
Graham Wilson, Publisher

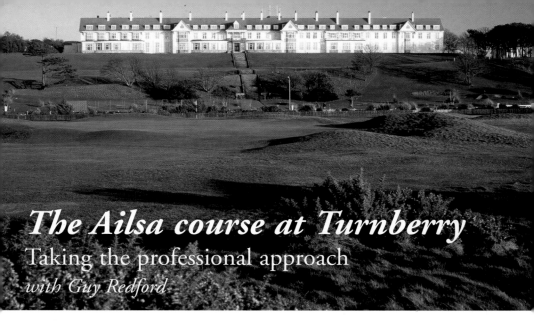

The Ailsa course at Turnberry
Taking the professional approach
with Guy Redford

The article in last year's edition, in which St.Andrews professional Jim Farmer took us around the Old Course and allowed us the most intimate of insights into the preparations and game management of the top tournament professionals, proved highly popular. The question then put by my publisher was not "Should we do another one?" but rather, "Where are you going this year?!" The choice was not an easy one. Carnoustie, Troon, Loch Lomond, Gleneagles, Muirfield and Turnberry were all thrown into the hat and, to be honest, we felt sure that our readers would lick their lips (not to mention the editor doing likewise!) at the thought of a report on any one of these.

At the end of the day, Turnberry got the vote, but by the narrowest of margins – hopefully the others will follow in future editions – and yours truly was granted the opportunity to accompany Guy Redford around the world-famous Ailsa course. Guy (by coincidence a former pupil of Jim Farmer) has enjoyed six years as a professional at Turnberry, and he put his mind and body into "Tournament Professional Mode" to give us an inside look at the preparation for, and execution of, these eighteen superb holes on the Ayrshire coast.

My host for our second "hands on" experience of a Scottish Championship course was born in Perth in 1971. His father, from whom he learned the basics of the game, soon had him a membership at King James VI and the new Murrayshall course up the road. At the age of sixteen, Guy was playing off one. Since 1990, he

has been under the eagle eye of the aforementioned Jim Farmer and he enjoyed golf at Boys and Youths level in Sweden, Italy, Belgium and then in the two years between January 1992 and December 1993, at Midland College, Texas, where he was a member of the National Junior College Championship winning team.

In 1994 he returned to Scotland – and to Turnberry – where, under the guidance of Bob Jamieson, he began a six month probationary period. Still playing amateur golf, he won the North East Open at Duff House, lowered his handicap to plus one, then turned professional in September. His PGA training continued at Turnberry and in 1997 he qualified as a PGA Professional, following which he visited China and the U.S.A. but never quite hit the high spots of Tour golf.

In 1999 he was offered the chance of rejoining the team at Turnberry as a qualified PGA Professional and in particular assisting the establishment of Colin Montgomerie's first Links Golf Academy. He now manages this exciting golfing development, which is already getting high praise from all who have ventured through the front door. Four more, throughout Europe, are in the pipeline. Despite the increasing workload and responsibility which accompanies such an onerous position, this delightful young man (how is it that golf consistently throws up the best behaved and most mannerly professionals compared to other sports where many earning small fortunes don't have the foggiest idea of how to conduct themselves?) was quick to take up my invitation to reveal to us lesser mortals exactly how the Ailsa would be tackled by the pro in a tournament situation.

Turnberry, for many years, was out of the Championship limelight despite some epic confrontations in the earlier half of the twentieth century. Many can still recall.

Then, in 1977, the Open Championship returned. The head-to-head final round duel between Nicklaus and Watson is now legend and the drama of the seventy-second hole was never equalled until Jean Van de Velde's Carnoustie disaster twenty five years later. The sun blazed down for four days on Turnberry during that Open, as it did too for Greg Norman in 1986 . In 1994, it was Nick Price who had the watching thousands in a frenzy as he put in an astonishing climax to steamroller past a stunned Jasper Parnevik in the dying minutes of that year's tournament.

So Turnberry has cemented itself into the world circuit again – and deservedly so. The architectural masterpiece re-created by Mackenzie Ross on the course after the Second World War is the perfect examination for the world's greatest exponents of the game. For lesser mortals it is a venue of sheer joy – and, at times,utter frustration as the average player tries to cope with the stern and constantly changing challenge presented to him. Inevitably, the presence of the Firth of Clyde and regular south-westerlies compound the difficulties (to enjoy a benign eighteen holes anywhere on the Ayrshire coast is a rare occurrence). Huge, undulating and at times steeply sloped greens just add insult to injury, although the stunning setting can compensate, in part at least, for any lack of success on the course.

But – tae oor tale; (with apologies to Rabbie Burns and Tam o' Shanter, but I couldn't resist that perfect local introduction to the task!) Guy Redford was quick to accept the challenge I put to him. Perhaps he saw some easy winnings ahead, but I would like to think that he agreed because it was something away from the ordinary. Not that he has a humdrum life now at this great Scottish venue; indeed, as the young man entrusted with the onerous task of getting the new Colin Montgomerie Golf Academy on its feet, he could easily have declined the request. Had he realised the horrendous conditions which were to accompany us for the whole round, he may well have had second thoughts!

You don't need a degree in Time Management to realise that his schedule is a packed one and carries heavy responsibility. As is so often the case, however, within a profession regarded across the world with great reverence, his acceptance was quick and his enthusiastic attitude exemplary. Mind you, I had to tell him that he would need a few hours of concentrated practice before he dared to take on an ageing, grey-haired "cricketing" golfer with a handicap of ten and a bad knee; I think that caused him more lost sleep than his job! Anyway, before we got down to destroying the course record, I needed answers to a few questions on the professional approach to the Ailsa challenge.

In answer to my first question on the basic preparation of mind and body for the job ahead, Guy reiterated almost exactly the words of Jim Farmer when I posed a similar query the year before. Long gone are the days of haphazard routines, irregular diet or sleep patterns and other things which, even in the slightest, might adversely affect the professional's performance over the four crucial rounds.

The Loch Lomond Invitational, held the week before the Open, has been ideal in timing, if not in course similarity, for many of the foreign-based players to immediately begin their acclimatisation to the Scottish weather and atmosphere. With Loch Lomond being parkland, rather than links, others have regularly taken themselves to Dornoch, Troon and the like to get the feel of links golf again. Their subsequent arrival at Turnberry will generally be on the Monday of Open week.

And what kind of physical or mental state will they be in? A dietician will, in all likelihood, have set their eating habits ages before and meals will be regular and energising, normally of the slow-release energy variety, with similar properties in fluids taken in. Physical Education advisers will have instructed fitness routines to suit and these will be followed religiously. (Whether the six hundred sit-ups which Tiger Woods is reputed to carry out on a daily basis is the norm or not, Guy could not confirm!) Work on the course or practice ground having gone well, they will call it a day around five or six o'clock, not really unlike the patterns of many ordinary mortals like you and I at our office desk or production line. Should there be problems, it is highly likely that the sound of club on ball will echo round Turnberry long after the majority have retired for the day!

A great deal, if not all, of technical preparation work on swing etc. will already have been taken care of in lengthy sessions with the individual coaches of each. Normally, therefore, the professional will be spending the great part of his lead-in to the tournament on the practice ground and, probably on two full rounds on the course itself. He is looking to"feel" his shots, to begin the final stages of his intimate acquaintance with the eighteen holes and it is likely – and what an interesting comment this was from Guy – that he will "play a round on the practice ground".

When I asked what exactly that meant, Guy explained that, with his caddy alongside, the pro would "play" the eighteen holes – from tee to green – in the precise order of shots he might expect during his round. The only difference is that he would not move from his allotted slot on the practice ground! I found it quite staggering that the degree of confidence which the top modern professional now has in himself could be reflected in such dedicated – and probably accurate – preparation of shot forecasting and execution.

Here we bring in the importance of having a right-hand man alongside; our old and much under-rated companion across every blade of Open grass, the Caddy. Guy confirmed that, nowadays, he is likely himself to be, or have been, a top quality player. He will, of course, know the capabilities and weaknesses, if any, of his boss. He will know the Ailsa intimately, having played, walked and measured it religiously.

His advice on club selection over four days will be based on a thorough research of hole lengths, bunker placements, pin positions and – inevitably on a course such as this – the effect that different wind directions and speeds will have on shot selection. "Let me just emphasise", confirmed Guy, "that it will be a team that wins the trophy. O.K. – the caddy won't strike a ball; but he will influence the vast majority of decisions taken by his charge over four days."

And so to round one, the first morning – or afternoon, depending on the draw. First of all, a weather check; having established the various constituent parts of the elements likely to be thrown at him over the probable time on the course, game plan"A" will start to formulate in the professional's mind. Should the conditions forecast be adverse, it might be that a defensive strategy is the order of the day. In other circumstances – for example a benign atmosphere with perhaps the merest of offshore breeze (some hope!) – and plan "B" will be the preferred option.

One way or another, when the pro steps onto the first tee, he will be as fully prepared, mentally, physically and in awareness of the course, as any golfer who has played in an Open Championship since that famous first occasion just up the road in 1860. He will know pin positions, he will know where he can attack or where he must defend, he will, to use the time-honoured cliche, "take one shot at a time".
Nevertheless, as Guy, Jim Farmer and countless others who play real golf have tried over the years to get into our thick ten-or-twenty handicap heads, he will – especially over links – constantly play the shot which makes the next one easier.

Turnberry's overall challenge, whether that be for amateurs or professionals, is a totally fair one, as Guy was keen to point out. There are few, if any, concealed traps or hazards – you see it all before you. Hidden pot bunkers that bear the James Braid hallmark are conspicuous by their absence. You therefore compete against this tremendous links course on ability alone. Lady Luck, of course, in the shape of draw timing or weather changes, can be an influence, but it surely could not be coincidence which resulted in the best golfer in the world, at that specific time, winning the open at Turnberry in 1977 (Watson), 1986 (Norman) and 1994 (Price).

Of course, it was the epic Watson/Nicklaus battle in the sun which captured the imagination of millions in July 1977; Nicklaus was never behind until the last few holes of the tournament. Few will forget Tom Watson's astonishing iron to three feet at the eighteenth, nor the enormous putt sunk by the Golden Bear which forced his great American opponent to sink a three-foot knee wobbler for the Claret Jug. Wonderful stuff and a memorable return to the Championship circuit for this great links.. "The further north they play this great Championship", said Jack, "the more I enjoy the course." In other words, east or west, Scotland's best!

Well, Scotland certainly was not best on the morning chosen by yours truly to find out exactly how the professional, courtesy of Guy Redford, would attack this course. The winds whistled in from the south-west, slackening occasionally, I must admit, to gale force! In regular doses, horrendous pulses of rain blew in from Ailsa Craig. Conditions weren't impossible, but sanity had to be questioned now and again as we battled with one of Turnberry's worst days of weather for months; trust me to pick a cracker! For these reasons, I unashamedly refuse to report the scores from the battlefield. Fortunately the purpose of the whole exercise was not diluted and I do hope that Guy's informative – at times precise – illumination of the right and wrong way to approach the Ailsa comes through bright and clear.

Hole 1: 'AILSA CRAIG'
350 yards – PAR 4 – STROKE INDEX 9

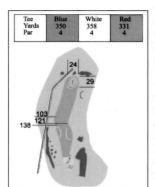

Tee	Blue	White	Red
Yards	350	358	331
Par	4	4	4

On the face of it, a straightforward and shortish first hole breaks you in gently for the task ahead. Club choice from the tee can be mixed and is dependent normally on wind speed and direction. Guy lined up on the bungalow with the off-white harling, found the semi-rough with his driver but avoided the three bunkers positioned to the right and left – precisely on the elbow of the dogleg – then put a six iron into a greenside trap (there are four lying in wait!). Bearing in mind the need for two perfect strikes against the gale, a four would be a real bonus, despite the modesty of length involved.

Hole 2: 'MAK SICCAR'
430 yards – PAR 4 – STROKE INDEX 13

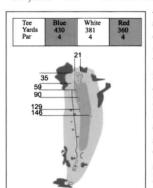

Tee	Blue	White	Red
Yards	430	381	360
Par	4	4	4

An immediate turn-about in direction creates pause for thought on the tee. With the strong following wind, club choice is a mid- to-long iron, on the line of the gorse-covered mound, to avoid any dicing with bunkers to left and right some two hundred and seventy yards out. This time the dogleg goes left and the vision of sand from the tee forces any thought of bravado out of the mind. Guy was subsequently left with a sand-iron for his second shot after a perfectly placed four iron(the wind was fierce!) Even that was a bit much, but a chip from the rear of the enormous green was superb and par was secured. The hole's title – 'Make sure' – instructs the player on how to approach club choice.

Hole 3: 'BLAW WEARIE'
462 yards – PAR 4 – STROKE INDEX 5

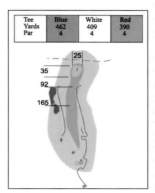

Tee	Blue	White	Red
Yards	462	409	390
Par	4	4	4

"Once more unto the breach, dear friends" as another 180 degree turn takes you back into the full force of the south-westerlies. A narrow fairway puts straightness at the very top of the priority list from the tee and yet again there's a subtle change of direction about three hundred yards from the back tee. Guy's perfectly struck drive into the gale found the left of the fairway; he was left with around 170 yards to the front of the green, although "it's playing about 200 yards today" Guy explained, as he then fired a three iron into the gale. Three big bunkers around the green await anything which is either off line or subject ed to wind-induced flight path variations! One such tugged his ball into the left-hand trap. (It was from the right-hand bunker that Greg Norman holed out in 1986 on his way to an epic Open triumph.) A superb hole and, against the wind, an early test of the professional's mettle.

Hole 4: 'WOE BE-TIDE'
165 yards – PAR 3 – STROKE INDEX 17

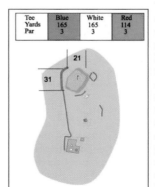

Tee	Blue	White	Red
Yards	165	165	114
Par	3	3	3

The fourth change of direction heralds the arrival of the first par three. The hole name tells you to be extremely careful as trouble is all about; never a truer word was spoken! This is all about choosing precisely the correct club and then ensuring that the left-hand side of the elevated green is avoided at all costs, as a thirty-foot drop awaits anything missing that edge of the putting surface. There's a steep slope up to the green and the sand hill out of which the green has been carved rears up to the right. For the amateur, it is not a big target; for the professional, as Guy convincingly reported, "he considers this a real birdie opportunity and will be disappointed not to get it."

Hole 5: 'FIN' ME OOT'
442 yards – PAR 4 – STROKE INDEX 3

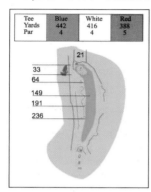

Tee	Blue	White	Red
Yards	442	416	388
Par	4	4	5

This is the first of four holes in the lee of the sand dunes which could determine the outcome of the whole round. All are, generally, wind assisted (on our adventure, they were gale-assisted!) which, with the pronounced left-handed curve on this one, makes the sight of a wooden club – on this tee at least – a rare one indeed. The pro is looking to put his teeshot on the right-hand-side of the fairway, having used the line of the shelter as his guide. Too much club? He will run out of fairway. Too tight to the left-hand side? He will find heavy rough or one of two bunkers and face a very difficult second to the heavily guarded green. Guy's one iron was perfection; a sand iron put him thirty feet from the cup.

This green is big, with undulations to match and nothing is guaranteed. It is not the third hardest hole on the course for nothing, although Sandy Lyle's potential nightmare here in 1979 when he hooked into the aforesaid rough and could only play out onto the fairway, culminated in triumph when he holed his approach! (Having birdied the third and fourth, he added three more to the seventh).

Hole 6: 'TAPPIE TOORIE'
231 yards – PAR 3 – STROKE INDEX 15

An elevated tee and an elevated, sloping green. You see it all and the simple requirement is for correct club choice and shot execution. The 215 yards we played from the red tee, with strengthening wind behind, reduced to about 180 yards, and Guy's five iron to the middle of the green was perfection. It is a cracker of a putting surface, mind you, and nothing should be taken for granted even though the teeshot finds the ideal green position. Four bunkers await anything miscued and if there's a strong crosswind, a horrendous drop on the right is death! On the face of it, this one should not cause problems.

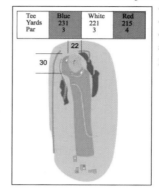

Tee	Blue	White	Red
Yards	231	221	215
Par	3	3	4

Hole 7: 'ROON' THE BEN'
529 yards – PAR 5 – STROKE INDEX 1

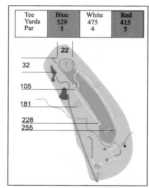

Tee	Blue	White	Red
Yards	529	475	415
Par	5	4	5

This is, quite simply, a beautiful golf hole, rated the hardest on the course, despite being a par five. Tom Watson's feat of hitting his driver from the tee and then again, bravely, from his perfect fairway lie in 1977, earned a precious birdie which was perhaps the key to his Open victory. The hole is open before you as you gaze from the tee. As it's name implies, it needs to be played as a long curve, with the teeshot being crucial to the outcome. Off the Championship tee the normal line is the bunkers to the right-hand side, the plan being to carry the mound and find fairway beyond. Too far right will end up in rough ; too far left is certain death among the sandhills. Guy's superb drive, which finished up some 340 yards from the tee, left him a mere nine iron (it's fifty yards shorter from the white tee!) from the putting surface. The correct conditions and ideal execution of the drive therefore destroy the dangers here; but otherwise you can take nothing for granted on a superb hole.

Hole 8: 'GOAT FELL'
431 yards – PAR 4 – STROKE INDEX 11

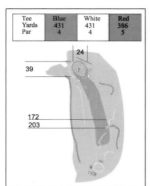

Tee Yards	Blue 431	White 431	Red 386
Par	4	4	5

The last of the "four-in-a-row" along the dunes and another of the outward par fours which features the right-to-left bend from the halfway point, this outwardly straightforward hole, generally wind assisted, should hold no terrors. The bunker on the right-hand edge of the fairway, however, regularly catches the amateur drive, while the pros will, in all probability, comfortably clear the obstacle and land up with a mere seven or eight iron's worth from the flag. Guy's enormous drive left him just such – he opted for the eight iron – and, hitting it low to prevent wind damage, left himself just off the big green. A lovely chip and single putt got his par. There ought to be no problem here if the teeshot is straight and true; the best players will have birdie in mind if they've got it remotely right.

Hole 9: 'BRUCE'S CASTLE'
454 yards – PAR 4 – STROKE INDEX 7

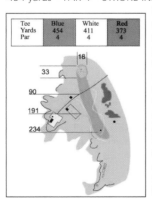

Tee Yards	Blue 454	White 411	Red 373
Par	4	4	4

Probably the Ailsa's signature hole, it is certainly the most photographed, either from the rocky promontory on which the Championship tee is set (with the old lighthouse a very badly hooked drive away across the bay) or from the crest of the fairway looking back to the tee with the telephoto lens pulling Ailsa Craig spectacularly close! It's the drive which will make it or break it. From the back tee it's 218 yards to the stone in mid-fairway. It ought to be comfortably cleared and a reasonably generous fairway should leave around 135 yards to the front edge of the green. Pulled teeshots will find a steep bank with heavy rough. Pushed drives will not allow the second to be at the best angle to attack the flag. (Guy offered another gem at this point about the professional's addiction to specific yardages, quoting Ladies' Champion Janice Moodie. She likes nothing better than giving herself ninety-four yards to the flag; she will drop three or four clubs just to provide that opportunity, since she knows herself to favour exactly that distance for an approach that will provide a birdie chance. You learn something every day!) For a change, the green is a touch flatter than the previous eight; with wind behind, birdies are expected.

A welcome cup of coffee awaited at the refreshment kiosk before the attack began on the inward half. Despite the horrendous weather, Guy had performed well. The thought of but one more hole with the elements in our favour did not appeal and I had a sneaky feeling that even the top professionals would find Ailsa's second nine a pretty daunting prospect in conditions such as these. Suitably refreshed, however, we returned to the fray; if anything, the wind was more fierce and the clouds yet more ominous!

Hole 10: 'DINNA FOUTER'
452 yards – PAR 4 – STROKE INDEX 6

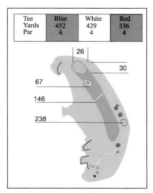

Tee Yards	Blue 452	White 429	Red 336
Par	4	4	4

There's another subtle change of angle here, although it is the drop in levels roughly halfway to the target which gives the professional cause for thought. As the hole title implies, however, you should not " dither about" on your decision making, especially with the second shot, which may well make or destroy this excellent and picturesque par four. Guy had the three iron out of his bag before he reached the tee. "You should be trying to play the approach shot from the flat bit of fairway about 170 yards from the green", he confirmed, "because if I go any further, my second, in all probability, will need to be struck from a down-slope." Of course, the fierce following wind also influenced his club selection, but the ball finished in perfect position 165 yards from the front of the green. His casually hit 9 iron , with assisting gale, was yet too much and he rolled off the back of a difficult, two-tier green. En route to our rescue attempts (I was at least two clubs too big!) I expressed my puzzlement at the placement of the huge 'ring' bunker some sixty yards short of the green. It does not appear to come into play at all, being too far from the tee, even for Tiger Woods, and then too far from the green to cause great anxiety for the approach. For the first time in about two hours, Guy was unable to offer an explanation. It seems odd, and is peculiarly out of place on this wonderfully created layout.

Hole 11: 'MAIDENS'
174 yards – PAR 3 – STROKE INDEX 18

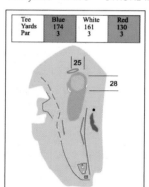

Tee Yards Par	Blue 174 3	White 161 3	Red 130 3

In normal circumstances – and as the stroke index confirms – this is a pretty comfortable short hole where the professional will expect to be giving himself a chance of a birdie with a precise teeshot. Normally, club choice would be six or seven iron; with the wind howling diagonally across the hole, Guy chose a nine iron, started it at least thirty yards right and it ended up twenty feet left of the flag – pin high. His birdie putt lipped the hole. As the rain showers wheeled in again, we turned south onto the twelfth tee.

Hole 12: 'MONUMENT'
446 yards – PAR 4 – STROKE INDEX 8

This is another of the Ailsa challenges where, as Guy reminded me, "you see it all before you." For a change, it's as straight as an arrow. There are two cleverly spaced bunkers at drive length to the left of the fairway, but just in case the wind is behind, rather than against, a third is sixty yards further on. On the first of the homeward holes into the teeth of the howling gale, Guy belted a low drive; it went left as the flight died and he caught the rough. He then struck a magnificent one

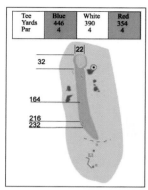

Tee Yards Par	Blue 446 4	White 390 4	Red 354 4

iron about two hundred yards, dead straight but just two yards short of glory as it caught the top of the left-hand greenside bunker. This is another of those Mackenzie Ross greens which don't look menacing, but are. There are few straightforward putts on the Ailsa, and good as his recovery was from the sand, he took two putts. (Just for the record, yours truly whacked one of his best drives of the day right down the middle. He repeated the dose with three wood, then closed the face of a six iron to hit a low approach into the green from about a hundred yards. It finished ten yards short!)

Hole 13: 'TICKLY TAP'
412 yards – PAR 4 – STROKE INDEX 14

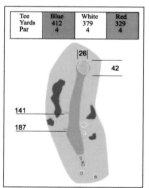

Tee Yards Par	Blue 412 4	White 379 4	Red 329 4

Played across the prevailing south-westerly, it is drive placement then shot execution to the big, elevated, two-tiered green which makes or breaks par. Firstly, the drive, which from the Championship Tee should be lined up over a gorse bush to find generous fairway space on the other side of the dogleg (yes, another one!) some two hundred and sixty yards out. It is then a six or seven iron – depending on pin position and wind – to a very tricky putting surface. In the right conditions – or rather, the wrong conditions – this can prove a real stinker, despite its rating on the card.

Hole 14: 'RISK-AN-HOPE'
449 yards – PAR 4 – STROKE INDEX 2

Rated the second hardest hole on the Ailsa, this apparently straightforward par four murdered the 1986

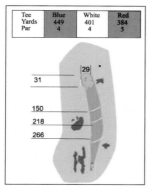

Tee Yards Par	Blue 449 4	White 401 4	Red 384 5

Open contenders. No fewer than 270 bogies or worse were recorded, while a paltry 12 birdies were plundered over the four days. Why should that be? Guy offered the two most plausible reasons; the first is the need for a bold, straight drive on the line of the shelter to hit a narrow fairway; the second is the essential requirement, as at thirteen, to pick exactly the right iron for the approach to the raised and well-protected green, which yet again is stepped and about six feet above fairway level – just enough to create a potential under-club and a resultant bogey. We both managed that, although Guy was again unlucky as the wind and rain contrived to push his clinically-struck drive into hellish rough down the right.

Hole 15: 'CA' CANNY'
209 yards – PAR 3 – STROKE INDEX 16

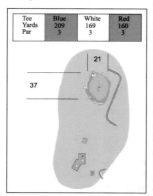

Tee Yards Par	Blue 209 3	White 169 3	Red 160 3

It is worth repeating, just in case it has not so far been apparent, that the conditions in which we were attempting to take on one of the world's best golf courses were rapidly becoming farcical. As we stood on the fifteenth tee, the rain which was whipping in at an angle of thirty degrees to the likely line of flight became a deluge and the gale ratcheted up another couple of notches. The normal five iron which Guy suggested would be struck to the heart of a fairly welcoming green became a three iron; he struck it fully thirty yards right of the aforesaid green and it failed to respond to the hurricane. It fell, or rather disappeared , into the abyss which falls steeply to the immediate right of the putting surface. Once again the title of the hole said it all; if you don't "take care" you will pay the penalty. But take nothing from the cunning architecture; should you be overly cautious about the cliff to the right, three bunkers await you if you are too far left. The form player will have no problem unless the gale is up; in 1977 Tom Watson pulled level with Nicklaus here for the first time in the tournament as he sank a long putt from the fringe of the green; the rest is history.

Hole 16: 'WEE BURN'
409 yards – PAR 4 – STROKE INDEX 10

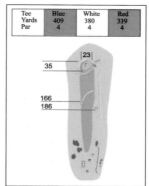

Tee Yards Par	Blue 409 4	White 380 4	Red 339 4

Jasper Parnevik arrived on this tee two strokes up on Nick Price in 1994 yet lost the Open. While it was probably the latter's putt at the seventeenth which did the damage, the Swede began to wilt at this lovely par four which is totally about success or failure with the second shot. The drive should ideally be down the right-hand side of the fairway on the line of the bridge. Pin placement may dictate otherwise, of course, but even into the wind, the selection of club and shot execution are the final essential ingredients of the approach. Wilson's Burn winds all around the front and right of the green; the putting surface sits fifty feet above the stream, and Edinburgh Castle-like grassy cliffs take anything short for a swim and a one shot penalty. If that wasn't enough, there is little depth to the green and there are more than a few wicked deviations on the surface. It's a great start to the Ailsa finish, if you will excuse the contradiction in terms!

Hole 17: 'LANG WHANG'
497 yards – PAR 5 – STROKE INDEX 4

The driving line at the penultimate hole is the shelter in the distance and it is always the driver which the professional asks from his caddy. The hole's title asks you for a "good whack" and, while there is a bunker some 275 yards from the tee, there is a broad enough fairway to accommodate you. It will probably be a three wood or long iron which sets off towards the

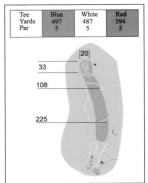

Tee	Blue	White	Red
Yards	497	487	394
Par	5	5	5

33
108
225
|20|

putting surface at the top of the rise a further 225 yards or so away. It needs length and carry to make up for the increase in levels from a low fairway lie. Of course, given the right conditions, two good strikes will get you aboard. Nick Price's legendary 50-foot putt for an eagle in 1994 will remain etched in the memories of all who saw it (most of all, sadly, in that of poor Jasper Parnevik, whose raffle ticket the Gods were certainly keen not to draw out of the hat on that astonishing final day.) A humble five, therefore, is probably unacceptable in the final throes of the big Turnberry tournament; the Big Guns are looking for birdies; Price's eagle – and the timing of it – was of a sports novelist's fantasy.

Hole 18: 'AILSA HAME'

434 yards – PAR 4 – STROKE INDEX 12

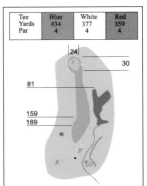

Tee	Blue	White	Red
Yards	434	377	359
Par	4	4	4

81
159
189
|24|
30

A finishing hole as clearly visible and simple as you could possibly imagine might well be criticised for not encouraging the bravado from a chasing pack; for even allowing the front runner to relax and enjoy the width of a broad landing area for his drive and an uncluttered,

straightforward eight or nine iron into a big, welcoming green. Bring final hole nerves and a bit of a breeze into the scheme of things, however, and watch the feathers fly! First, the drive; from the Championship tee it will be lined up on the left-hand tower of the Spa. If it flies straight, it will leave an eight or nine iron into the green. A low iron can 'bump and run' ideally into pole position for a birdie chance – there is no sand in the way, as such, if that be the choice. If the wind dictates a longer second, there's lots of room on the big green; Jack Nicklaus found that out in 1977. To the astonishment of the watching millions, he rolled a huge birdie putt into the cup. Tom Watson, either through the grace of God or consummate skill, had stuck his approach three feet from the hole and the Golden Bear's final piece of unnerving bravado was all to no avail.

It is appropriate that we conclude this round of the Ailsa in the company of Guy Redford with a word on that epic 1977 Open finish. Without the slightest doubt, it put Turnberry on the map again and on the lips of thousands who, until then, had barely given it a second glance. Twenty four years later, the greatness of the place is assured. It did not need Colin Montgomerie's Golf Academy to cement the respect in which it is held in the minds of golf lovers everywhere, but the addition of this brilliant new facility can only bring even more appreciation. The Open will be back soon – make no mistake – and so will thousands of golf lovers from across the world for whom the ambience of Turnberry is magnetic.

Then there is the newly opened and totally revamped second course – the Kintyre – no slouch at 6481 yards from the boxes and another potential winner for this renowned sanctuary of Scottish links golf. It all adds up to a future of guaranteed golfing pleasure – and, no doubt, further Championship drama – at a favourite location for the lowly amateur and the top professional alike. In thanking Guy Redford for his insight into the intimacies of this beautiful place, we wish both he and Turnberry all the success they so richly deserve in the years ahead of them.

DONALD FORD

An even greater magnet – but at what price?

by Donald Ford

It was anticipated that the end of the Second Millennium (remember that the beginning of the new one is 2001) would bring yet more memorable feats in the world of golf and that, because the year 2000 was such a special one, a few more names and events would become etched in the mind for a long time to come. We were not disappointed.

Tiger Woods, of course, stole the show, as many expected him to. Quite apart from his enormous victory at St.Andrews in the Millennium Open, he made it abundantly obvious that his was a very special talent. His golfing skills apart, the mental application and near-perfect management of the psychological demands of top level competition golf are simply, for one so young, staggering. The comparisons with earlier 'greats' are inevitable and only time will tell if he can continue to excel at the very top of the sport, but the maturity of his game at such a tender age must be unique.

The glories of an unusually benign St.Andrews last July were beamed around the world into trillions of homes and it has to be said that the Old Girl looked fantastic. There were murmurings, of course, about the severity of the bunkers but it would be a dull four days without a gripe or two from someone. At the end of the day, arguably the world's most famous annual sporting extravaganza was a total success for the R and A; let's hope that the unseemly scenes at the seventy-second hole as the Champion Elect made his way across the Swilcan Burn were a one-off and will not become the norm. Afficionados of golf here in Scotland have a very high reputation which must be upheld.

The rest of Scotland basked in the reflected glory from St.Andrews, but few courses let it go at that. Once again the advancement of course presentation was in ample evidence as the most modest pulled out all the stops to vie for attention from members and visitors who put their golfing acumen to the test across the length and breadth of Scotland. New courses like the one at Kingsbarns, just up the road from the Old Course, came on stream to open up new markets, although in the case of this latest Fife offering, it is a pretty expensive one, classic old links setting or no.

It was not all sweetness and light, however. A pronounced dip in reported visitors to these shores in 1999, together with forecasts of another slide in numbers for 2000, prompted the Scottish Executive to fire a broadside at the Tourist Board and, in particular, to alert Scotland's golfing people to the Government's disenchantment with the apparent complacency which had set in. At best brushing aside, at worst ignoring, the appalling effects of a ridiculously strong pound, First Minister for Scotland, Henry MacLeish, wheeled in Colin Montgomerie in an attempt to beef up the marketing of Scotland's golfing assets.

Now I know how much time the publisher of this annual handbook on Scottish golf agonises about reaching a wider market; about spreading the Gospel further; about introducing new features or dangling carrots or just whetting appetites abroad that little bit more. Furthermore, I believe that similar thought and discussion takes priority in golf club committee rooms around Scotland every year, especially those who depend on visitors for a great slice of their club's annual income.

While I am not for one minute arguing that the marketing and publicity of Scottish golf is perfect - indeed some clubs, in this new age of e-mail, internet and desktop publishing have been very slow to react to the fresh opportunities afforded by modern technology - I do not believe that bad marketing is preventing people coming here to play golf. Rising costs, however, are certainly a factor, and in this context, the Government - and some clubs - stand accused.

One of my trips with the camera last year mirrored the above point. Four out of six club officials, whose courses I visited in May, all ruefully reported poor bookings for the coming season. Two of them are of Championship standard, while four are typical of the clubs whose Balance Sheet glows or dims through the strength or weakness of outings and holiday golfers. The 'big' clubs had increased their charges for visitors over two years by an average of 25%; the smaller by around 16%. Over the same period, the value of the pound against major foreign currencies had gone up by around 30%. In one case, that meant that the cost to an American golfer, for instance, had increased by around 24 dollars – and that was just for one round. If he were here for a fortnight . . . well, work it out for yourself.

There is no doubt that many clubs are not getting revenue as they once did from the bar or dining room. Members resist the treasurer's demands at an A.G.M. for increased subscriptions.What remains available, therefore, to generate money to fund the additional costs to be incurred in the coming season's desire to present ever-improving facilities to the golfer? Answer – fees from non-members.

In its basic form, a fee from a visiting player is rent. There are no additional costs incurred whether thirty holiday golfers turn up for a day's golf, or none do so. The costs of preparing course and clubhouse are fixed, irrespective of the numbers who play. Bearing in mind the comments above on decreasing revenues in food and drink, therefore, why not reduce, rather than raise, fees?

Why not entice potential American, Japanese, Spanish or even English visitors by a cut in 'rent' rather than discouraging or even dissuading them by the double whammy of increased fees and a strong currency? Ten fees at fifteen pounds make an impact. Zero fees at twenty pounds make none. There are, too, some very high charges being levied at some of the bigger clubs. We must be careful not to price ourselves out of the market; the clubs therefore have to tread warily. If we in Scotland ever reach a stage where we automatically assume that golfers will pour into the country, irrespective of prices or standards, we will be in real trouble.

Anyway, before my publisher sacks me for slating too many people (which is not why I am here!) let us return to happier topics. Despite the problems mentioned above, Scotland's courses have never been better. The pride which is so obviously taken by green staff up and down the country in preparing their beloved turf has

"Scotland's courses have never been better. The pride which is so obviously taken by green staff up and down the country in preparing their beloved turf has never been in greater evidence."

For its part, this Government's apathy over the huge impact of the rising pound on tourism has been deplorable. It is to be for ever regretted that few, if any, politicians have the proper qualities to take the responsibility for running the country. They cannot - perhaps dare not – plan or use foresight. They merely react to things that happen or to headlines they see and repeat time-honoured phrases to appease a skeptical public. Real action is therefore conspicuous by its absence. Stern words put together by spin doctors are the solitary, but hollow offerings.

It would not take the brains of a rocket scientist to come up with a few solutions. Indeed, the costs to the Government, bearing in mind the extra VAT which would be collected from an increase in tourists, would be negligible. In the continuing deafening silence within the Scottish Executive, constructive suggestions are therefore highly unlikely. So we are back to the Clubs.

never been in greater evidence. From shaped fairways, to manicured bunkers and river banks, beautifully mown greens and eye catching stripes everywhere, one club after another leaps on the bandwagon of cosmetic course maintenance. The effects are stunning.

There's a little nine-hole course not far from my house. It is maintained by 'one and a half' people. it looks like Augusta minus the sand and water and the thrills generated for members and visitors are immeasurable. That is happening all over Scotland and, boring as it may be to repeat in each year's introduction, the courses are looking better than ever.

Our featured round on the Old Course with St.Andrews' professional Jim Farmer was very well received in last year's edition. This time around, I was lucky enough to enjoy the might and beauty of Turnberry in the company of Guy Redford, a delightful young man who has had the onerous task of getting

Colin Montgomerie's Academy of Golf away to a flying start. Once again the huge gulf between amateur and professional golf in thinking, never mind playing, your way around a Championship links was in ample evidence; but what an experience (in spite of the weather!) – I hope the report does it justice.

When I approached Catriona Matthew, she was quick to take up the invitation to produce an article, despite a heavy schedule which has seen her grace many of the world's top courses over the past two years or so, but more importantly make her mark among the world's leading lady golfers. She has never lost her love or admiration for her North Berwick home nor the native courses where she shaped and developed her professional career. I think that comes over loud and clear from her comments.

As we witness the arrival of the Third Millennium around our Scottish courses and wonder at the pace of their development, improvement and appearance, the question has to be asked – what next? It is hard for me to imagine, when I look through the viewfinder, that the great numbers of clubs who now exude near-perfection in course presentation and are willing to adopt whatever new practices or inventions come along could possibly make them even better. Yet experience tells you that the golf course research specialists will inevitably produce more wizardry for stressed greenkeepers to adopt. Higher standards having been achieved, members and visitors simply expect more to come along on the next bus. It will be fascinating to see what develops!

A final word of thanks, as always, must go to the aforementioned green staff who have consistently produced quite magnificent golfing panoramas for the camera. If I occasionally forgot to replace a pin, or a teebox or interrupted in the midst of grasscutting, I do apologise! To club members and visitors across Scotland, I also express my gratitude for, on the whole, accepting me on the course and taking such an interest in what I was doing. To the couple of members who asked for a fee for my capturing them putting out (no names, no pack drill!) I would refer them to Equity for advice.

I look forward to meeting you all again next season somewhere in the 'Home of Golf.' Meantime, I do hope you enjoy this edition and get all you need to tempt you back for more sport in the greatest country in the world in which it is on offer.

From the Ladies' Tee

by Catriona Matthews

Over the past ten years I have been lucky enough to have spent most of my time travelling the world to play golf. Starting as an amateur, I represented Scotland then Great Britain and Ireland in various tournaments, while most recently I have been playing as a tournament professional on the LPGA and Ladies' European Tours.

I have been lucky enough to have played on many of the world's best known courses – from Pebble Beach, Pine Valley and Seminole in the U.S.A. to Royal Melbourne in Australia, Sotogrande in Spain, Vilamoura in Portugal, Morfortaine in France – and not forgetting Royal Lytham and Sunningdale in England. That's an exciting itinerary for any golfer.

However, home is where the heart is, and I don't honestly believe anything quite compares to the variety of courses which are on offer here in my native Scotland. I have picked out a few of my own favourite venues, all of which have a special meaning to me, despite the fact that some may not have the glamourous names which some people associate with Scottish golf.

East Lothian is where I was brought up; I learned the game over the classic links of North Berwick (West). The course has many great holes; the 15th – Redan – has been copied by golf architects all over the world yet it doesn't rank in my top five holes on the course! That gives you some idea of the calibre of the course and if, on a sunny day, you can lift your head long enough to enjoy the views of the Firth of Forth, the Bass Rock, Fidra, Lamb and Craigleith islands are stunning. It is no wonder the place inspired Robert Louis Stevenson to write *Treasure Island*.

Gullane, but a few miles along the coast, is where I won my third – and last – Scottish Amateur title, shortly before I turned professional. It too is a classic links with holes going in every direction to fully test

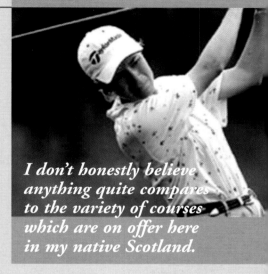

how you can play in the wind. With the severest of rough to cope with as well, if you are not hitting it straight you better have stocked up with balls from Jimmy Hume's shop first!

Heading further up the east coast, your next stop has to be the legendary St Andrews. I have been lucky enough to play there quite a bit and there is no other feeling in golf to equal that of playing the eighteenth. Everyone (from the top professional to the highest handicapped) is guaranteed a gallery down the home hole so I hope it doesn't put you off!

Across the Firth of Tay to Carnoustie, where I won my first Scottish Amateur title, and which is tough from hole one. As we all know, it was widely criticised for being too tough for the 1999 Open Championship contenders – isn't it great to hear the top pros in the world whinge?! My countryman Paul Lawrie simply remained patient (if you are going to tame this course that's the watchword) and came through to win in dramatic style. If you haven't been yet, put it at the top of your agenda.

Half an hour or so up the coast is Montrose, another links course carved out among the sand dunes and as the fifth oldest course in the world is well worth a visit.

I have not yet played any further north than Nairn, which hosted the 1999 Walker Cup (another home win – sorry if I offend my American friends!) I played in a Vagliano Trophy match here (Great Britain and Ireland versus Continent of Europe). Nairn is a tough course for the visitor, but nonetheless a thrill especially if the seaside winds are blowing. Low scoring is a bit of a rarity here. Hopefully the day is not too far off when I will get the opportunity to get that bit further north and manage a tilt at Dornoch, about whose special qualities I have heard nothing but good.

Heading south again, my next stop is Gleneagles, where, on the King's Course in 1998 I won the McDonalds Womens' Professional Championship of Europe, to date my most memorable achievement. It was so special to win in front of a home crowd and being cheered onto every green was a wonderful feeling. This course is just awesome; it has everything a great course should, from its excellent design to its acceptability of golfers at all levels – providing you choose the right tees – plus superb views over the Perthshire countryside.

I don't honestly believe anything quite compares to the variety of courses which are on offer here in my native Scotland.

Just a little to the south-west is Stirling, where I went to University and which is, of course, the land of 'Braveheart' William Wallace. While studying there we played and practised at Glenbervie, a very attractive inland course some twenty minutes away and well worth a visit. It is where the Scottish PGA has its headquarters and you will find me here every time I am home for a lesson or two from my teaching pro John Chillas.

Heading south-west into Ayrshire we find another course overshadowed by a better-known neighbour at the other end of the town. Prestwick St.Nicholas, the more southerly of the two, is where I won my middle Scottish Amateur title. This is a fun golf course with many interesting and unusual holes and at just under 6000 yards can be a real test in the wind.

My final port of call on this short Scottish tour is Royal Troon. We used to play an Amateur tournament here in April when the weather was always unkind to us – if you broke 80 you really felt as if you had achieved something! That, however, is part of the challenge of playing golf in Scotland. You have to cope with whatever the weatherman throws at you and adapt your game to suit.

I have not yet had the chance to pit my wits against Tom Weiskopf's Loch Lomond course but I hope that it's not too far distant. Indeed there are so many other great courses in Scotland that you could easily spend a lifetime going round them all. Why not come to Scotland soon and test your game . . .

. . . perhaps we may meet up at Dornoch?

Eyemouth

The extension of the course to eighteen holes has created a spectacular location on the clifftops above the North Sea. At 6472 yards – and with the inevitable presence of anything between a breeze and a howling gale, this is no pushover. There's plenty of room, mind you, and loads of variety in the layout. When the course reaches full maturity, it will be one of the busiest in the Borders.

15th, Eyemouth.

HOLE	NAME	WHITE YARDS	YELLOW YARDS	PAR	STROKE INDEX
1	Gunsgreen	524	–	5	6
2	White House	439	–	4	3
3	Puddocks Pond	155	–	3	12
4	Auld Hill	308	–	4	17
5	Hurkurs	380	–	4	9
6	A-Still-No-Ken	170	–	3	16
7	Gullies	331	–	4	14
8	Stane Dykes	379	–	4	8
9	Presidents	352	–	4	10

HOLE	NAME	WHITE YARDS	YELLOW YARDS	PAR	STROKE INDEX
10	Pishymere	512	–	5	4
11	Smugglers Brae	288	–	4	11
12	Scooties Flet	172	–	3	13
13	Hawk Ness	607	–	5	2
14	Luff Hard	353	–	4	15
15	Baine's Burn	457	–	4	1
16	Pitchers Well	357	–	4	7
17	The Loanin'	147	–	3	18
18	Home At Last	541	–	5	5

No. of holes: 18	Yardage: 6520	SSS: 72	
GREEN FEES	Weekdays		
Individual round	£20	Gaz ref: Page 113	
Daily rates	£25	Map ref: Page 156, E3	
Are visitors free to play?	Yes		
Nearest Airport: Edinburgh, 57 miles		Nearest Rail Station: Berwick-upon-Tweed, 8.6 miles	

EYEMOUTH GOLF CLUB

Gunsgreenhill,
Eyemouth TD14 5SE

Clubhouse (01890) 750551
Pro Shop (01890) 750004
Annual closure No
Weekly closure No

TO LOCATE THIS GOLF COURSE ON THE MAPS (p154-158) LOOK FOR THE FLAG WITH THIS PAGE NUMBER.

Duns

I had looked forward to my visit to Duns (another course recently extended to a full eighteen holes) and I was not disappointed. It winds its way across lovely, lush parkland to the north-west of the town and while 5700 yards will not exert you, club selection, shot placement and accuracy will all play a vital role in this highly pleasurable foray around some lovely Berwickshire countryside.

hidden gem

11th and 15th greens, Duns.

HOLE	NAME	WHITE YARDS	YELLOW YARDS	PAR	STROKE INDEX	HOLE	NAME	WHITE YARDS	YELLOW YARDS	PAR	STROKE INDEX
1	The Rain	400	395	4	9	10	Roon' the Bend	545	523	5	10
2	Cheviots	398	346	4	3	11	Harden's Way	390	383	4	4
3	Pouterlynie	368	307	4	15	12	Borthwick Brae	204	196	3	12
4	Scotston	171	163	3	7	13	The Quarry	366	360	4	2
5	Hole in the Wa'	387	350	4	11	14	The Field	326	320	4	14
6	Woodend	500	405	5/4	1	15	Double Trouble	116	107	3	18
7	The Gully	163	157	3	17	16	Hay's Castle	369	337	4	6
8	Postie's Walk	390	363	4	5	17	Wellrig Burn	195	190	3	5
9	Green Knowe	388	354	4	13	18	Dinger's Dyke	533	507	5	8

No. of holes: 18	Yardage: 6209	SSS: 70
GREEN FEES	Weekdays	
Individual round	On application	Gaz ref: Page 113
Daily rates	On application	Map ref: Page 156, D4
Are visitors free to play?	Yes	
Nearest Airport: Edinburgh, 51.7 miles	Nearest Rail Station: Berwick-upon-Tweed, 16 miles	

DUNS GOLF CLUB

Hardens Road, Duns

Clubhouse   (01361) 882194
Pro Shop   -
Annual closure No
Weekly closure No

TO LOCATE THIS GOLF COURSE ON THE MAPS (p154-158) LOOK FOR THE FLAG WITH THIS PAGE NUMBER.

Innerleithen

Constructed around the meanderings of Leithen Water, a couple of miles up the B709 from the town, this nine-holer remains a highly popular alternative to the busier Borders venues. Unusually, there are no hills to worry about – they merely provide a spectacular backdrop to almost every shot. Straightness is crucial,and there's not a better par three anywhere than the 175 yard first.

1st green, Innerleithen.

HOLE	NAME	WHITE YARDS	YELLOW YARDS	PAR	STROKE INDEX
1	Bridge	177	–	3	13
2	Cauld	343	–	4	11
3	Pirn Craig	474	–	4	1
4	Clubhouse	378	–	4	7
5	Hill	100	–	3	17
6	Common	485	–	5	3
7	Lea Pool	180	–	3	15
8	Dyke	524	–	5	5
9	Hame	372	–	4	9

HOLE	NAME	WHITE YARDS	YELLOW YARDS	PAR	STROKE INDEX
10	Bridge	177	–	3	14
11	Cauld	343	–	4	12
12	Pirn Craig	474	–	4	2
13	Clubhouse	378	–	4	8
14	Hill	100	–	3	18
15	Common	485	–	5	4
16	Lea Pool	180	–	3	16
17	Dyke	524	–	5	6
18	Hame	372	–	4	10

No. of holes: 9	Yardage: 6066	SSS: 69	
GREEN FEES	Weekdays		
Individual round	-	Gaz ref: Page 133	
Daily rates	£16	Map ref: Page 156, B4	
Are visitors free to play?		Yes	
Nearest Airport: Edinburgh, 35.8 miles		Nearest Rail Station: Waverley, 30.8 miles	

INNERLEITHEN GOLF CLUB

Leithen Water

Clubhouse (01896) 830951
Pro Shop -
Annual closure No
Weekly closure No

TO LOCATE THIS GOLF COURSE ON THE MAPS (p154-158) LOOK FOR THE FLAG WITH THIS PAGE NUMBER.

West Linton

I enjoyed my first round here in 1962. The course simply improves with age – I wish I could say the same! – and the delightful setting to the south of the western end of the Pentlands is just idyllic. The rough will be especially punitive, but the condition of the course is superb and pure enjoyment of heathland golf is guaranteed, with putting on velvet greens a sheer delight.

hidden **gem**

17th green, West Linton.

HOLE	NAME	WHITE YARDS	YELLOW YARDS	PAR	STROKE INDEX
1	Medwyn	307	–	4	14
2	Lynedale	143	–	3	18
3	Syke Burn	353	–	4	7
4	Lucky Dip	525	–	5	3
5	Muckle Knock	470	–	4	5
6	Mendrick	360	–	4	9
7	Windy Gowl	330	–	4	11
8	Woolfe's Wood	447	–	4	1
9	Kittley Knowe	162	–	3	16

HOLE	NAME	WHITE YARDS	YELLOW YARDS	PAR	STROKE INDEX
10	Slipperfield	348	–	4	10
11	Kettles Hill	469	–	4	4
12	Balnabruach	203	–	3	17
13	Mackellar's Wood	295	–	4	13
14	Westwater	376	–	4	2
15	Lang Whang	503	–	5	8
16	Crooked Jock	415	–	4	6
17	Wee Knock	196	–	3	15
18	Home	230	–	3	12

No. of holes: 18	Yardage: 6132	SSS: 70

GREEN FEES	Weekdays	
Individual round	£19	Gaz ref: Page 133
Daily rates	£28	Map ref: Page 156, A4
Are visitors free to play?	Yes	

Nearest Airport: Edinburgh, 21.7 miles   Nearest Rail Station: Waverley, 17.7 miles

WEST LINTON GOLF CLUB

West Linton

Clubhouse	(01986) 660463
Pro Shop	-
Annual closure	No
Weekly closure	No

TO LOCATE THIS GOLF COURSE ON THE MAPS (p154-158) LOOK FOR THE FLAG WITH THIS PAGE NUMBER.

Peebles

You never hear a bad word about this magnificent golf course. It looks immaculate and it is a joy to play. Its hillside location inevitably involves a few climbs but the slopes are cleverly used to add to the enjoyment. Plenty change of direction adds variety, and the gorgeous setting of the course in the heart of Tweeddale is breathtaking, especially in autumn. The new clubhouse is the icing on the cake.

6th green, Peebles.

HOLE	NAME	WHITE YARDS	YELLOW YARDS	PAR	STROKE INDEX	HOLE	NAME	WHITE YARDS	YELLOW YARDS	PAR	STROKE INDEX
1	Firknowe	–	196	3	9	10	Kitleyknowe	–	365	4	5
2	Sunny Acres	–	440	4	1	11	Windyridge	–	326	4	12
3	Wraes Burn	–	359	4	7	12	The Rushes	–	173	3	17
4	Jedderfield	–	295	4	15	13	CA' Canny	–	319	4	14
5	Meiklehope	–	342	4	13	14	Stey Brae	–	377	4	2
6	Glensax	–	401	4	3	15	Randles Park	–	431	4	8
7	Colts Choice	–	135	3	18	16	The Whaum	–	193	3	16
8	Peggys Lea	–	359	4	11	17	Langie	–	411	4	4
9	Hearthstanes	–	497	5	6	18	Green Mantle	–	541	5	10

No. of holes: 18	Yardage: 6160	SSS: 70
GREEN FEES	Weekdays	
Individual round	£20	Gaz ref: Page 133
Daily rates	£27	Map ref: Page 156, A4
Are visitors free to play?		Yes
Nearest Airport: Edinburgh, 27.7 miles	Nearest Rail Station: Waverley, 23.1 miles	

PEEBLES GOLF CLUB

Kirkland Street, Peebles

Clubhouse	(01721) 720197
Pro Shop	-
Annual closure	No
Weekly closure	No

TO LOCATE THIS GOLF COURSE ON THE MAPS (p154-158) LOOK FOR THE FLAG WITH THIS PAGE NUMBER.

Torwoodlee

The sylvan setting of the original nine holes remains; the course extension on the higher ground has created a layout of great interest and no mean challenge either. Willie Park would be pleased to see how his original design has blended with the new, but his greatest pleasure would have been in seeing the loveliness of it all as modern course presentation has made it so picturesque.

hidden gem

18th green, Torwoodlee.

HOLE	NAME	WHITE YARDS	YELLOW YARDS	PAR	STROKE INDEX
1	Meigleview	378	–	4	9
2	Park's Brae	401	–	4	3
3	Waverley Line	124	–	3	17
4	Torwood	293	–	4	15
5	Summit	418	–	4	1
6	Bowland View	355	–	4	13
7	The Whin	152	–	3	11
8	Fish Farm	512	–	5	5
9	Sunset	367	–	4	7

HOLE	NAME	WHITE YARDS	YELLOW YARDS	PAR	STROKE INDEX
10	Hame Turn	176	–	3	10
11	Monkey Puzzle	425	–	4	2
12	Postage Stamp	139	–	3	18
13	Buckholm View	420	–	4	8
14	Ryehaugh	546	–	5	12
15	Gala Water	336	–	4	16
16	William Law	420	–	4	4
17	Auld First	234	–	3	6
18	The Brig	325	–	4	14

No. of holes: 18	Yardage: 6021	SSS:		**TORWOODLEE GOLF CLUB**
GREEN FEES	Weekdays			Edinburgh Road,
Individual round	£20	Gaz ref: Page 140		Galashiels TD1 2NE
Daily rates	£27	Map ref: Page 156, B4		Clubhouse (01896) 752260
Are visitors free to play?		Yes		Pro Shop -
				Annual closure No
Nearest Airport: Edinburgh, 46.4 miles		Nearest Rail Station: Waverley, 30.6 miles		Weekly closure No

TO LOCATE THIS GOLF COURSE ON THE MAPS (p154-158) LOOK FOR THE FLAG WITH THIS PAGE NUMBER.

KING'S HOTEL

56 Market Street, Galashiels TD1 3AN

Tel: 01896 755497 Fax: 01896 755497 Email: kingshotel@talk21.com

Centrally situated in the Scottish Borders to allow you to take advantage of the many courses available, this family-run, town centre hotel is ideally placed for the golfer who is looking for first class accomodation and good value, freshly prepared food. There is also a small, friendly lounge bar, which is the ideal place to relax over a quiet drink and contemplate those missed putts!

STB ★ ★   AA ★ ★   P

ASHLYN GUEST HOUSE

7 Abbotsford Road, Galashiels TD1 3DP

Tel: 01896 752416 Fax: 01896 752416 Email: ashlyn7@hotmail.com

Ashlyn Guest House, situated on the south side of Galashiels, just two minutes walk from the city centre, was built in the 1850s.
Residents are eligible for special rates at Torwoodlee Golf Club
and there are plenty of other outdoor activities in the surrounding area.

AA ★ ★   P

Abbotsford Arms Hotel

63 Stirling Street, Galashiels
Telephone: 01896 752 517

SMALL, FRIENDLY FAMILY HOTEL WITH
GOOD FOOD AT REASONABLE PRICES.

CENTRAL SITUATION FOR 20 GOLF COURSES IN THE AREA.

Mintole Classic Gold   STB ★ ★

SCOTLAND
HOME OF GOLF
online

www.scotland-for-golf.com

The Roxburghe

The longest – and unquestionably the stiffest – challenge in Borders' golf. Of course, the Duke intended it to be just that and Dave Thomas didn't let him down. It can be a daunting experience for anyone not striking the ball well, but there's compensation in another glorious Border setting beside the Teviot. A sunny, late afternoon autumn round here will prove unforgettable.

Looking across the 13th, The Roxburghe.

HOLE	NAME	WHITE YARDS	YELLOW YARDS	PAR	STROKE INDEX	HOLE	NAME	WHITE YARDS	YELLOW YARDS	PAR	STROKE INDEX
1	Home Farm	–	385	4	6	10	Monument	–	469	4	1
2	Whinny Braes	–	396	4	10	11	Old Plantation	–	526	5	7
3	Beeches	–	364	4	18	12	House Park	–	399	4	9
4	Azalea	–	188	3	12	13	Scott-Kerr	–	216	3	15
5	Mount	–	546	5	2	14	Viaduct	–	523	5	11
6	Roundel	–	382	4	14	15	Quarry	–	177	3	17
7	Teviot View	–	520	5	8	16	Kerr's Cleuch	–	394	4	3
8	Badger Sett	–	181	3	16	17	Floors	–	382	4	13
9	Deer Park	–	403	4	4	18	Sunlaws	–	422	4	5

No. of holes: 18	Yardage: 6925	SSS: 74
GREEN FEES	Weekdays	
Individual round	£35	Gaz ref: Page 139
Daily rates	£50	Map ref: Page 156, C5
Are visitors free to play?		Yes

Nearest Airport: Edinburgh, 55.2 miles   Nearest Rail Station: Berwick-upon-Tweed, 26.3 miles

THE ROXBURGHE GOLF COURSE

Kelso, Roxburghshire TD5 8JZ

Clubhouse   (01573) 450331
Pro Shop   -
Annual closure No
Weekly closure No

TO LOCATE THIS GOLF COURSE ON THE MAPS (p154-158) LOOK FOR THE FLAG WITH THIS PAGE NUMBER.

Twenty seven holes are on offer at this lovely location beneath the east end of the Ochil Hills. It regularly enjoys a lot of outings and, once you have tasted it, you will understand why. When the 'second' nine was completed across the road, Muckhart was made. Heathland, with the requirement for straightness off the tee and a sound short game essential, it is on many lists for a second visit.

13th green, Muckhart.

HOLE	NAME	WHITE YARDS	YELLOW YARDS	PAR	STROKE INDEX
1	Duncan's Grace	221	221	4	7
2	Cauldron Lim	378	404	4	3
3	The Bogle's Birk	194	223	3	6
4	Wildboarclough	339	345	4	5
5	Andrew's Law	289	311	4	8
6	Cantie Knowes	436	457	4	1
7	The Wee Skellum	176	190	3	9
8	Lang Stravaig	533	562	5	2
9	Whitewisp	394	411	4	4

HOLE	NAME	WHITE YARDS	YELLOW YARDS	PAR	STROKE INDEX
10	The Sheugh	278	288	4	7
11	The Road Hole	287	307	4	5
12	The Auld Quarry	290	290	4	4
13	The Ewe Buchts	165	168	3	9
14	Top of the World	361	361	4	2
15	The Lonesome Pine	192	195	3	8
16	Fire Hill	469	530	5	1
17	The Hare's Clap	475	487	5	3
18	Stewart's Prospect	201	209	3	6

No. of holes: 27	Yardage: 5778	SSS: 70

GREEN FEES	Weekdays	
Individual round	£16	Gaz ref: Page 114
Daily rates	£23	Map ref: Page 156, E2
Are visitors free to play?		Yes

Nearest Airport: Edinburgh, 31.5 miles   Nearest Rail Station: Gleneagles, 11.4 miles

MUCKHART GOLF CLUB

by Dollar, Clackmannanshire

Clubhouse	(01259) 781423
Pro Shop	-
Annual closure	No
Weekly closure	No

TO LOCATE THIS GOLF COURSE ON THE MAPS (p155-159) LOOK FOR THE FLAG WITH THIS PAGE NUMBER.

Glenbervie

This highly regarded course just exudes class, from the lovely hilltop clubhouse to the glories of a superb parkland course with one of the hardest finishes in Scottish inland golf. A wealth of broad-leafed trees presents more than a few problems as well as lighting up the setting – especially in autumn, and you'll need good long irons to make any impact. Classic golf in a classic ambience.

Looking up the 14th, Glenbervie.

HOLE	NAME	WHITE YARDS	YELLOW YARDS	PAR	STROKE INDEX
1	Yetts O'Bervie	356	–	4	11
2	Geans	534	–	5	5
3	The Manor	332	–	4	15
4	Copse	153	–	3	17
5	Ben Cleugh	386	–	4	9
6	Scotch Corner	401	–	4	3
7	Auchengaw	211	–	3	7
8	Blairs	339	–	4	13
9	Bluebell Wood	436	–	4	1

HOLE	NAME	WHITE YARDS	YELLOW YARDS	PAR	STROKE INDEX
10	The Neuk	168	–	3	12
11	The Pines	331	–	4	18
12	The Well	424	–	4	2
13	Treetops	198	–	3	8
14	Braid's	407	–	4	4
15	Joug Tree	506	–	5	16
16	Torwood	373	–	4	10
17	The Oaks	500	–	5	14
18	Todhill	368	–	4	6

No. of holes: 18	Yardage: 6423	SSS: 71
GREEN FEES	Weekdays	
Individual round	£30	Gaz ref: Page 141
Daily rates	£40	Map ref: Page 156, D2
Are visitors free to play?	Yes	
Nearest Airport: Edinburgh, 23.9 miles	Nearest Rail Station: Larbert, 1.2 miles	

GLENBERVIE GOLF CLUB

Stirling Road, Larbert, FK5 4SJ

Clubhouse	(01324) 562605
Pro Shop	-
Annual closure	No
Weekly closure	No

TO LOCATE THIS GOLF COURSE ON THE MAPS (p155-159) LOOK FOR THE FLAG WITH THIS PAGE NUMBER.

Stirling

Many still rate the first hole here as one of the hardest starts in Scottish golf. Whatever your fate, the rest of the course is enthralling, not just for the challenge it presents, but for a setting which Hollywood directors would die for. Henry Cotton was involved here and "Cotton's Fancy" is one of the great par fours. Your first round at Stirling will prove unforgettable – whatever your performance.

15th green, Stirling.

HOLE	NAME	WHITE YARDS	YELLOW YARDS	PAR	STROKE INDEX
1	Polmaise	–	462	5	5
2	Towers	–	268	4	15
3	Rocking Stone	–	300	4	13
4	Elms	–	344	4	9
5	Tree Out	–	489	5	3
6	Flagstaff	–	138	3	17
7	Craigforth	–	432	4	7
8	Gillieshill	–	180	3	11
9	The Butts	–	418	4	1

HOLE	NAME	WHITE YARDS	YELLOW YARDS	PAR	STROKE INDEX
10	Quarry	–	170	3	16
11	Spires	–	400	4	10
12	Ben Lomond	–	367	4	4
13	Mound	–	483	5	8
14	Ballengeich	–	152	3	18
15	Cotton's Fancy	–	365	4	2
16	Ben Venue	–	297	4	14
17	Tree In	–	361	4	12
18	Castle	–	497	5	6

No. of holes: 18	Yardage: 6400	SSS: 69
GREEN FEES	Weekdays	
Individual round	£25	Gaz ref: Page 141
Daily rates	£35	Map ref: Page 156, D2
Are visitors free to play?		Yes (by arrangement)
Nearest Airport: Edinburgh, 30.9 miles		Nearest Rail Station: Stirling, 1.4 miles

STIRLING GOLF CLUB

Queen's Road, Stirling, FK8 3AA
Clubhouse   (01786) 473801
Pro Shop   -
Annual closure   No
Weekly closure   No

TO LOCATE THIS GOLF COURSE ON THE MAPS (p155-159) LOOK FOR THE FLAG WITH THIS PAGE NUMBER.

Lanark

In the company of a dozen former footballing colleagues (perhaps 'adversaries' is more apt!), I had the pleasure of my first round here last year. It is a vastly understated course of heathland, much change of direction and a potential nightmare if you cannot be straight. James Braid created it, and his trademark is evident in tee and green placement to make full use of the landscape: brilliant!

Short 18th, Lanark.

HOLE	NAME	WHITE YARDS	YELLOW YARDS	PAR	STROKE INDEX	HOLE	NAME	WHITE YARDS	YELLOW YARDS	PAR	STROKE INDEX
1	Loch	–	360	4	13	10	Tintock Tap	–	152	3	17
2	Dodger	–	467	4	3	11	Butts	–	397	4	4
3	Newlands	–	409	4	9	12	Valley	–	362	4	12
4	Houston	–	457	4	1	13	Drove Road	–	362	4	8
5	Stanmore	–	318	4	15	14	Quarry Knowe	–	399	4	6
6	North Faulds	–	377	4	7	15	Vassie	–	470	4	2
7	Gorstone	–	141	3	18	16	Anstruther	–	337	4	14
8	Tinto	–	530	5	5	17	Whitelees	–	309	4	10
9	Whinney Knowe	–	360	4	11	18	Home	–	216	3	16

No. of holes: 18	Yardage: 6306	SSS: 71
GREEN FEES	Weekdays	
Individual round	£26	Gaz ref: Page 126
Daily rates	£40	Map ref: Page 156, D3
Are visitors free to play?	Yes	
Nearest Airport: Glasgow, 37.9 miles	Nearest Rail Station: Lanark, 1.3 miles	

LANARK GOLF CLUB

The Moor, Whiteless Road, Lanark, ML11 7RX

Clubhouse   (01555) 663219
Pro Shop   -
Annual closure No
Weekly closure No

TO LOCATE THIS GOLF COURSE ON THE MAPS (p155-159) LOOK FOR THE FLAG WITH THIS PAGE NUMBER.

Hands up if you have never heard of it; note well the name for a future visit. Lying south of Hamilton alongside Chatelherault Country Park, this is a lovely place where the arboreal surroundings are not just magnificent but also influential in decision-making at almost every hole. The phrase "hidden gem" is greatly overused, but is a perfect description of a very modest club enjoying an idyllic setting.

hidden **gem**

15th, Hamilton.

HOLE	NAME	WHITE YARDS	YELLOW YARDS	PAR	STROKE INDEX	HOLE	NAME	WHITE YARDS	YELLOW YARDS	PAR	STROKE INDEX
1	Cadzow Castle	–	354	4	11	10	Belvidere	–	312	4	16
2	Avonbraes	–	382	4	3	11	Plateau	–	417	4	4
3	Hoolet Row	–	138	3	18	12	Perfection	–	218	3	12
4	Lang Gait	–	491	5	9	13	The Oaks	–	398	4	6
5	Woodyett	–	492	5	5	14	Dalzell	–	404	4	10
6	Spinney	–	417	4	7	15	Mount Zion	–	167	3	17
7	Devil's Elbow	–	416	4	1	16	The Wham	–	459	4	2
8	Tinto	–	296	4	15	17	Chatelherault	–	359	4	14
9	The Pen	–	176	3	13	18	Riccarton	–	347	4	8

No. of holes: 18	Yardage: 6472	SSS:
GREEN FEES	Weekdays	
Individual round	On application	Gaz ref: Page 125
Daily rates	On application	Map ref: Page 156, D3
Are visitors free to play?	Yes	
Nearest Airport: Glasgow, 24.9 miles		Nearest Rail Station: Hamilton Central, 1.9 miles

HAMILTON GOLF CLUB

Riccarton, Ferniegair, by Hamilton

Clubhouse	(01698) 282872
Pro Shop	-
Annual closure	No
Weekly closure	No

TO LOCATE THIS GOLF COURSE ON THE MAPS (p155-159) LOOK FOR THE FLAG WITH THIS PAGE NUMBER.

Cawder

Handily placed just outside Glasgow's north-east corner, Cawder sports two courses which endow a stretch of rolling parkland on an estate dating from 1624. The Keir is shorter; the Cawder is a tough nut. James Braid, initially, then Donald Steel more recently have combined to create a varied layout which beautifully combines a flat start with a plateau on which a score will be made or wasted.

Short 8th, Cawder.

HOLE	NAME	WHITE YARDS	YELLOW YARDS	PAR	STROKE INDEX
1	The Brig	361	361	4	11
2	Corrie Corner	409	409	4	5
3	Magh Mor	427	399	4	2
4	Cowden Ridge	399	378	4	9
5	Boundary Beeches	385	363	4	13
6	Campsie	164	164	3	15
7	Hilton	532	498	5	7
8	Mickle Bin	144	144	3	18
9	Wilderness	373	364	4	3

HOLE	NAME	WHITE YARDS	YELLOW YARDS	PAR	STROKE INDEX
1	Balmore	358	348	4	6
2	Antonine Wall	524	512	5	10
3	Mavis Vale	506	496	5	17
4	Bearsden	158	141	3	12
5	Kelvin	454	423	4	1
6	The Gardens	390	365/338	4	4
7	Golden Jubilee	157	147	3	16
8	Cawder Wood	355	345	4	8
9	Hame	201	191	3	14

No. of holes: 18	Yardage: 6244	SSS: 71/68
GREEN FEES	Weekdays	
Individual round	£26	Gaz ref: Page 124
Daily rates	£31	Map ref: Page 156, C2
Are visitors free to play?	Yes	
Nearest Airport: Glasgow, 15 miles		Nearest Rail Station: Bishopbriggs, 2.1 miles

CAWDER GOLF CLUB

Cadder Road, Bishopbriggs

Clubhouse	(0141) 772 5167
Pro Shop	-
Annual closure	No
Weekly closure	No

TO LOCATE THIS GOLF COURSE ON THE MAPS (p155-159) LOOK FOR THE FLAG WITH THIS PAGE NUMBER.

Douglas Park

Milngavie and Bearsden support eight clubs between them; this has to be one of the most attractive with the spectacular view down the eighteenth among the finest in the west of Scotland. It's not long – just under 6000 yards – but there's a fine mix of holes with five par threes, high tees/low greens and vice versa, and the most beautiful backdrop of trees; steer clear of them, or else!

hidden gem

18th, Douglas Park.

HOLE	NAME	WHITE YARDS	YELLOW YARDS	PAR	STROKE INDEX	HOLE	NAME	WHITE YARDS	YELLOW YARDS	PAR	STROKE INDEX
1	Kilmardinny	403	389	4	11	10	Burnbrae	484	476	5	2
2	Neck	343	325	4	7	11	Island	310	303	4	10
3	Firs	133	125	3	17	12	Whin Hill	101	101	3	18
4	Boclair	447	433	4	3	13	Roman Wall	478	468	5	6
5	Hedge	239	226	3	15	14	Dyke	379	369	4	4
6	Victorious VIth	307	303	4	13	15	Mount	197	197	3	12
7	Dougalston	381	370	4	5	16	Braes	399	371	4	8
8	Knowe	430	420	4	1	17	Wood	136	124	3	16
9	Haugh	465	449	4	9	18	Home	330	312	4	14

No. of holes: 18	Yardage: 5982	SSS: 69
GREEN FEES	Weekdays	
Individual round	£22	Gaz ref: Page 116
Daily rates	£30	Map ref: Page 156, C2
Are visitors free to play?	Yes	
Nearest Airport: Glasgow, 9.6 miles	Nearest Rail Station: Hillfoot, 0.4 miles	

DOUGLAS PARK GOLF CLUB

Hillfoot, Bearsden, G 61 2TJ

Clubhouse (0141) 942 2220
Pro Shop (0141) 942 1482
Annual closure No
Weekly closure No

TO LOCATE THIS GOLF COURSE ON THE MAPS (p155-159) LOOK FOR THE FLAG WITH THIS PAGE NUMBER.

Windyhill

An apt name for the club's location on the rising ground north west of Bearsden, but don't let it put you off a visit! This is a cracker of a course, where tight fairways and smallish greens cry out for accuracy. There are highs and lows which force the golfer to think all the time about the next shot, nowhere more so than on the ninth – "Perfection" – stroke index one and deservedly so!

1st green, Windyhill.

HOLE	NAME	WHITE YARDS	YELLOW YARDS	PAR	STROKE INDEX	HOLE	NAME	WHITE YARDS	YELLOW YARDS	PAR	STROKE INDEX
1	Baljaffry	–	358	4	9	10	Craters	–	163	3	10
2	Orr's Rest	–	152	3	17	11	Nest	–	281	4	14
3	Elbow	–	414	4	7	12	Rocky Gait	–	447	4	2
4	Westward Ho'	–	357	4	11	13	Switchback	–	489	5	4
5	Whins	–	375	4	13	14	De'ils Crag	–	144	3	18
6	Hogg's Back	–	416	4	3	15	Muir	–	476	5	6
7	Port Lucy	–	183	3	15	16	Happy Valley	–	312	4	8
8	Road	–	451	4	5	17	Cottage	–	290	4	16
9	Perfection	–	414	4	1	18	Home	–	246	3	12

No. of holes: 18	Yardage: 6254	SSS: 70

GREEN FEES	Weekdays	
Individual round	£20	Gaz ref: Page 116
Daily rates	£20	Map ref: Page 156, C2
Are visitors free to play?	Yes	

Nearest Airport: Glasgow, 11.3 miles | Nearest Rail Station: Bearsden, 2.1 miles

WINDYHILL GOLF CLUB

Baljaffray Road, Bearsden, G61 4QQ

Clubhouse	(0141) 942 2349
Pro Shop	(0141) 942 7157
Annual closure	No
Weekly closure	No

TO LOCATE THIS GOLF COURSE ON THE MAPS (p155-159) LOOK FOR THE FLAG WITH THIS PAGE NUMBER.

Helensburgh

Traditionally one of the most affluent of the towns on the north bank of the Clyde estuary, the golf course and, particularly, the clubhouse, perfectly reflects the ambience. The top of the course opens up superb vistas over the Clyde, but you've a bit of work to do before you can relax and enjoy them. This is a lovely heathland course of great variety and almost guaranteed enjoyment.

5th green, Helensburgh.

HOLE	NAME	WHITE YARDS	YELLOW YARDS	PAR	STROKE INDEX	HOLE	NAME	WHITE YARDS	YELLOW YARDS	PAR	STROKE INDEX
1	High Hopes	283	264	4	13	10	Clyde View	447	416	4	2
2	Fruin	429	402	4	1	11	Clyde Arran	210	172	3	16
3	Mirror of the Moor	182	151	3	11	12	The Dell	339	280	4	14
4	Ben Bouie	372	365	4	7	13	Lang Stracht	508	486	5	8
5	Bunker Hill	300	298	4	15	14	Baillie's Brig	408	393	4	6
6	Loch Lomond	412	405	4	5	15	Churchill	371	355	4	12
7	Seaward	408	397	4	3	16	The Quarry	150	147	3	18
8	Sundowner	371	359	4	9	17	Due West	379	365	4	10
9	Old Luss Road	131	126	3	17	18	Rolling Home	404	392	4	4

No. of holes: 18	Yardage: 6104	SSS:
GREEN FEES	Weekdays	
Individual round	On application	Gaz ref: Page 117
Daily rates	On application	Map ref: Page 156, C2
Are visitors free to play?		Yes
Nearest Airport: Glasgow, 21.5 miles		Nearest Rail Station: Helensburgh Central, 1 mile

HELENSBURGH GOLF CLUB

25 East Abercromby Street, Helensburgh

Clubhouse   (01436) 674173
Pro Shop   -
Annual closure No
Weekly closure No

TO LOCATE THIS GOLF COURSE ON THE MAPS (p155-159) LOOK FOR THE FLAG WITH THIS PAGE NUMBER.

Cardross

I had heard and read about Cardross and, as usual, was annoyed that it had taken me so long to get there with the camera. A stunning course and a stern examination of golfing elan – at all handicap levels – James Braid has again been at it here; he is immortalised at the fifteenth (Braid's Bend) which features a 90-degree right turn only 180 yards out. It makes this a true three-shot par five and is but one of nine difficult challenges on the much longer inward half of a first class venue.

hidden gem

1st green, Cardross.

HOLE	NAME	WHITE YARDS	YELLOW YARDS	PAR	STROKE INDEX
1	Fernie's First	398	388	4	6
2	Auchenfroe	351	340	4	13
3	Bloomhill	256	248	4	16
4	Carman	393	378	4	8
5	Burn's Loup	131	121	3	18
6	Dinger	397	354	4	1
7	Clyde View	367	355	4	12
8	Killoeter	371	365	4	10
9	Argyll	399	371	4	4

HOLE	NAME	WHITE YARDS	YELLOW YARDS	PAR	STROKE INDEX
1	Kilmahew	458	454	4	7
2	Avenue	432	381	4	2
3	Cairniedrouth	163	145	3	17
4	Castle	502	463	5	11
5	Kirkton	404	395	4	3
6	Tall o' the Bank	196	190	3	15
7	Braid's Bend	512	504	5	5
8	Boquhomrie	285	249	4	14
9	Douggie's Mound	474	461	4	9

No. of holes: 18	Yardage: 6469	SSS: 72
GREEN FEES	Weekdays	
Individual round	£25	Gaz ref: Page 117
Daily rates	£35	Map ref: Page 156, C2
Are visitors free to play?		Yes (weekdays)
Nearest Airport: Glasgow, 15.7 miles		Nearest Rail Station: Cardross, 0.4 miles

CARDROSS GOLF CLUB

Main Road, Cardross, Dumbarton, G82 5LB

Clubhouse (01389) 841213
Pro Shop -
Annual closure No
Weekly closure No

TO LOCATE THIS GOLF COURSE ON THE MAPS (p155-159) LOOK FOR THE FLAG WITH THIS PAGE NUMBER.

Irvine Bogside

There are few clubs in Scotland whose names can rival this one as a complete contradiction of its characteristics. The nearest of the town's courses to the sea, this is links golf at its best, with a succession of cracking holes set amidst gorse, heather and the usual tough seaside terrain which makes staying on the straight and narrow imperative. Perhaps in the shadow of the Gailes courses at the other end of the town, but in the same league as a test of golf, without a doubt.

3rd green, Irvine Bogside.

HOLE	NAME	WHITE YARDS	YELLOW YARDS	PAR	STROKE INDEX	HOLE	NAME	WHITE YARDS	YELLOW YARDS	PAR	STROKE INDEX
1	Eglinton	418	–	4	7	10	Braid	373	–	4	10
2	Winton	476	–	5	5	11	Grandstand	465	–	4	2
3	Fullarton	358	–	4	9	12	Arran	368	–	4	14
4	The Moor	289	–	4	11	13	Snodgrass	429	–	4	4
5	Sandface	279	–	4	15	14	The Specs.	382	–	4	12
6	Cannon Hill	411	–	4	1	15	Bartonholm	337	–	4	8
7	The Cup	322	–	4	13	16	Redburn	156	–	3	18
8	Saddle Back	165	–	3	17	17	The Warren	391	–	4	6
9	Racecourse	456	–	4	3	18	Flagstaff	333	–	4	16

No. of holes: 18	Yardage: 6408	SSS: 71	
GREEN FEES	Weekdays		
Individual round	On application	Gaz ref: Page 110	
Daily rates	On application	Map ref: Page 156, B3	
Are visitors free to play?		Yes (by arrangement)	
Nearest Airport: Prestwick, 10.5 miles		Nearest Rail Station: Irvine, 2.2 miles	

THE IRVINE GOLF CLUB

Bogside, Irvine

Clubhouse	(01294) 275979
Pro Shop	(01294) 275626
Annual closure	No
Weekly closure	No

TO LOCATE THIS GOLF COURSE ON THE MAPS (p155-159) LOOK FOR THE FLAG WITH THIS PAGE NUMBER.

Prestwick St Nicholas

Like Bogside, this longstanding club has not found fame to match its counterpart at the north end of the town. Despite a modest 6000 yard length, it loses nothing in stiffness, with a tight layout which features several blind teeshots and a remarkable emphasis on plateau greens – all guarded by intimidating bunkers. There's room to stray, mind you, as the rough is kinder than normal, and three par threes will keep you on your toes in an exciting finishing stretch.

hidden gem

13th green, Prestwick St. Nicholas.

HOLE	NAME	WHITE YARDS	YELLOW YARDS	PAR	STROKE INDEX
1	Well	342	–	4	7
2	Bruce	172	–	3	17
3	Maryborough	281	–	4	13
4	Dyke	420	–	4	3
5	St. Ninians	406	–	4	9
6	Bellrock	326	–	4	11
7	Midfield	454	–	4	1
8	Quarry	360	–	4	5
9	Cock O' Bendy	338	–	4	12

HOLE	NAME	WHITE YARDS	YELLOW YARDS	PAR	STROKE INDEX
10	Lady Isle	165	–	3	15
11	Pladda	498	–	5	2
12	Pans	139	–	3	18
13	Tam Jack's	456	–	4	8
14	New Prestwick	412	–	4	6
15	Kingcase	276	–	4	10
16	Coila	379	–	4	4
17	Grangemuir	301	–	4	16
18	Home	227	–	3	14

No. of holes: 18	Yardage: 5952	SSS: 69

GREEN FEES	Weekdays	
Individual round	£30	Gaz ref: Page 111
Daily rates	£50	Map ref: Page 156, C4
Are visitors free to play?	Yes	

Nearest Airport: Prestwick, 1.7 miles — Nearest Rail Station: Prestwick, 0.8 miles

ST NICHOLAS GOLF CLUB

Grangemuir Road, Prestwick, KA9 1SN

Clubhouse (01292) 477608
Pro Shop (01292) 473904
Annual closure No
Weekly closure No

TO LOCATE THIS GOLF COURSE ON THE MAPS (p155-159) LOOK FOR THE FLAG WITH THIS PAGE NUMBER.

40 SCOTLAND **HOME OF GOLF**

The essential guide for fishing in Scotland

If you enjoy fishing, you'll love **Scotland for Fishing 2001/2002.** Edited by award-winning fisherman and journalist Mike Shepley, Scotland for Fishing contains all you need to know to get on the water at Scotland's best fishing sites.

If you order your copy direct from Pastime Publications, you can save £1 off the cover price. For just **£5.99** including post and packaging, we'll deliver the guide to your door anywhere in the UK.

Send your cheque, made payable to: Pastime Publications, Golf Reader Offer, 5 Dalgety Avenue, Edinburgh EH7 5UF, along with your address details. Then sit back and start planning your Scottish fishing holiday.

Allow 28 days for delivery.

Portpatrick

Next stop is Ireland; you can't find a Scottish course further from the main belt than this one, but what a way to go! For years this club has been a magnet for visiting golfers and it remains one of the most heavily played in the south of Scotland. A lovely setting above the Irish Sea and the unfailing quality of presentation – not to mention fine clubhouse fare – all combine to create a classic.

hidden **gem**

Ladies' tee, 13th, Portpatrick.

HOLE	NAME	WHITE YARDS	YELLOW YARDS	PAR	STROKE INDEX	HOLE	NAME	WHITE YARDS	YELLOW YARDS	PAR	STROKE INDEX
1	St Maden	393	387	4	7	10	Erinview	329	319	4	10
2	Dasher's Den	375	331	4	11	11	Puddle Hole	163	138	3	12
3	Muckle Skelp	544	534	5	1	12	Dunskey	388	370	4	2
4	Captain's Leap	160	156	3	15	13	Sandeel	293	285	4	14
5	Plateau	405	365	4	3	14	Glenside	293	293	4	6
6	Portree	382	345	4	9	15	Campbell's Gamble	101	99	3	18
7	Gorsebank	165	160	3	13	16	Rickwood	393	379	4	4
8	Flyover	377	288	4	5	17	Greenfield	301	285	4	16
9	Hillcrest	311	298	4	17	18	Journey's End	535	506	5	8

No. of holes: 18	Yardage: 5908	SSS: 69
GREEN FEES	Weekdays	
Individual round	£22	Gaz ref: Page 142
Daily rates	£33	Map ref: Page 156, A6
Are visitors free to play?		Yes

Nearest Airport: Prestwick, 63.1 miles   Nearest Rail Station: Stranraer, 8.5 miles

PORTPATRICK GOLF CLUB

Portpatrick, DG9 8TB

Clubhouse	(01776) 810273
Pro Shop	-
Annual closure	No
Weekly closure	No

TO LOCATE THIS GOLF COURSE ON THE MAPS (p155-159) LOOK FOR THE FLAG WITH THIS PAGE NUMBER.

Here is another beautifully manicured and highly entertaining eighteen holes which you rarely hear about in the wider circles of golf. The course is set around the loch to the west of the town and interest never wanes as man-made features combine with nature to provide a highly pleasurable round. Ideally situated for English visitors, who enjoy great value for their green fees.

1st green, Lochmaben.

HOLE	NAME	WHITE YARDS	YELLOW YARDS	PAR	STROKE INDEX
1	The Key	314	–	4	14
2	Bruce's Motte	188	–	3	4
3	The Moats	190	–	3	8
4	Braid's First	311	–	4	12
5	Queensberry	359	–	4	6
6	The Beeches	404	–	4	2
7	Swans Nest	291	–	4	10
8	Kirk Loch	120	–	3	18
9	Skelvieland	295	–	4	16

HOLE	NAME	WHITE YARDS	YELLOW YARDS	PAR	STROKE INDEX
10	Ancient Domain	445	–	4	1
11	Broadchapel	522	–	5	9
12	Cockies Knowe	143	–	3	13
13	Larks Rise	425	–	4	3
14	Mark's Way	343	–	4	7
15	The Neuk	141	–	3	17
16	Vendace Burn	426	–	4	5
17	Cormorant's Rest	328	–	4	11
18	Castlehill Gait	132	–	3	15

No. of holes: 18	Yardage: 5336	SSS: 66	
GREEN FEES	Weekdays		
Individual round	On application	Gaz ref: Page 115	
Daily rates	On application	Map ref: Page 156, E5	
Are visitors free to play?		Yes	
Nearest Airport: Prestwick, 70.7 miles		Nearest Rail Station: Lockerbie 4.4 miles	

LOCHMABEN GOLF CLUB

Castlehillgate, Lochmaben,
Lockerbie, DG11 1NT

Clubhouse   (01387) 810552
Pro Shop   -
Annual closure No
Weekly closure No

TO LOCATE THIS GOLF COURSE ON THE MAPS (p155-159) LOOK FOR THE FLAG WITH THIS PAGE NUMBER.

Colvend

The success story of this little club goes on and on. Another which is regularly invaded by visitors from the north of England, the original nine holes lie south of the main road and overlook the bay of Sandyhill. Across the way, rolling parkland has yielded the new holes which, together with the friendliest of welcomes in the clubhouse, has made this a regular stop for holiday golfers.

hidden gem

3rd, Colvend.

HOLE	NAME	WHITE YARDS	YELLOW YARDS	PAR	STROKE INDEX
1	Torrs Hill	258	241	4	10
2	Portling	118	109	3	18
3	Solway View	360	340	4	4
4	Whinny Bank	171	160	3	16
5	The Rowan	318	290	4	12
6	Teugh Brae	335	328	4	2
7	Douglas Hall	365	318	4	14
8	The Burn	192	173	3	6
9	Drumburn	300	293	4	8

HOLE	NAME	WHITE YARDS	YELLOW YARDS	PAR	STROKE INDEX
10	Newbarns	253	221	4	11
11	The Ruin	371	282	4	5
12	Devil's Elbow	431	393	4	1
13	The Water Hole	183	122	3	13
14	Fairgirth	413	391	4	3
15	Barnhourie	513	500	5	7
16	Wee Dunt	139	104	3	17
17	Roon The Bend	226	188	4	15
18	The Oaks	274	263	4	9

No. of holes: 18	Yardage: 4716	SSS: 67
GREEN FEES	Weekdays	
Individual round	£20	Gaz ref: Page 123
Daily rates	£20	Map ref: Page 156, D6
Are visitors free to play?	Yes	
Nearest Airport: Prestwick, 66.1 miles		Nearest Rail Station: Dumfries 19.7 miles

COLVEND GOLF CLUB

Sandyhills, Colvend, by Dalbeattie, DG5 4PY

Clubhouse	(01556) 630398
Pro Shop	-
Annual closure	Apr–Sep
Weekly closure	Tues, Thurs (early)

TO LOCATE THIS GOLF COURSE ON THE MAPS (p155-159) LOOK FOR THE FLAG WITH THIS PAGE NUMBER.

Wigtownshire County

Ladies' medal day was in full swing when I visited Glenluce last year – and how they were enjoying it! Granted, the weather was perfect, but the course was, as ever, in splendid condition and there was nothing but smiles from those doing battle with the eighteen holes. It's not true links, despite the proximity of the sea, but indisputably a super test of golf in a lovely spot.

hidden
gem

4th tee, Wigtownshire County.

HOLE	NAME	WHITE YARDS	YELLOW YARDS	PAR	STROKE INDEX	HOLE	NAME	WHITE YARDS	YELLOW YARDS	PAR	STROKE INDEX
1	The Ditch	332	–	4	9	10	The Mound	332	–	4	6
2	The Quarry	350	–	4	15	11	The Viaduct	294	–	4	12
3	The Bowl	402	–	4	2	12	Cunninghams Best	392	–	4	1
4	St Helena	301	–	4	11	13	The Target	152	–	3	17
5	Wee Dunt	162	–	3	18	14	The Mains	341	–	4	8
6	Blackthorn	491	–	5	7	15	Piltanton	372	–	4	5
7	The Runnel	363	–	4	3	16	Pees Weep	325	–	4	14
8	Balcarry	300	–	4	13	17	The Bay	196	–	3	16
9	The Castle	341	–	4	10	18	The Crook	397	–	4	4

No. of holes: 18	Yardage: 5847	SSS: 68
GREEN FEES	Weekdays	
Individual round	£18.50	Gaz ref: Page 142
Daily rates	£24	Map ref: Page 156, B6
Are visitors free to play?		Yes (except Weds after 5.30pm)
Nearest Airport: Prestwick, 61 miles		Nearest Rail Station: Stranraer, 9.1 miles

WIGTOWNSHIRE COUNTY GOLF CLUB

Mains of Park, Glenluce, Newton Stewart

Clubhouse	(01581) 300420
Pro Shop	-
Closure	No

TO LOCATE THIS GOLF COURSE ON THE MAPS (p155-159) LOOK FOR THE FLAG WITH THIS PAGE NUMBER.

Dumfries & County

The first voices I heard on my trip to Dumfries and County were again English. The popularity of these southern venues is amazing, but those visitors to whom I spoke were fulsome in their praise of a smashing course, looking, as ever, an absolute picture. The course may be a hole or two short of greatness, but its tightness is daunting, as many who regularly enjoy it will testify.

hidden gem

Short 6th, 'The Dell', Dumfries & County.

HOLE	NAME	WHITE YARDS	YELLOW YARDS	PAR	STROKE INDEX
1	Dhucorse	291	287	4	11
2	The Gully	395	380	4	5
3	The Rowans	329	253	4	9
4	Queensberry	327	313	4	15
5	Spion Kop	374	274	4	3
6	The Dell	178	164	3	17
7	Burns Walk	519	496	5	7
8	Lea Rig	433	406	4	1
9	Halfway Hill	172	165	3	13

HOLE	NAME	WHITE YARDS	YELLOW YARDS	PAR	STROKE INDEX
10	Straight Away	278	266	4	16
11	Lincluden	332	317	4	12
12	Nunholm	428	393	4	4
13	Edinburgh Road	450	413	4	2
14	The Wee Yin	90	90	3	18
15	Braid's Tree	371	352	4	8
16	The Rhodies	201	179	3	14
17	The Chesters	381	370	4	6
18	Doonhamer	379	289	4	10

No. of holes: 18	Yardage: 5928/5407	SSS: 69
GREEN FEES	Weekdays	
Individual round	£26	Gaz ref: Page 115
Daily rates	£26	Map ref: Page 156, E6
Are visitors free to play?		Yes (except Sat)
Nearest Airport: Prestwick, 63.2 miles		Nearest Rail Station: Dumfries 0.9 miles

DUMFRIES AND COUNTY GOLF CLUB

Nunfield, Edinburgh Road, Dumfries

Clubhouse	(01387) 253585
Pro Shop	(01387) 268918
Annual closure	No
Weekly closure	No

TO LOCATE THIS GOLF COURSE ON THE MAPS (p155-159) LOOK FOR THE FLAG WITH THIS PAGE NUMBER.

Lockerbie

It really is a pleasure to visit the lesser known Scottish venues and see the quality which is now evident in course presentation and appearance. Here is another which, despite having a few restrictions imposed by roads or difficult terrain, steadily matures and improves as the years go on and offers all who play a really good game of golf – and inevitably at a good price too; and the setting . . .

Short 8th, Lockerbie.

HOLE	NAME	WHITE YARDS	YELLOW YARDS	PAR	STROKE INDEX
1	Mounthoolie	357	–	4	3
2	Curling Pond	249	–	4	15
3	Drove Road	366	–	4	7
4	Braids Special	407	–	4	6
5	Hunstmans Way	218	–	3	10
6	The Beeches	375	–	4	9
7	Quhytewoolen	410	–	4	2
8	Little Ponds	121	–	3	16
9	The Butts	338	–	4	13

HOLE	NAME	WHITE YARDS	YELLOW YARDS	PAR	STROKE INDEX
10	Mid Annandale	360	–	4	11
11	The Brae	369	–	4	4
12	Wyllies Way	360	–	4	8
13	Lockerbie House	131	–	3	18
14	The Haas	401	–	4	1
15	St Blanes	326	–	4	12
16	Queensberry View	171	–	3	5
17	The Gully	334	–	4	14
18	Home	200	–	3	17

No. of holes: 18	Yardage: 5614	SSS: 67
GREEN FEES	Weekdays	
Individual round	£16	Gaz ref: Page 115
Daily rates	£16	Map ref: Page 156, E5
Are visitors free to play?	Yes	
Nearest Airport: Prestwick, 86.7 miles		Nearest Rail Station: Lockerbie, 0.4 miles

LOCKERBIE GOLF CLUB

Corrie Road, Lockerbie

Clubhouse	(01576) 203363
Pro Shop	-
Annual closure	No
Weekly closure	No

TO LOCATE THIS GOLF COURSE ON THE MAPS (p155-159) LOOK FOR THE FLAG WITH THIS PAGE NUMBER.

PLACES TO STAY AND EAT

Kirkcudbright

I encountered ten junior members at Kirkcudbright last year. Not one was over twelve and, with a couple of exceptions, they had swings I would die for. They were enjoying an after-school "quickie" on another busy Dumfries-shire venue, laid out above the town with lovely views of the Dee. Some hilly bits, a few blind shots, but smashing fun at the friendliest of locations.

14th green and The Dee, Kirkcudbright.

HOLE	NAME	WHITE YARDS	YELLOW YARDS	PAR	STROKE INDEX
1	Oppenheimer	330	310	4	9
2	Knowes	367	355	4	5
3	Banks	273	261	4	13
4	Hastings	327	301	4	7
5	Whins	429	384	4	3
6	Valley	135	134	3	17
7	Avenue	380	378	4	1
8	Jessie Robertson	469	477	5	11
9	Pond	190	176	3	15

HOLE	NAME	WHITE YARDS	YELLOW YARDS	PAR	STROKE INDEX
10	Boreland	344	330	4	8
11	Burn	326	279	4	12
12	Plantation	449	439	4/5	4
13	Spire View	167	161	3	16
14	Piggery	327	295	4	10
15	Clingans	228	213	3	14
16	Glebe	185	174	3	18
17	Glendroit	400	362	4	2
18	Galloway	391	383	4	6

No. of holes: 18	Yardage: 5739	SSS: 69
GREEN FEES	Weekdays	
Individual round	On application	Gaz ref: Page 123
Daily rates	On application	Map ref: Page 156, D6
Are visitors free to play?	Yes	
Nearest Airport: Prestwick, 59.3 miles	Nearest Rail Station: Dumfries, 27.3 miles	

KIRKCUDBRIGHTSHIRE GOLF CLUB

Stirling Crescent, Kirkcudbright
Clubhouse (01557) 330314
Pro Shop -
Annual closure No
Weekly closure No

TO LOCATE THIS GOLF COURSE ON THE MAPS (p155-159) LOOK FOR THE FLAG WITH THIS PAGE NUMBER.

Powfoot

I have made the point about the modesty of many of the D & G venues. Now here is one whose reputation goes before it and which rightly gets regular rave notices. It is a James Braid creation, where clever tee locations, in particular, force the player to concentrate on placement with the driver. With not one easy putt on any of the eighteen big greens, this is the epitome of links golf.

Short 12th, Powfoot.

HOLE	NAME	WHITE YARDS	YELLOW YARDS	PAR	STROKE INDEX
1	Corner	349	340	4	11
2	Fish House	474	459	5	9
3	Shore	442	428	4	1
4	Whins	357	331	4	13
5	Ridge	272	258	4	17
6	Dog Leg	349	341	4	3
7	Sand Hole	154	148	3	15
8	Warren	360	349	4	5
9	Crater	402	388	4	7

HOLE	NAME	WHITE YARDS	YELLOW YARDS	PAR	STROKE INDEX
10	Prairie	428	418	4	2
11	Sahara	313	300	4	10
12	Hogsback	156	135	3	18
13	Rushes	339	339	4	12
14	Long	498	489	5	6
15	Lake	200	181	3	16
16	Ryehill	427	380	4	4
17	Summit	332	322	4	14
18	Home	403	374	4	8

No. of holes: 18	Yardage: 6010	SSS: 70

POWFOOT GOLF CLUB

Powfoot, Annan, DG12 5QE

GREEN FEES	Weekdays	
Individual round	£23	Gaz ref: Page 115
Daily rates	£30	Map ref: Page 156, E6
Are visitors free to play?		Yes

Clubhouse	(01461) 700276
Pro Shop	(01461) 700327

Annual closure No
Weekly closure No

Nearest Airport: Prestwick, 76.3 miles   Nearest Rail Station: Annan, 4.2 miles

TO LOCATE THIS GOLF COURSE ON THE MAPS (p155-159) LOOK FOR THE FLAG WITH THIS PAGE NUMBER.

It is appropriate that we end our Galloway golf tour at this splendid club. The western shores of Loch Ryan and the parkland above yielded the Stranraer course, and on a warm summer day, there is nothing to beat a tussle with James Braid's final work of art. The great man never saw it completed (it opened in 1952), but the eighteenth, so aptly titled 'Braid's Last', brings a lump to your throat. His architectural genius is again so obvious as he links nature's gifts with man's needs in golf.

hidden **gem**

15th green, Stranraer.

HOLE	NAME	WHITE YARDS	YELLOW YARDS	PAR	STROKE INDEX
1	Garroway	319	281	4	16
2	Lea Rig	338	330	4	14
3	The Burn	420	403	4	4
4	Dandy Napper	324	317	4	12
5	Corunna	397	382	4	6
6	The Wig	160	149	3	10
7	The Heugh	381	369	4	8
8	Hillhead	315	308	4	18
9	Halfway Howff	458	417	4	2

HOLE	NAME	WHITE YARDS	YELLOW YARDS	PAR	STROKE INDEX
10	Craw's Nest	346	336	4	11
11	Bluidy Burn	377	372	4	3
12	Tattie Bogle	185	180	3	13
13	Lochswad	335	325	4	17
14	Lang Whang	513	496	5	7
15	Drums Tap	165	162	3	9
16	Creachmore	470	441	4	1
17	Kilmorrie	462	452	4	5
18	Braid's Last	343	336	4	15

No. of holes: 18	Yardage: 6308	SSS: 72	
GREEN FEES	Weekdays		
Individual round	£20	Gaz ref: Page 143	
Daily rates	£20	Map ref: Page 156, A6	
Are visitors free to play?		Yes	
Nearest Airport: Prestwick, 57.6 miles		Nearest Rail Station: Stranraer, 3 miles	

STRANRAER GOLF CLUB

Creachmore, Leswalt, Stranraer, DG9 OLF

Clubhouse	(01776) 870245
Pro Shop	-
Annual closure	No
Weekly closure	No

TO LOCATE THIS GOLF COURSE ON THE MAPS (p155-159) LOOK FOR THE FLAG WITH THIS PAGE NUMBER.

Leven

The first of the tough links courses as you reach the East Neuk of Fife (Leven has been an Open Qualifier for a long number of years) makes for a splendid start to a seaside golfing bonanza in 'The Kingdom'. If you happen to catch it on a calm day, you'll wonder how so many find a course with plenty room and big greens such a problem . Hang about until the wind gets up and you'll find out!

Looking down the 7th, Leven.

HOLE	NAME	WHITE YARDS	YELLOW YARDS	PAR	STROKE INDEX
1	Table	413	386	4	5
2	Knowe	381	329	4	9
3	Bents	343	314	4	11
4	Sea	449	392	4	3
5	Valley	158	140	3	17
6	Silverburn N	567	549	5	1
7	Corriemar	184	151	3	15
8	Bing	348	350	4	7
9	Pavillion	164	173	3	18

HOLE	NAME	WHITE YARDS	YELLOW YARDS	PAR	STROKE INDEX
10	Cattle Creep	325	303	4	13
11	Boundary	363	333	4	10
12	Silverburn S	482	444	4	2
13	Seg	482	458	4	4
14	Dykeneuk	332	302	4	8
15	Railway	188	166	3	16
16	Circus	386	371	4	6
17	Howe	414	404	4	14
18	Scoonie	457	448	4	12

No. of holes: 18	Yardage: 6436	SSS: 70
GREEN FEES	Weekdays	
Individual round	On application	Gaz ref: Page 119
Daily rates	On application	Map ref: Page 157, B2
Are visitors free to play?	Yes	
Nearest Airport: Edinburgh, 34 miles	Nearest Rail Station: Markinch, 6.4 miles	

LEVEN LINKS GOLF COURSE

The Promenade, Leven, KY8 4HS

Clubhouse   (01333) 428859
Pro Shop   -
Annual closure No
Weekly closure No

TO LOCATE THIS GOLF COURSE ON THE MAPS (p155-159) LOOK FOR THE FLAG WITH THIS PAGE NUMBER.

Lundin Links

I find it quite impossible to omit this wonderful links – "joined at the waist" with Leven – from my annual look at Fife. Leaving out the Open venues, I consider the first four holes here to be the hardest start in Scottish links golf. It doesn't get a lot easier, although the top of the course offers a brief respite from the links. Superb entertainment is guaranteed on yet another Open Qualifying test.

8th green, Lundin.

HOLE	NAME	WHITE YARDS	YELLOW YARDS	PAR	STROKE INDEX	HOLE	NAME	WHITE YARDS	YELLOW YARDS	PAR	STROKE INDEX
1	High	424	–	4	5	10	Thorn Tree	353	–	4	10
2	Quarry	346	–	4	9	11	Racecourse	466	–	4	6
3	Bents	335	–	4	15	12	Sunnybraes	150	–	3	17
4	Mile Dyke	452	–	4	3	13	Neil Shaw	512	–	5	2
5	Silverburn	140	–	3	18	14	Perfection	175	–	3	16
6	Spectacles	330	–	4	11	15	Heather	418	–	4	4
7	Burn	273	–	4	13	16	Trows	314	–	4	14
8	Aithernie	364	–	4	7	17	Station	345	–	4	8
9	Long	555	–	5	1	18	Home	442	–	4	12

No. of holes: 18	Yardage: 6394	SSS: 71
GREEN FEES	Weekdays	
Individual round	£32	Gaz ref: Page 120
Daily rates	£40	Map ref: Page 157, B1
Are visitors free to play?	Yes	
Nearest Airport: Edinburgh, 35.7 miles		Nearest Rail Station: Markinch, 7.8 miles

LUNDIN GOLF CLUB

Golf Road, Lundin Links, KY8 6BA

Clubhouse	(01333) 320202
Pro Shop	-
Annual closure	No
Weekly closure	No

TO LOCATE THIS GOLF COURSE ON THE MAPS (p155-159) LOOK FOR THE FLAG WITH THIS PAGE NUMBER.

Elie

The immortal James Braid's home course – he learned all he knew here – this ancient links boasts not one par five. Do not let that lull you into any false sense of security. Pot bunkers galore, typical heughs and howes, clever tee and green positions (particularly the latter on which, over eighteen holes, not one easy putt is offered) combine to provide the epitome of Scottish links golf.

13th green, Elie.

HOLE	NAME	WHITE YARDS	YELLOW YARDS	PAR	STROKE INDEX	HOLE	NAME	WHITE YARDS	YELLOW YARDS	PAR	STROKE INDEX
1	Stacks	420	–	4	12	10	Lundar Law	288	–	4	9
2	High Hole	284	–	4	3	11	Sea Hole	131	–	3	12
3	Wickets	214	–	3	17	12	Bents	466	–	4	2
4	Provost	378	–	4	6	13	Croupie	380	–	4	11
5	Doctor	365	–	4	13	14	Suckielea	414	–	4	5
6	Quarries	316	–	4	7	15	Coalhill	338	–	4	16
7	Peggy's	252	–	4	15	16	Grange	407	–	4	4
8	Neuk	382	–	4	1	17	Ferry	439	–	4	14
9	Martin's Bay	440	–	4	10	18	Home	359	–	4	8

No. of holes: 18	Yardage: 6273	SSS: 70
GREEN FEES	Weekdays	
Individual round	On application	Gaz ref: Page 118
Daily rates	On application	Map ref: Page 157, B2
Are visitors free to play?		Yes
Nearest Airport: Edinburgh, 42.5 miles		Nearest Rail Station: Markinch, 14.5 miles

THE GOLF HOUSE CLUB

Elie, Fife, KY9 1AS

Clubhouse	(01333) 330301
Pro Shop	(01333) 330955

Annual closure No
Weekly closure No

TO LOCATE THIS GOLF COURSE ON THE MAPS (p155-159) LOOK FOR THE FLAG WITH THIS PAGE NUMBER.

Still one of Scotland's most heavily visited venues, now with the Craighead course as a second offering to the legendary Balcomie Links, Crail's popularity grows year-on-year. The Craighead is different in all respects from the old course; it's much longer, reveals modern design features and doesn't have the scenic bit. It's a great foil,though, and fulfills the demand for more room at a fine club.

hidden gem

14th green, Balcomie Links, Crail.

HOLE	NAME	WHITE YARDS	YELLOW YARDS	PAR	STROKE INDEX
1	–	328	319	4	17
2	–	494	453	5	5
3	–	184	167	3	13
4	–	346	317	4	7
5	–	459	449	4	1
6	–	186	170	3	9
7	–	349	288	4	11
8	–	442	425	4	3
9	–	306	253	4	15

HOLE	NAME	WHITE YARDS	YELLOW YARDS	PAR	STROKE INDEX
10	–	336	287	4	12
11	–	496	428	5	8
12	–	528	519	5	4
13	–	219	208	3	6
14	–	150	140	3	16
15	–	270	260	4	18
16	–	163	156	3	14
17	–	463	418	4	2
18	–	203	196	3	10

No. of holes: 18	Yardage: 5922	SSS: 69
GREEN FEES	Weekdays	
Individual round	£25	Gaz ref: Page 118
Daily rates	£38	Map ref: Page 157, C1
Are visitors free to play?		Yes
Nearest Airport: Edinburgh, 53.4 miles		Nearest Rail Station: Leuchars, 17.2 miles

CRAIL GOLFING SOCIETY

Balcomie Club House, Fifeness,
Crail, KY10 3XN

Clubhouse   (01333) 450686
Pro Shop   (01333) 450278
Annual closure No
Weekly closure No

TO LOCATE THIS GOLF COURSE ON THE MAPS (p155-159) LOOK FOR THE FLAG WITH THIS PAGE NUMBER.

Kingsbarns

The newcomer to links golf in Fife, this wonderfully scenic layout could be destined for great things. In a couple of years, the world will be raving about it – already the Dunhill Cup is booked in for next year. It has been carefully nurtured with no acceleration of growth from artificial means, and Kyle Phillips' design is stunning. It's not cheap, but it is certain to attract golfers in their thousands over the next few years. Remember the name – and watch this space!

Short 13th, Kingsbarns.

HOLE	NAME	WHITE YARDS	YELLOW YARDS	PAR	STROKE INDEX
1	–	388	370	4	7
2	–	190	165	3	13
3	–	502	471	5	11
4	–	389	365	4	5
5	–	370	350	4	9
6	–	318	287	4	15
7	–	436	421	4	1
8	–	154	132	3	17
9	–	536	500	5	3

HOLE	NAME	WHITE YARDS	YELLOW YARDS	PAR	STROKE INDEX
10	–	373	353	4	14
11	–	425	369	4	8
12	–	566	538	5	2
13	–	135	123	3	18
14	–	335	307	4	16
15	–	185	151	3	10
16	–	504	481	5	12
17	–	432	408	4	6
18	–	414	383	4	4

No. of holes: 18	Yardage: 6652	SSS: -	
GREEN FEES	Weekdays		
Individual round	£105	Gaz ref: Page 120	
Daily rates	£155	Map ref: Page 157, C1	
Are visitors free to play?		Yes	
Nearest Airport: Edinburgh, 54.3 miles		Nearest Rail Station: Leuchars, 13.8 miles	

KINGSBARNS GOLF LINKS

Kingsbarns, St Andrews

Clubhouse   (01334) 460860
Pro Shop   (01334) 460865
Annual closure Dec–Mar
Weekly closure

TO LOCATE THIS GOLF COURSE ON THE MAPS (p155-159) LOOK FOR THE FLAG WITH THIS PAGE NUMBER.

Duke's Course

This great golfing test above St Andrews is suddenly not the newcomer to Fife golf, with Kingsbarns and St Andrews Bay now on stream. Yet Peter Thomson's cracking layout is a splendid test for all, if a bit on the tough side for the higher handicaps. The 'remoteness' of the second half is a possible negative if form lapses, but a round to handicap is a fine effort on the Duke's.

8th green, Duke's Course.

HOLE	NAME	WHITE YARDS	YELLOW YARDS	PAR	STROKE INDEX
1	Highland	479	472	5	12
2	Drumcarrow	421	336	4	4
3	Denhead	140	151	3	18
4	Roundel	404	397	4	14
5	Beeches	343	336	4	16
6	Badgers	510	455	5	8
7	Denbrae	431	400	4	6
8	Fair Dunt	185	161	3	2
9	Craigtoun	393	327	4	10

HOLE	NAME	WHITE YARDS	YELLOW YARDS	PAR	STROKE INDEX
10	Burn Brig	403	396	4	7
11	Feddinch	578	547	5	15
12	Double Dyke	192	134	3	3
13	Braw View	366	359	4	9
14	Well	435	408	4	1
15	Steading	501	465	5	11
16	Lumbo	410	403	4	17
17	Melville	177	167	3	13
18	Ice House	381	350	4	5

No. of holes: 18	Yardage: 6749	SSS: 73
GREEN FEES	Weekdays	
Individual round	£50	Gaz ref: Page 120
Daily rates	£90	Map ref: Page 157, B1
Are visitors free to play?	Yes	
Nearest Airport: Edinburgh, 46.8 miles	Nearest Rail Station: Leuchars, 7 miles	

DUKE'S COURSE

Craigton, St Andrews, KY16 8NS

Clubhouse	(01334) 470214
Pro Shop	(01334) 470214
Annual closure	No
Weekly closure	No

TO LOCATE THIS GOLF COURSE ON THE MAPS (p155-159) LOOK FOR THE FLAG WITH THIS PAGE NUMBER.

Scotscraig

Sixteen visiting American golfers were waiting to tee off as we completed our round here last July. Secretary Barry Liddle told me that twelve more beat us to it earlier! That says it all about a terrific – and underestimated – Fife venue, where one superb hole follows another. Be erratic off the tee at your peril; think your way around and you'll score. Play it when it's fast; it is a pure treat.

7th, Scotscraig.

HOLE	NAME	WHITE YARDS	YELLOW YARDS	PAR	STROKE INDEX
1	Admiral	402	–	4	9
2	Wood	374	–	4	15
3	Gully	214	–	3	5
4	Westward Ho	366	–	4	1
5	Whins	402	–	4	13
6	Pond	150	–	3	17
7	Plateau	401	–	4	3
8	High	387	–	4	7
9	Flagstaff	484	–	5	11

HOLE	NAME	WHITE YARDS	YELLOW YARDS	PAR	STROKE INDEX
10	Cricket	404	–	4	12
11	Shanwell	459	–	4	4
12	Rushes	389	–	4	8
13	Island	165	–	3	18
14	Garpit	523	–	5	2
15	Burn	175	–	3	14
16	Railway	479	–	5	6
17	Road	380	–	4	16
18	Home	396	–	4	10

No. of holes: 18	Yardage: 6550	SSS: 72
GREEN FEES	Weekdays	
Individual round	On application	Gaz ref: Page 121
Daily rates	On application	Map ref: Page 155, B7
Are visitors free to play?	Yes	
Nearest Airport: Edinburgh, 54.6 miles	Nearest Rail Station: Leuchars, 6 miles	

SCOTSCRAIG GOLF CLUB

Golf Road, Tayport, DD6 9DZ

Clubhouse	(01382) 552515
Pro Shop	-
Annual closure	No
Weekly closure	No

TO LOCATE THIS GOLF COURSE ON THE MAPS (p155-159) LOOK FOR THE FLAG WITH THIS PAGE NUMBER.

Burntisland

One of Fife's friendliest clubs proudly boasts one of its most spectacular golfing offerings into the bargain. This little adventure has a stiffish and unspectacular start but from the fourth to the eighteenth, the challenge, the vistas on offer across the Forth, the continuous change of direction and the need to be in total control of your game combine to provide a memorable day's golf.

hidden **gem**

Looking down the 4th, Burntisland.

HOLE	NAME	WHITE YARDS	YELLOW YARDS	PAR	STROKE INDEX	HOLE	NAME	WHITE YARDS	YELLOW YARDS	PAR	STROKE INDEX
1	Farm Cottage	303	–	4	16	10	Kingswood	342	–	4	11
2	Low Binn	534	–	5	3	11	Hawthorns	350	–	4	5
3	Whinnyhall	223	–	3	8	12	The Quarry	491	–	5	1
4	Grangehill	363	–	4	10	13	Dodhead	369	–	4	7
5	The Pond	146	–	3	18	14	The Delves	361	–	4	9
6	Inchkeith	161	–	3	13	15	High Binn	317	–	4	17
7	Langbank	349	–	4	6	16	The Gully	400	–	4	4
8	Black Rock	393	–	4	2	17	The Bottle	151	–	3	12
9	Crow Wood	347	–	4	15	18	Coronation '53	365	–	4	14

No. of holes: 18	Yardage: 5897	SSS: 70
GREEN FEES	Weekdays	
Individual round	£15	Gaz ref: Page 117
Daily rates	£25	Map ref: Page 157, A2
Are visitors free to play?		Yes
Nearest Airport: Edinburgh, 18.6 miles		Nearest Rail Station: Burntisland, 1 mile

BURNTISLAND GOLF HOUSE CLUB

Dodhead, Burntisland

Clubhouse	(01592) 874093
Pro Shop	(01592) 872116
Annual closure	No
Weekly closure	No

TO LOCATE THIS GOLF COURSE ON THE MAPS (p155-159) LOOK FOR THE FLAG WITH THIS PAGE NUMBER.

PLACES TO STAY AND EAT

Tell them you saw them in Scotland Home of Golf

Less than five minutes from the famous Royal Aberdeen Golf Club, the Patio Hotel can boast 20 golf courses within 30 minutes drive. Scotland's premier drive range and largest golf superstore is two minutes drive from the Hotel. 124 beautifully appointed double and twin rooms, some with stunning sea views. Indulge in delicious, freshly prepared meals served in one of our award-winning restaurants or a light lunch in our Cafe bar. Complimentary membership of Breakers' Leisure Club with indoor pool, saunas, Turkish steam and spa baths, solarium, treatment room and fully equipped gym.

PATIO HOTEL

★ ★ ★ ★

STB 4-Star Highly Commended   AA 4-Star

BEACH BOULEVARD, ABERDEEN AB24 5EF
TEL: 01224 633339 • FAX: 01224 638833

www.patiohotels.com
e-mail: patiosales@globalnet.co.uk

THE SPIRES

executive apartments

We have all your accomodation needs down to a tee.

Our luxury, fully furnished two bedroom apartments are ideal for your golfing break or business trip.

With bookings available from one night upward we guarantee a warm Aberdonian welcome.

All that we ask is that you remember to take your golf clubs.

For further details or to make a booking please contact Liam or Susan on Aberdeen (01224) 209991.

The Spires executive apartments, 531 Great Western Road, Aberdeen. www.thespires.co.uk

---

Open every day of the week,
12.00 - 2.00pm and 6.30 - 10.00pm
400 wines, 100 malts, 70 cognacs

The finest Aberdeenshire Steak, Scottish Lobster and seafood restaurant in North East Scotland

The Marcliffe at Pitfodels

North Deeside Road, Pitfodels, Aberdeen AB15 9YA
Tel: 01244 861000 Fax: 01224 868860
http://www.marcliffe.com
E-mail: enquiries@marcliffe.com

Royal Aberdeen

Carnoustie's Bob Simpson was responsible for the original design of Balgownie while the great James Braid latterly had a hand in it too. The greatest contributor, however, was Mother Nature, who donated the most glorious succession of dunes and sandhills through which the architects have threaded this great course. One of the most natural links in Scotland – and one of the best.

Short 8th, Royal Aberdeen.

HOLE	NAME	WHITE YARDS	YELLOW YARDS	PAR	STROKE INDEX	HOLE	NAME	WHITE YARDS	YELLOW YARDS	PAR	STROKE INDEX
1	First	409	–	4	9	10	Shelter	342	–	4	8
2	Pool	530	–	5	11	11	Short	166	–	3	16
3	Cottage	223	–	3	13	12	Plateau	383	–	4	4
4	Valley	423	–	4	1	13	Blind	375	–	4	10
5	Road	326	–	4	15	14	Dyke	390	–	4	2
6	Scotson	486	–	5	7	15	Well	341	–	4	14
7	Blackdog	375	–	4	3	16	Hill	389	–	4	6
8	Ridge	147	–	3	17	17	Pots	180	–	3	18
9	End	453	–	4	5	18	Home	434	–	4	12

No. of holes: 18	Yardage: 6403	SSS: 71
GREEN FEES	Weekdays	
Individual round	£60	Gaz ref: Page 103
Daily rates	£85	Map ref: Page 155, D3
Are visitors free to play?		Yes

Nearest Airport: Aberdeen, 7.2 miles	Nearest Rail Station: Aberdeen, 3.8 miles

ROYAL ABERDEEN GOLF CLUB

Links Road, Bridge of Don,
Aberdeen, AB23 8AT

Clubhouse (01224) 702571
Pro Shop (01224) 702221
Annual closure No
Weekly closure No

TO LOCATE THIS GOLF COURSE ON THE MAPS (p155-159) LOOK FOR THE FLAG WITH THIS PAGE NUMBER.

You can shake hands with Royal Aberdeen members at the southern end of this terrific, buttesting links. It is not a place to spray the ball and newcomers inevitably find themselves a club short of the correct choice. Again this is such a natural course that devious tee and green placements (several of the latter being hidden for approach shots) seem superfluous, but it's fun on typical coastal terrain.

hidden gem

3rd green, Murcar.

HOLE	NAME	WHITE YARDS	YELLOW YARDS	PAR	STROKE INDEX
1	Bothy	322	300	4	13
2	Pond	367	340	4	9
3	Ice House	401	380	4	4
4	Pool	489	423	5	7
5	Plateau	162	152	3	17
6	Seaton	447	421	4	2
7	Serpentine	423	411	4	6
8	Park Hill	383	362	4	11
9	Black Dog	323	280	4	15

HOLE	NAME	WHITE YARDS	YELLOW YARDS	PAR	STROKE INDEX
10	Tarbothill	402	385	4	1
11	Railway	338	312	4	10
12	Strabathie	155	144	3	16
13	Point	386	365	4	3
14	Mundurno	482	442	5	12
15	Field	351	332	4	8
16	Nipper	160	139	3	18
17	H'mm'cks	367	307	4	5
18	Home	329	314	4	14

No. of holes: 18	Yardage: 6287	SSS: 71	
GREEN FEES	Weekdays		
Individual round	On application	Gaz ref: Page 103	
Daily rates	On application	Map ref: Page 155, D3	
Are visitors free to play?		Yes	
Nearest Airport: Aberdeen, 8.3 miles		Nearest Rail Station: Aberdeen, 5.3 miles	

MURCAR GOLF CLUB

Bridge of Don, Aberdeen, AB23 8BD

Clubhouse   (01224) 704354
Pro Shop   -
Annual closure No
Weekly closure No

TO LOCATE THIS GOLF COURSE ON THE MAPS (p155-159) LOOK FOR THE FLAG WITH THIS PAGE NUMBER.

Newburgh-On-Ythan

Extended to eighteen holes within the last couple of years, here is a smashing alternative to the more weel-kent links in this part of Buchan. Basically it divides in two; a flat section around the south bank of the Ythan and the new holes on rising ground behind the big new clubhouse (a community effort incorporating squash as well.) If the committee get this right, it must turn out to be the perfect complement to illustrious neighbours. At 6162 yards, it is ideal leisure golf.

8th green, Newburgh-on-Ythan.

HOLE	NAME	WHITE YARDS	YELLOW YARDS	PAR	STROKE INDEX
1	Forswiftit	385	–	4	1
2	Neebra	224	–	3	5
3	Pitscaff	467	–	5	14
4	Drovers	285	–	4	16
5	St Peter's Well	201	–	3	10
6	Forvie	343	–	4	6
7	Funs Gap	288	–	4	11
8	Puddock's Pond	313	–	4	7
9	Corf House	482	–	5	4

HOLE	NAME	WHITE YARDS	YELLOW YARDS	PAR	STROKE INDEX
10	Gallows Hill	338	–	4	12
11	Pavilion	390	–	4	8
12	Home	428	–	4	2
13	Majuba	316	–	4	17
14	Prince Charlie	347	–	4	15
15	Boathouse	305	–	4	18
16	Short	148	–	3	9
17	Billow's Lime	354	–	4	13
18	Springbok	548	–	5	3

No. of holes: 18	Yardage: 6162	SSS: 70
GREEN FEES	Weekdays	
Individual round	£16	Gaz ref: Page 105
Daily rates	£21	Map ref: Page 155, E3
Are visitors free to play?	Yes	
Nearest Airport: Aberdeen, 17.5 miles		Nearest Rail Station: Aberdeen, 13.7 miles

NEWBURGH-ON-YTHAN GOLF CLUB

Beach Road, Newburgh, AB41 6BE

Clubhouse	(01358) 789058
Pro Shop	-
Annual closure	No
Weekly closure	No

TO LOCATE THIS GOLF COURSE ON THE MAPS (p155-159) LOOK FOR THE FLAG WITH THIS PAGE NUMBER.

Royal Tarlair

There's a par three here which would not be out of place at Pebble Beach. The tee is high above the cliffs east of Macduff; the green is 152 yards below on a little oasis of clifftop grass. Do not underclub! Royal Tarlair's 5800 yards or so are modest and roomy. There are no trees, plenty of open space and, unless you are really wild, rough is forgiving. It's a lovely, lush holiday course.

hidden gem

Short 13th, Tarlair.

HOLE	NAME	WHITE YARDS	YELLOW YARDS	PAR	STROKE INDEX
1	Duff	292	270	4	11
2	Leys	363	355	4	7
3	Quarry	125	120	3	17
4	Braes	477	476	5	3
5	Plateau	289	292	4	13
6	Hillock	410	402	4	5
7	Fife	176	167	3	15
8	Langshank	483	483	5	1
9	Gamrie	351	334	4	9

HOLE	NAME	WHITE YARDS	YELLOW YARDS	PAR	STROKE INDEX
10	Park	353	340	4	8
11	Cornhill	345	348	4	10
12	Morven	331	319	4	12
13	Clivet	152	144	3	18
14	Moray	276	271	4	14
15	Monument	363	353	4	6
16	Lang Stracht	477	454	5	2
17	Howe	221	214	3	16
18	Doune	380	374	4	4

No. of holes: 18	Yardage: 5866	SSS: 68	
GREEN FEES	Weekdays		
Individual round	£10	Gaz ref: Page 113	
Daily rates	£15	Map ref: Page 155, C1	
Are visitors free to play?	Yes		
Nearest Airport: Aberdeen, 41.6 miles		Nearest Rail Station: Keith, 23.1miles	

ROYAL TARLAIR GOLF CLUB

Buchan Street, Macduff, AB44 1TA

Clubhouse   (01261) 832897
Pro Shop   -
Annual closure No
Weekly closure No

TO LOCATE THIS GOLF COURSE ON THE MAPS (p155-159) LOOK FOR THE FLAG WITH THIS PAGE NUMBER.

Hopeman

In May, this haven of seaside golf is spectacular. Gorse and broom cover almost the entire acreage and you see nothing but a blaze of yellow all around. The modest 5600 yards conceal some tricky challenges, with narrow fairways, smallish greens and the aforesaid rough stuff only too eager to grab the strays. An epic par three, but 106 yards from the tee to a prospective watery grave, is classic. It's the epitome of Scottish holiday golf, with the warmest of welcomes in a lovely, homely clubhouse.

hidden gem

Looking down 14th, Hopeman.

HOLE	NAME	WHITE YARDS	YELLOW YARDS	PAR	STROKE INDEX	HOLE	NAME	WHITE YARDS	YELLOW YARDS	PAR	STROKE INDEX
1	Morven	371	–	4	7	10	More	299	–	4	16
2	Munro	352	–	4	1	11	Warren	365	–	4	5
3	Picklelaw	174	–	3	13	12	Prieshach	152	–	3	14
4	Road	471	–	5	17	13	Lodge	344	–	4	8
5	Williamston	342	–	4	11	14	Doon Hill	383	–	4	6
6	Morras Woodie	397	–	4	3	15	Nesses	106	–	3	18
7	Ditches	198	–	3	10	16	Daisy Rock	384	–	4	2
8	Heathery	346	–	4	9	17	Braemou	194	–	3	12
9	Quarry	302	–	4	15	18	Bagley	410	–	4	4

No. of holes: 18	Yardage: 5590	SSS: 67
GREEN FEES	Weekdays	
Individual round	On application	Gaz ref: Page 133
Daily rates	On application	Map ref:Page 155, A1
Are visitors free to play?	Yes	
Nearest Airport: Inverness, 39 miles		Nearest Rail Station: Elgin, 7.7 miles

HOPEMAN GOLF CLUB

Hopeman, Elgin, IV30 5YA

Clubhouse   (01343) 830578
Pro Shop   -
Annual closure No
Weekly closure No

TO LOCATE THIS GOLF COURSE ON THE MAPS (p155-159) LOOK FOR THE FLAG WITH THIS PAGE NUMBER.

Nairn Dunbar

One is always open to criticism for being over-generous to a town or region. I make no apologies for including Nairn's two great courses this time around. You will get nary a glimpse of the sea from this one, although the terrain is mainly links, with heath and a bit of parkland thrown in. It is longer than its neighbour and has a great finish; three fives might well win the sweep! Fierce rough and plenty other natural hazards are cleverly brought into play on an outstanding layout.

hidden **gem**

Looking to the 10th, Nairn Dunbar.

HOLE	NAME	WHITE YARDS	YELLOW YARDS	PAR	STROKE INDEX
1	Moray Firth	418	404	4	5
2	Hilton	333	300	4	15
3	Lochloy	189	173	3	13
4	Braids	448	423	4	8
5	View Hill	453	445	4	1
6	Table	419	412	4	7
7	King Steps	395	384	4	3
8	Brodie	163	134	3	17
9	Old Bar	501	479	5	10

HOLE	NAME	WHITE YARDS	YELLOW YARDS	PAR	STROKE INDEX
10	Westward Ho	414	367	4	2
11	Bents	126	114	3	18
12	Birches	381	360	4	9
13	Long Peter	529	511	5	6
14	The Flats	346	342	4	14
15	Harbour	161	154	3	16
16	Spires	503	476	5	11
17	Burn	442	337	4	4
18	Merryton	499	477	5	12

No. of holes: 18	Yardage: 6720	SSS: 73
GREEN FEES	Weekdays	
Individual round	£25	Gaz ref: Page 133
Daily rates	£33	Map ref: Page 154, E4
Are visitors free to play?		Yes

Nearest Airport: Inverness, 17.8 miles   Nearest Rail Station: Nairn, 0.9 miles

NAIRN DUNBAR GOLF COURSE

Lochloy Road, Nairn, IV12 5AE

Clubhouse   (01667) 452741
Pro Shop   (01667) 453964
Annual closure No
Weekly closure No

TO LOCATE THIS GOLF COURSE ON THE MAPS (p155-159) LOOK FOR THE FLAG WITH THIS PAGE NUMBER.

Nairn

The reputation of the west course, host to the last Walker Cup, goes before it. One magnificent golf hole follows another; the outward opening stretch is invariably into the teeth of the wind and the contest could be finished by the turn if you struggle to keep straight. Huge greens can play all sort of tricks on you (stand up James Braid and Old Tom Morris!) It is just magical seaside golf.

2nd green, Nairn.

HOLE	NAME	WHITE YARDS	YELLOW YARDS	PAR	STROKE INDEX
1	Sea	–	400	4	10
2	Anchareidh	–	474	4	2
3	Nest	–	377	4	6
4	Bunker	–	146	3	18
5	Nets	–	390	4	4
6	Ben Wyvis	–	185	3	8
7	Long	–	494	5	16
8	Deinies	–	330	4	14
9	Icehouse	–	325	4	12

HOLE	NAME	WHITE YARDS	YELLOW YARDS	PAR	STROKE INDEX
10	Cawdor	–	500	5	15
11	Gate	–	163	3	17
12	Table	–	445	4	5
13	Crown	–	430	4	1
14	Kopjes	–	206	3	7
15	Sutors	–	309	4	13
16	Road	–	418	4	3
17	Burn	–	364	4	9
18	Home	–	516	5	11

No. of holes: 18	Yardage: 6745	SSS: 74
GREEN FEES	Weekdays	
Individual round	£70	Gaz ref: Page 133
Daily rates	-	Map ref: Page 154, E4
Are visitors free to play?	Yes	
Nearest Airport: Inverness, 17.8 miles	Nearest Rail Station: Nairn, 1.4 miles	

THE NAIRN GOLF CLUB

Seabank Road, Nairn

Clubhouse   (01667) 453208
Pro Shop   (01667) 452787
Annual closure No
Weekly closure No

TO LOCATE THIS GOLF COURSE ON THE MAPS (p155-159) LOOK FOR THE FLAG WITH THIS PAGE NUMBER.

Fraserburgh

My publisher raised his eyebrows when told I was including Scotland's most north-easterly course. Naturally, like many others, he had never heard it mentioned. That's the way the locals like it, but this tremendous, narrow course where only two holes don't run on a direct north to south axis is cracking. Brilliantly carved from huge dunes, it can be windy, which necessitates straightness, but if it should fall apart, enjoy the experience and the terrific views of Fraserburgh and the North Sea.

hidden gem

Short 17th, Fraserburgh

HOLE	NAME	WHITE YARDS	YELLOW YARDS	PAR	STROKE INDEX
1	Corbie Hill	–	404	4	2
2	Braid's Bellow	–	363	4	4
3	Whyte's Shelter	–	295	4	16
4	The Plateau	–	307	4	8
5	The Hump	–	180	3	15
6	The Cottage	–	497	5	12
7	The Well	–	131	3	13
8	The Spruces	–	360	4	9
9	Lang Whang	–	450	4	1

HOLE	NAME	WHITE YARDS	YELLOW YARDS	PAR	STROKE INDEX
10	Solitude	–	277	4	17
11	Elsie's	–	310	4	6
12	The Castle	–	364	4	5
13	The Hillocks	–	305	4	18
14	Homeward	–	189	3	14
15	The Bent's	–	508	5	11
16	The Valley	–	345	4	10
17	Peninsula	–	154	3	7
18	The Bridge	–	378	4	3

No. of holes: 18	Yardage: 6279	SSS: 70
GREEN FEES	Weekdays	
Individual round	£20	Gaz ref: Page 104
Daily rates	£20	Map ref: Page 155, E1
Are visitors free to play?		Yes

Nearest Airport: Aberdeen, 44.7 miles   Nearest Rail Station: Aberdeen, 41.1 miles

FRASERBURGH GOLF CLUB

Fraserburgh, Aberdeenshire

Clubhouse	(01346) 518287
Pro Shop	-
Annual closure	No
Weekly closure	No

TO LOCATE THIS GOLF COURSE ON THE MAPS (p155-159) LOOK FOR THE FLAG WITH THIS PAGE NUMBER.

The Isle of Arran extraordinarily sports seven courses. Most are probably better known than Corrie, but none offers the friendliness of welcome or amazing setting of the nine holes here at the foot of Glen Sannox. You head straight up the glen towards the Goat Fell range in a progression of par threes and fours on heathland, aiming for pretty small but velvet greens. It is thrilling stuff of which the most entertaining holiday golf is made and the memories of a round here will last a lifetime.

hidden gem

2nd green, Corrie.

HOLE	NAME	WHITE YARDS	YELLOW YARDS	PAR	STROKE INDEX	HOLE	NAME	WHITE YARDS	YELLOW YARDS	PAR	STROKE INDEX
1	–	139	128	3	17	10	–	139	128	3	18
2	–	199	135	3	3	11	–	199	135	3	4
3	–	251	230	4	5	12	–	251	230	4	6
4	–	171	121	3	13	13	–	171	121	3	14
5	–	128	114	3	11	14	–	128	114	3	12
6	–	320	270	4	1	15	–	320	270	4	2
7	–	306	300	4	9	16	–	360	300	4	10
8	–	160	110	3	15	17	–	160	110	3	16
9	–	274	230	4	7	18	–	274	230	4	8

No. of holes: 9	Yardage: 1948	SSS: 61		**CORRIE GOLF CLUB**
GREEN FEES	Weekdays			Sannox, Isle of Arran, KA27 8JD
Individual round	On application	Gaz ref: Page 143		Clubhouse (01770) 810223
Daily rates	On application	Map ref:		Pro Shop -
Are visitors free to play?		Yes		Annual closure No
Nearest Airport: Prestwick, 25 miles		Nearest Rail Station: Ardrossan, by ferry		Weekly closure No

TO LOCATE THIS GOLF COURSE ON THE MAPS (p155-159) LOOK FOR THE FLAG WITH THIS PAGE NUMBER.

Navidale House Hotel

Country House Hotel with gardens and grounds set in a spectacular cliff-top
location with outstanding views across Moray Firth.
Recently refurbished to a high standard, the hotel is ideally located for exploring
the north of Scotland or as a base for fishing, golf, hillwalking or birdwatching.
Restaurant featuring fresh local produce including fish, seafood and game.
A warm welcome awaits the discerning traveller.

Dinner, bed and breakfast from £60 per person.

– Two newly completed self catering lodges –
Helmsdale, Sutherland KW8 6JS

www.contact-my-idea.com/navidale/navidalehouse.htm.

Tel: 01431 821258 Fax: 01431 821531

Glenaveron is a luxurious Edwardian house set in extensive mature gardens only a few minutes walk from
Brora's challenging *James Braid golf course*. Other courses close by include the famous *Royal Dornoch*, the lovely
Golspie course and the exclusive *Carnegie Club* at Skibo Castle. When not golfing, Glenaveron is a superb base for touring the
Northern Highlands. We are close to *wonderful beaches* and great sites of historical interest. We can offer you safe parking
and our facilities are some of the best in the Highlands. *Golf in some of the most beautiful scenery in Scotland.*

GLENAVERON

Golf Road, Brora, Sutherland KW9 6QS
Tel/Fax: 01408 621601, E-mail: glenaveron@hotmail.com, www.glenaveron.co.uk

STB ★ ★ ★ ★   AA ♦ ♦ ♦ ♦

PITGRUDY
CARAVAN PARK

Poles Road, Dornoch, Sutherland IV25 3HY
Tel: 01862 821253 Fax: 01862 821382
www.host.co.uk

OPEN: May - September
40 touring pitches. £7.50-9 per pitch per night.
10 holiday caravans, sleeping 2-5. £95-£295 per week.

Enjoy the peace and quiet with panoramic views over the
Dornoch Firth. A golfer's paradise with several golf courses and
distilleries within a short drive. Enjoy the beautiful scenery and
splendid beaches in Sutherland. Shops nearby.

Directions: 35 miles north of Inverness, leave A9 at Evelix. Follow
A949 to war memorial 1 mile. Turn left onto B9186 signposted
Pitgrundy Park half a mile on the right.

STB ★ ★ ★ ★ ★

SCOTLAND
HOME OF GOLF
online

www.scotland-for-golf.com

Royal Dornoch

Far from the madding crowd, this magnificent links remains the jewel in the crown of Scotland's most northerly venues. The most famous names in golf have been here; Fred Couples is but one who almost missed an Open because he didn't want to go. Steeped in tradition, the folklore can grip you as much as the ambience of the seaside dunes and marram grass. Wonderfully created from nature's gifts, these links will grant you a succession of unforgettable golfing memories.

3rd green, Royal Dornoch.

HOLE	NAME	WHITE YARDS	YELLOW YARDS	PAR	STROKE INDEX	HOLE	NAME	WHITE YARDS	YELLOW YARDS	PAR	STROKE INDEX
1	First	331	300	4	7	10	Fuaran	147	142	3	16
2	Ord	177	167	3	15	11	A'chlach	446	434	4	4
3	Earl's Cross	414	398	4	11	12	Sutherland	507	489	5	12
4	Achinchanter	427	403	4	3	13	Bents	166	148	3	18
5	Hilton	354	317	4	9	14	Foxy	445	439	4	2
6	Whinny Brae	163	163	3	17	15	Stulaig	319	298	4	2
7	Pier	463	423	4	1	16	High Hole	402	395	4	6
8	Dunrobin	396	386	4	5	17	Valley	405	390	4	8
9	Craiglaith	496	491	5	13	18	Home	456	446	4	14

No. of holes: 18	Yardage: 6514	SSS: 70
GREEN FEES	Weekdays	
Individual round	On application	Gaz ref: Page 141
Daily rates	On application	Map ref: Page 154, E3
Are visitors free to play?	Yes	
Nearest Airport: Inverness, 47 miles	Nearest Rail Station: Golspie, 9.9 miles	

ROYAL DORNOCH GOLF CLUB

Golf Road, Dornoch, IV25 3LW

Clubhouse	(01862) 810219
Pro Shop	-
Annual closure	No
Weekly closure	No

TO LOCATE THIS GOLF COURSE ON THE MAPS (p155-159) LOOK FOR THE FLAG WITH THIS PAGE NUMBER.

Brora

Another from the architectural locker of the great James Braid, Brora enjoys a reputation built up over the years as a masterpiece in links golf. At its northern extremity, you marvel how such a narrow strip of coastal land could yield such sport. Year upon year, like Dornoch – but perhaps not quite with the same proliferation of numbers – Brora attracts regular golfing adventurers; little wonder!

hidden **gem**

1st green, Brora.

HOLE	NAME	WHITE YARDS	YELLOW YARDS	PAR	STROKE INDEX
1	First	–	280	4	13
2	Bents	–	334	4	9
3	Canal	–	447	4	1
4	White Post	–	313	4	15
5	Burn	–	400	4	3
6	Witch	–	164	3	7
7	2nd Burn	–	340	4	11
8	Long	–	501	5	5
9	Sea Hole	–	149	3	17

HOLE	NAME	WHITE YARDS	YELLOW YARDS	PAR	STROKE INDEX
10	Greenhill	–	425	4	6
11	Dry Burn	–	412	4	8
12	Dalchalm	–	314	4	10
13	Snake	–	108	3	18
14	Trap	–	305	4	16
15	Sahara	–	399	4	2
16	Plateau	–	335	4	12
17	Tarbatness	–	438	4	4
18	Home Hole	–	190	3	14

No. of holes: 18	Yardage: 6110	SSS: 69
GREEN FEES	Weekdays	
Individual round	£25	Gaz ref: Page 141
Daily rates	£35	Map ref: Page 154, E2
Are visitors free to play?	Yes	
Nearest Airport: Inverness, 60.8 miles		Nearest Rail Station: Brora, 0.3 miles

BRORA GOLF CLUB

Golf Road, Brora, KW9 6QS

Clubhouse	(01408) 621417
Pro Shop	-
Annual closure	No
Weekly closure	No

TO LOCATE THIS GOLF COURSE ON THE MAPS (p155-159) LOOK FOR THE FLAG WITH THIS PAGE NUMBER.

You won't get any further north than this amazing place to play golf. Within sight of the Orkneys, yet another Braid creation spreads itself between the main road and Sandside Bay. Some have called it 'exacting'; if the wind is about, there could not be a better description. You need accuracy, ingenuity, luck and, above all, iron play of the highest class to defeat the 5831 yards, which includes four par threes on the way out; the 196-yard seventh is stroke one, which surely is unique!

hidden **gem**

17th green, Reay.

HOLE	NAME	WHITE YARDS	YELLOW YARDS	PAR	STROKE INDEX
1	Beinn Ratha	235	–	3	7
2	Sandside	428	–	4	5
3	Loch An Eoin	369	–	4	15
4	Sahara	581	–	5	3
5	Cnocstanger	144	–	3	17
6	Braids Choice	477	–	5	9
7	Pilkington	196	–	3	1
8	Machar	399	–	4	11
9	Chapel	176	–	3	13

HOLE	NAME	WHITE YARDS	YELLOW YARDS	PAR	STROKE INDEX
10	Isauld	351	–	4	6
11	Torran	406	–	4	2
12	Chimneys	348	–	4	14
13	Spring Lochy	305	–	4	16
14	Mary's Cottage	476	–	5	4
15	Vikings Grave	136	–	3	18
16	Reay Kirk	314	–	4	12
17	Dossie's Dyke	328	–	4	8
18	Clachan	162	–	3	10

No. of holes: 18	Yardage: 5876	SSS: 69	
GREEN FEES	Weekdays		
Individual round	£15	Gaz ref: Page 114	
Daily rates	£15	Map ref: Page 154, E1	
Are visitors free to play?		Yes	
Nearest Airport: Inverness, 115.3 miles		Nearest Rail Station: Thurso, 11.3 miles	

REAY GOLF CLUB

Thurso, Caithness, KW14 7RE

Clubhouse	(01847) 811288
Pro Shop	-
Annual closure	No
Weekly closure	No

TO LOCATE THIS GOLF COURSE ON THE MAPS (p155-159) LOOK FOR THE FLAG WITH THIS PAGE NUMBER.

Gairloch

Hidden away at the western edge of the great Torridon region, this beautifully present-ed little nine-hole golf course is the last thing you would expect to find. It measures 2228 yards, with the majority of the challenges par threes, and combines links with some parkland to provide an idyllic golfing haven miles from the beaten track. Climbers and walkers predominate, but put it on your list.

hidden
gem

Gairloch Golf Club.

HOLE	NAME	WHITE YARDS	YELLOW YARDS	PAR	STROKE INDEX
1	The Leabaidh	320	312	4	10
2	Oakwood	185	179	3	7
3	Kirkhill	162	152	3	14
4	Blind Piper	233	209	3	6
5	Caberfeidh	317	312	4	4
6	Westward Ho!	194	187	3	11
7	An Dun	91	88	3	18
8	Traigh Mor	526	488	5	2
9	Mo Dhachaidh	119	119	3	17

HOLE	NAME	WHITE YARDS	YELLOW YARDS	PAR	STROKE INDEX
10	The Leabaidh	327	312	4	9
11	Oakwood	182	179	3	8
12	Kirkhill	184	152	3	5
13	Blind Piper	244	209	4	16
14	Caberfeidh	423	312	4	1
15	Westward Ho!	194	187	3	12
16	An Dun	143	89	3	15
17	Traigh Mor	526	488	5	3
18	Mo Dhachaidh	144	119	3	13

No. of holes: 9	Yardage: 4250	SSS: 63
GREEN FEES	Weekdays	
Individual round	On application	Gaz ref: Page 139
Daily rates	On application	Map ref: Page 154, B3
Are visitors free to play?	Yes	
Nearest Airport: Inverness, 71.3 miles	Nearest Rail Station: Achnasheen, 28.8 miles	

GAIRLOCH GOLF CLUB

Gairloch, Ross-shire, IV21 2BQ

Clubhouse	(01445) 712407
Pro Shop	-
Annual closure	No
Weekly closure	No

TO LOCATE THIS GOLF COURSE ON THE MAPS (p155-159) LOOK FOR THE FLAG WITH THIS PAGE NUMBER.

HIGHLANDS & ISLANDS

Traigh

They say that you have never lived until you've seen a sunset over the Western Isles. This lovely course is exactly the location to enjoy it. First, though, enjoy the thrill of tackling this gem of a holiday course; shortish, granted, at 2456 yards, it has still conjured up one of the great holes in Scottish golf, the long second. Briefly, the panoramas to Rhum, Eigg and Skye disappear behind sixty-foot sandhills, but the ninth tee reinstates one of the finest viewpoints of any Scottish Club.

hidden **gem**

1st green, Traigh.

HOLE	NAME	WHITE YARDS	YELLOW YARDS	PAR	STROKE INDEX	HOLE	NAME	WHITE YARDS	YELLOW YARDS	PAR	STROKE INDEX
1	Captain's Caper	130	130	3	12	10	Tobar an Steallain	130	130	3	14
2	Spion Kop	452	452	5	4	11	An Sgurr	452	452	5	2
3	Road to the Isles	173	173	3	18	12	Rathad nan Eilean	173	173	3	13
4	Jimmy's Choice	257	249	4	8	13	Tagadh Sheumais	257	249	4	10
5	The Bridge	135	125	3	15	14	Allt an Asaidh	135	125	3	17
6	McEachen's Leap	283	264	4	9	15	Leum MhicEachainn	283	264	4	6
7	The Lang Whang	479	446	5	1	16	Strac Fada	479	446	5	3
8	Local Hero	367	337	4	5	17	Gaisgeach Lonadail	367	337	4	7
9	Traigh Mhor	180	170	3	11	18	Machair Thraigh	180	170	3	16

No. of holes: 9 Yardage: 2456 SSS: 65

GREEN FEES	Weekdays	
Individual round	£12	Gaz ref: Page 121
Daily rates	£12	Map ref: Page 154, B6
Are visitors free to play?	Yes	

Nearest Airport: Inverness, 154.6 miles   Nearest Rail Station: Arisaig, 2.3 miles

TRAIGH GOLF COURSE
Arisaig, Inverness-shire
Clubhouse   (01687) 450337
Pro Shop   -
Annual closure No
Weekly closure No

TO LOCATE THIS GOLF COURSE ON THE MAPS (p155-159) LOOK FOR THE FLAG WITH THIS PAGE NUMBER.

Rothesay

The island of Bute was, for many years, one of the favourite Glasgow Fair holiday destinations. With a course like this, it has never lost its magnetism for golfers, irrespective of the foreign holiday takeover of the mainstream population. Built around Canada Hill, with fabulous views in every direction, a stiff climb at the first gets you up to the main challenge. It's a mix of heath and parkland and there are yet some climbs and a few blind shots, but it's a lovely layout certain to please.

hidden **gem**

13th green, Rothesay.

HOLE	NAME	WHITE YARDS	YELLOW YARDS	PAR	STROKE INDEX	HOLE	NAME	WHITE YARDS	YELLOW YARDS	PAR	STROKE INDEX
1	Glebelands	268	–	4	14	10	Cumbrae	261	–	4	8
2	Road Hole	399	–	4	3	11	Striven	148	–	3	18
3	The Whins	342	–	4	7	12	Panorama	306	–	4	6
4	Barone	202	–	3	9	13	The Tank	174	–	3	12
5	The Bush	269	–	4	13	14	The Pines	256	–	4	15
6	Bogany	512	–	5	1	15	Eastlands	277	–	4	17
7	Canada Hill	365	–	4	5	16	Sleeping Warrior	523	–	5	2
8	Ardbrannan	209	–	3	10	17	The Burn	374	–	4	4
9	Clandale	269	–	4	16	18	Westering Home	243	–	3	11

No. of holes: 18	Yardage: 5395	SSS: 66		**ROTHESAY GOLF CLUB**
GREEN FEES	Weekdays			Canada Hill, Rothesay, Isle of Bute
Individual round	On application	Gaz ref: Page 143		Clubhouse (01700) 502244
Daily rates	On application	Map ref: Page 156, B3		Pro Shop -
Are visitors free to play?		Yes		Annual closure No
Nearest Airport: Glasgow, 25 miles		Nearest Rail Station: Wemyss Bay, by ferry		Weekly closure No

TO LOCATE THIS GOLF COURSE ON THE MAPS (p155-159) LOOK FOR THE FLAG WITH THIS PAGE NUMBER.

Broomieknowe

My first visit here since 1972 left me aghast that I had left it so long. Here is a quite beautiful course which rarely gets a mention when golf in the Lothians is aired. I did not see a better presented eighteen holes anywhere last year and the maturity of shrubs and trees – of all varieties – lights up the course. This 6000 yards of blissful golf is the most under-rated venue around Edinburgh.

hidden **gem**

Short 5th, Broomieknowe.

HOLE	NAME	WHITE YARDS	YELLOW YARDS	PAR	STROKE INDEX
1	Fairway	316	306	4	17
2	Eldindean	347	319	4	10
3	Hawthorns	369	348	4	6
4	Cedar Tree	321	306	4	11
5	Dalhousie	167	160	3	18
6	Mary's Dyke	401	384	4	9
7	Cockpen	468	453	4	2
8	Harry Smith's	470	455	5	8
9	Brough's Dub	350	332	4	5

HOLE	NAME	WHITE YARDS	YELLOW YARDS	PAR	STROKE INDEX
10	Trig Point	402	375	4	3
11	Old Barn	183	165	3	13
12	Melville Gully	441	430	4	1
13	The Gap	430	417	4	7
14	Kyesturn	408	394	4	4
15	Robin's Nest	153	153	3	16
16	St Margarets	297	287	4	15
17	Pittendreich	309	309	4	14
18	Knowesend	318	318	4	12

No. of holes: 18	Yardage: 6150	SSS: 69	
GREEN FEES	Weekdays		
Individual round	£17	Gaz ref: Page 127	
Daily rates	£25	Map ref: Page 157, B3	
Are visitors free to play?		Yes	
Nearest Airport: Edinburgh, 13.7 miles		Nearest Rail Station: Waverley, 7.9 miles	

BROOMIEKNOWE GOLF CLUB

36 Golf Course Road, Bonnyrigg

Clubhouse (0131) 663 9317
Pro Shop (0131) 660 2035
Annual closure No
Weekly closure No

TO LOCATE THIS GOLF COURSE ON THE MAPS (p155-159) LOOK FOR THE FLAG WITH THIS PAGE NUMBER.

Edinburgh is lucky to have such a varied landscape. Just a few hills – and the odd extinct volcano! – create the contrast; Murrayfield enjoys just this on the eastern sideof Corstorphine Hill. The climb up the first three holes affords a fabulous view of the city, which can be distracting if you are successfully negotiating arguably the hardest part of the course. It's a fine (and busy) golf club.

Short 2nd, Murrayfield.

HOLE	NAME	WHITE YARDS	YELLOW YARDS	PAR	STROKE INDEX
1	Highland Muir	378	370	4	5
2	Witches' Knoll	131	125	3	13
3	Rest and be Thankful	420	416	4	1
4	Auld Reekie	364	351	4	11
5	King's Step	331	323	4	3
6	Sky Park	287	278	4	17
7	Dykeside of Belmont	180	167	3	9
8	Law Park	322	315	4	7
9	Forth View	258	252	4	15

HOLE	NAME	WHITE YARDS	YELLOW YARDS	PAR	STROKE INDEX
10	Old Quarry	196	161	3	6
11	The Rigs	392	386	4	2
12	Craigcrook	309	306	4	18
13	Ravelston	129	126	3	16
14	King's Seat	503	469	5	14
15	West Bog	349	349	4	4
16	Fountain Head	357	357	4	8
17	Buchtknowe	337	313	4	12
18	Haining Brae	523	465	5/4	10

No. of holes: 18	Yardage: 5765	SSS: 69	
GREEN FEES	Weekdays		
Individual round	On application	Gaz ref: Page 129	
Daily rates	On application	Map ref: Page 157, A3	
Are visitors free to play?		Yes	
Nearest Airport: Edinburgh, 5.8 miles		Nearest Rail Station: Haymarket, 1.4 miles	

MURRAYFIELD GOLF CLUB

43 Murrayfield Rd, Edinburgh
EH12 6EU

Clubhouse	(0131) 337 0721
Pro Shop	-
Annual closure	No
Weekly closure	No

TO LOCATE THIS GOLF COURSE ON THE MAPS (p155-159) LOOK FOR THE FLAG WITH THIS PAGE NUMBER.

Braids No.1

There's always concern when Local Authority courses are mentioned. Will they suffer from overplay by golfers who don't yet know the etiquette of golf? Do they get the same attention by green staff? Here's a cracker of a course which continues to defy the odds, and yields unmatched pleasure to many. The stunning location apart, it will test all areas of your golfing ability; it is beautifully kept.

hidden **gem**

2nd green, Braids No. 1.

HOLE	NAME	WHITE YARDS	YELLOW YARDS	PAR	STROKE INDEX	HOLE	NAME	WHITE YARDS	YELLOW YARDS	PAR	STROKE INDEX
1	–	303	280	4	13	10	–	549	524	5	4
2	–	147	141	3	17	11	–	522	464	5	10
3	–	328	287	4	5	12	–	292	281	4	16
4	–	264	243	4	15	13	–	205	173	3	6
5	–	518	444	4	3	14	–	386	354	4	2
6	–	430	419	4	1	15	–	351	311	4	14
7	–	343	330	4	7	16	–	307	291	4	8
8	–	329	269	4	11	17	–	165	153	3	18
9	–	185	172	3	9	18	–	268	254	4	12

No. of holes: 18	Yardage: 6472	SSS:
GREEN FEES	Weekdays	
Individual round	On application	Gaz ref: Page 128
Daily rates	On application	Map ref: Page 157, A3
Are visitors free to play?		Yes
Nearest Airport: Edinburgh, 9.6 miles		Nearest Rail Station: Haymerket, 3.2 miles

BRAID HILLS GOLF CLUB

Braid Hills Approach, Edinburgh EH10 6FY

Clubhouse	(0131) 447 6666
Pro Shop	-
Annual closure	No
Weekly closure	No

TO LOCATE THIS GOLF COURSE ON THE MAPS (p155-159) LOOK FOR THE FLAG WITH THIS PAGE NUMBER.

The Original Old Club House at Gullane

Lounge Bar, Wine Bar and Brasserie.
Food served all day......till very late!!
Lunch or evening dinner.
Wide selection of food and wine.

East Links Road, Gullane. Telephone: (01620) 842008.
Proprietors: Guy and Brenda Campanile
Email: info@oldclubhouse.com   Website: http://www.oldclubhouse.com

Warm up for your round in East Lothian

* 24 covered floodlit bays   * Top quality balls
* 9 hole par 3 course   * Putting Green
* Short game practice area
* Open 9am to 9pm 7 days

THE JANE CONNACHAN GOLF CENTRE LTD

We are on the B1345 Drem to Dirleton Road, 21/2 miles from North Berwick, East Lothian. Telephone: (01620) 850475

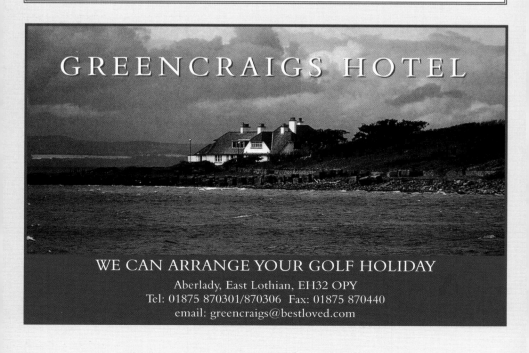

GREENCRAIGS HOTEL

WE CAN ARRANGE YOUR GOLF HOLIDAY

Aberlady, East Lothian, EH32 0PY
Tel: 01875 870301/870306 Fax: 01875 870440
email: greencraigs@bestloved.com

Gullane No.1

It goes without saying that any Open Qualifying course could be daunting. Climb up through the second hole here (it's a cracker) and when the wind coming down the Forth hits you on the third tee, prepare for battle! This is arguably the hardest links course in the Lothians, thousands of hopefuls having perished over the years on a quite superb eighteen holes. Join the list this year?

2nd, Gullane No. 1.

HOLE	NAME	WHITE YARDS	YELLOW YARDS	PAR	STROKE INDEX	HOLE	NAME	WHITE YARDS	YELLOW YARDS	PAR	STROKE INDEX
1	First	–	302	4	14	10	Thucket Knowe	–	466	4	7
2	Windygate	–	379	4	4	11	Maggie's Loup	–	471	4	2
3	Racecourse	–	496	5	8	12	The Valley	–	480	5	11
4	Island	–	144	3	18	13	Hole Across	–	170	3	15
5	Murrays Hill	–	450	4	1	14	The Shelter	–	435	4	3
6	Roundel	–	324	4	16	15	Pumphouse	–	537	5	9
7	Queen's Head	–	398	4	6	16	Traprain	–	186	3	13
8	King's Chair	–	332	4	10	17	Hilltop	–	390	4	5
9	Corbie	–	151	3	12	18	Kirklands	–	355	4	17

No. of holes: 18	Yardage: 6466	SSS: 72

GREEN FEES	Weekdays	
Individual round	£58	Gaz ref: Page 130
Daily rates	£87	Map ref: Page 157, B2
Are visitors free to play?	Yes	

Nearest Airport: Edinburgh, 27.3 miles	Nearest Rail Station: Longniddry, 6 miles

GULLANE NO.1 GOLF COURSE

East Lothian EH31 2BB

Clubhouse (01620) 842255
Pro Shop (01620) 843111
Annual closure No
Weekly closure No

TO LOCATE THIS GOLF COURSE ON THE MAPS (p155-159) LOOK FOR THE FLAG WITH THIS PAGE NUMBER.

North Berwick

North Berwick members who read this editorial will not be pleased that I put Gullane on a pedestal (see above!) Let me escape the brickbats by saying that here we have the finest natural seaside links anywhere in the Lothians (sometimes it's the hardest!) It is a tremendous course, stretching some two miles from the heart of the town, creating one challenge after another.

15th, 'Redan', North Berwick.

HOLE	NAME	WHITE YARDS	YELLOW YARDS	PAR	STROKE INDEX
1	Point Garry (out)	–	328	4	9
2	Sea	–	431	4	11
3	Trap	–	464	4	1
4	Carlekemp	–	175	3	15
5	Bunkershill	–	373	4	5
6	Quarry	–	162	3	17
7	Eli Burn	–	354	4	3
8	Linkhouse	–	495	5	13
9	Mizzentop	–	510	5	7

HOLE	NAME	WHITE YARDS	YELLOW YARDS	PAR	STROKE INDEX
10	Eastward Ho!	–	176	3	18
11	Bos'ns Locker	–	550	5	2
12	Bass	–	389	4	8
13	Pit	–	365	4	12
14	Perfection	–	376	4	6
15	Redan	–	192	3	14
16	Gate	–	381	4	4
17	Point Garry (in)	–	425	4	10
18	Home	–	274	4	16

No. of holes: 18	Yardage: 6420	SSS: 71

GREEN FEES	Weekdays	
Individual round	£40	Gaz ref: Page 131
Daily rates	£60	Map ref: Page 157, C2
Are visitors free to play?	Yes	

Nearest Airport: Edinburgh, 31.8 miles   Nearest Rail Station: North Berwick, 0.2 miles

NORTH BERWICK GOLF CLUB

Beach Road, North Berwick

Clubhouse   (01620) 895040
Pro Shop   (01620) 893233
Annual closure   No
Weekly closure   No

TO LOCATE THIS GOLF COURSE ON THE MAPS (p155-159) LOOK FOR THE FLAG WITH THIS PAGE NUMBER.

Dunbar

Regular home of the Scottish Boys' Championship, here we have another perfect links course whose popularity, season upon season, remains unrivalled. Always in lovely condition, the layout winds its way south-east from the clubhouse and supplies all the tried-and-tested requirements of a natural seaside course. As ever, the wind will play a part, but it will not spoil a memorable day's golf.

15th green and the town, Dunbar.

HOLE	NAME	WHITE YARDS	YELLOW YARDS	PAR	STROKE INDEX	HOLE	NAME	WHITE YARDS	YELLOW YARDS	PAR	STROKE INDEX
1	Broxmouth Wood	474	460	5	9	10	Sheiling	202	202	3	12
2	Deer Park	492	490	5	3	11	Girgie Mire	418	406	4	8
3	Jackson's Pennies	173	152	3	15	12	The Point	457	445	4	2
4	Shore	353	340	4	5	13	Pot	377	359	4	14
5	Doon Hill	147	162	3	17	14	Mill Stone Den	432	413	4	4
6	Broxburn	347	338	4	1	15	Skerries	338	322	4	18
7	Vaults	382	371	4	13	16	Narrows	163	145	3	16
8	Cromwell	370	323	4	11	17	Fluke Dub	338	320	4	6
9	Longbanks	506	506	5	7	18	Hame	435	421	4	10

No. of holes: 18	Yardage: 6404	SSS: 71	
GREEN FEES	Weekdays		
Individual round	£28	Gaz ref: Page 127	
Daily rates	£35	Map ref: Page 157, C3	
Are visitors free to play?		Yes	
Nearest Airport: Edinburgh, 36.9 miles		Nearest Rail Station: Dunbar, 0.8 miles	

DUNBAR GOLF CLUB

East Links, Dunbar EH42 1LL

Clubhouse   (01368) 862317
Pro Shop   (01368) 862086
Annual closure No
Weekly closure No

TO LOCATE THIS GOLF COURSE ON THE MAPS (p155-159) LOOK FOR THE FLAG WITH THIS PAGE NUMBER.

Dunbar Winterfield

At the west end of Dunbar, the lesser-known but highly popular Winterfield course never gets the same plaudits as its older brother. It is of different character; links there are, but a large part of the course is flat parkland and it is much shorter than the Championship course. Nevertheless, the setting is superb, there is great variety around the fringes of the layout and it attracts many visitors.

15th, Dunbar Winterfield.

HOLE	NAME	WHITE YARDS	YELLOW YARDS	PAR	STROKE INDEX	HOLE	NAME	WHITE YARDS	YELLOW YARDS	PAR	STROKE INDEX
1	Whelkie Haugh	238	230	3	11	10	Traprain	212	203	3	14
2	Promenade	369	348	4	3	11	Muir's View	183	130	3	17
3	Pin Cod	287	280	4	8	12	Clancy's	303	293	4	6
4	Craigengelt	140	125	3	18	13	Targets	368	356	4	2
5	Pencraik	307	297	4	5	14	The Point	202	182	3	16
6	Lauderdale	322	300	4	10	15	Blocks	234	221	3	12
7	Kirk Park	438	396	4	1	16	Bass Rock	311	293	4	7
8	The May	250	240	3	13	17	Doon Hill	490	480	5	4
9	The School	236	226	3	15	18	St Margaret's	265	260	4	9

No. of holes: 18	Yardage: 5155	SSS: 65
GREEN FEES	Weekdays	
Individual round	On application	Gaz ref: Page 128
Daily rates	On application	Map ref: Page 157, C3
Are visitors free to play?	Yes	
Nearest Airport: Edinburgh, 36 miles	Nearest Rail Station: Dunbar, 1 mile	

WINTERFIELD GOLF CLUB

North Road, Dunbar

Clubhouse	(01368) 862280
Pro Shop	(01368) 863362
Annual closure	No
Weekly closure	No

TO LOCATE THIS GOLF COURSE ON THE MAPS (p155-159) LOOK FOR THE FLAG WITH THIS PAGE NUMBER.

Greenburn

It is odd that the courses in West Lothian get little publicity outside their own region. In Fauldhouse, the old mining town at the extreme southern edge of the county, is Greenburn, a modest 6000 yards off the back tees, but a first-class golf course where the dissection by the railway has created the need for players to think, rather than thrash, their way around a fine test of their skills.

4th green and viaduct, Greenburn.

HOLE	NAME	WHITE YARDS	YELLOW YARDS	PAR	STROKE INDEX	HOLE	NAME	WHITE YARDS	YELLOW YARDS	PAR	STROKE INDEX
1	Falla Hill	270	–	4	12	10	Muldron	219	–	3	13
2	The Plum	282	–	4	8	11	The Ruins	322	–	4	11
3	Greenhill	342	–	4	10	12	Race Track	460	–	4	2
4	Bent Head	514	–	5	3	13	Levenseat	494	–	5	4
5	The Pond	431	–	4	1	14	Eldrick	374	–	4	6
6	Bridge End	172	–	3	14	15	The Buchs	213	–	3	15
7	Tarry Dews	495	–	5	5	16	The Knowes	373	–	4	7
8	Wellhill	164	–	3	16	17	The Viaduct	250	–	4	18
9	Powder House	308	–	4	17	18	The Greenburn	363	–	4	9

No. of holes: 18	Yardage: 6046	SSS: 70
GREEN FEES	Weekdays	
Individual round	On application	Gaz ref: Page 130
Daily rates	On application	Map ref: Page 156, E3
Are visitors free to play?	Yes	
Nearest Airport: Edinburgh, 19.9 miles	Nearest Rail Station: Fauldhouse, 1 mile	

GREENBURN GOLF CLUB

Greenburn, Bridge Street,
Fauldhouse

Clubhouse   (01501) 770292
Pro Shop   -
Annual closure No
Weekly closure No

TO LOCATE THIS GOLF COURSE ON THE MAPS (p155-159) LOOK FOR THE FLAG WITH THIS PAGE NUMBER.

King's Acre

The farming industry's devastation in recent years has, on occasion, had unexpected benefits. Here at Lasswade, golfers have reaped the rewards of one disenchanted farmer creating a new course. It's a beauty, too, with a contrast of testing holes on a chunk of converted farmland and clever use of old parkland and trees elsewhere. It works well, is maturing nicely and is great-value golf.

18th, King's Acre.

HOLE	NAME	WHITE YARDS	YELLOW YARDS	PAR	STROKE INDEX	HOLE	NAME	WHITE YARDS	YELLOW YARDS	PAR	STROKE INDEX
1	Sandy Brae	327	318	4	10	10	Jacqui's Gallop	378	352	4	3
2	Pentlands	449	440	5	18	11	John's Dyke	186	171	3	11
3	Bunkered	553	545	5	2	12	Rye Hill	506	484	5	5
4	Forth View	153	145	3	12	13	Lizzie's Leap	343	322	4	17
5	Mayfield	367	357	4	4	14	Willie's Temple	177	169	3	15
6	Park Burn	198	184	3	16	15	Thro' the Pines	501	498	5	1
7	England's Hill	356	346	4	8	16	The Haugh	217	202	3	7
8	Moorfoots	172	133	3	14	17	Nancy's Knowe	302	294	4	13
9	Tom's Track	389	366	4	6	18	Last Splash	361	340	4	9

No. of holes: 18	Yardage: 5935	SSS: 70
GREEN FEES	Weekdays	
Individual round	£16	Gaz ref: Page 130
Daily rates	£16	Map ref: Page 156, B3
Are visitors free to play?	Yes	
Nearest Airport: Edinburgh, 13.5 miles		Nearest Rail Station: Waverley, 6.2 miles

KING'S ACRE GOLF COURSE

Lasswade, Midlothian EH18 1AV

Clubhouse   (0131) 663 3456
Pro Shop   -
Annual closure No
Weekly closure No

TO LOCATE THIS GOLF COURSE ON THE MAPS (p155-159) LOOK FOR THE FLAG WITH THIS PAGE NUMBER.

Royal Musselburgh

The East Lothian links courses tend to hog the limelight, so for a change why not visit this cracking parkland course at Prestonpans? Gloriously set amidst old broad-leaved trees, the course presentation is up with the best in the Lothians. Lush fairway lies are guaranteed, greens are smooth and beautifully cut, while the old clubhouse exudes a perfect aura of grandeur.

hidden gem

13th, Royal Musselburgh.

HOLE	NAME	WHITE YARDS	YELLOW YARDS	PAR	STROKE INDEX	HOLE	NAME	WHITE YARDS	YELLOW YARDS	PAR	STROKE INDEX
1	Carriage Way	349	309	4	8	10	Morrison's Haven	356	343	4	7
2	Stables	295	280	4	18	11	Pony Park	370	351	4	15
3	Easter Yett	368	349	4	10	12	The Gap	362	329	4	11
4	Laurels	365	352	4	4	13	Blink o' Forth	452	435	4	1
5	Orchard	329	311	4	16	14	The Gully	149	127	3	17
6	Mary Wright	176	147	3	6	15	The Glebe	440	419	4	3
7	Arthur's Seat	391	363	4	2	16	Hole Across	176	148	3	9
8	Suthren Yett	420	410	4	12	17	Auld Reekie	352	334	4	13
9	Jimmy Braid	477	465	5	14	18	Prestongrange	410	377	4	5

No. of holes: 18	Yardage: 6237	SSS: 70
GREEN FEES	Weekdays	
Individual round	£20	Gaz ref: Page 130
Daily rates	£35	Map ref: Page 157, B3
Are visitors free to play?	Yes	
Nearest Airport: Edinburgh, 16.8 miles	Nearest Rail Station: Prestonpans, 1.2 miles	

ROYAL MUSSELBURGH GOLF CLUB

Preston Grange House, Prestonpans
EH32 9RP

Clubhouse   (01875) 810276
Pro Shop   (01875) 810139
Annual closure No
Weekly closure No

TO LOCATE THIS GOLF COURSE ON THE MAPS (p155-159) LOOK FOR THE FLAG WITH THIS PAGE NUMBER.

Ratho Park

Think of Ratho Park and trees will come first to mind. Thousands of them there are, too, of all varieties and most very old. Hundreds will affect or influence your round, from club selection to shot placement, but all combine to provide the most sumptuous arboreal setting for golf. The course is always immaculate, the greens superb and an autumn outing to Ratho could not be bettered.

hidden **gem**

Looking down the 7th, Ratho Park.

HOLE	NAME	WHITE YARDS	YELLOW YARDS	PAR	STROKE INDEX
1	Corstorphine	–	258	4	11
2	The Doocot	–	359	4	13
3	Wrath-o	–	282	4	15
4	The Avenue	–	386	4	5
5	The Plateau	–	421	4	1
6	Criss Cross	–	389	4	7
7	The Lodge	–	383	4	3
8	The Captain	–	169	3	17
9	The Spinney	–	379	4	9

HOLE	NAME	WHITE YARDS	YELLOW YARDS	PAR	STROKE INDEX
10	Rest and be Thankful	–	308	4	12
11	The Long Hole	–	519	5	6
12	Seven Sisters	–	170	3	16
13	The Roondel	–	164	3	14
14	Braid's Test	–	463	4	2
15	Sandy Hollow	–	161	3	18
16	The Glade	–	380	4	8
17	Paddock Holm	–	381	4	4
18	The Terrace	–	360	4	10

No. of holes: 18	Yardage: 5900	SSS: 68
GREEN FEES	Weekdays	
Individual round	£25	Gaz ref: Page 129
Daily rates	£35	Map ref: Page 157, A3
Are visitors free to play?	Yes	
Nearest Airport: Edinburgh, 4 miles		Nearest Rail Station: Haymarket, 6.8 miles

RATHO PARK GOLF CLUB

Ratho, Newbridge,
Midlothian EH28 8NX

Clubhouse	(0131) 333 2566
Pro Shop	(0131) 333 1406
Annual closure	No
Weekly closure	No

TO LOCATE THIS GOLF COURSE ON THE MAPS (p155-159) LOOK FOR THE FLAG WITH THIS PAGE NUMBER.

Uphall

Here is a modest West Lothian venue which is probably unknown to most visiting golfers, but the pleasure of whose eighteen holes is a constant source of fun to members. There is a fascinating start and finish, a main road to cross to reach the flatter part of the course but loads of variety in a not overly-taxing round. The clubhouse and surrounds are lovely, and it's as sociable as any around.

17th and Club House, Uphall.

HOLE	NAME	WHITE YARDS	YELLOW YARDS	PAR	STROKE INDEX	HOLE	NAME	WHITE YARDS	YELLOW YARDS	PAR	STROKE INDEX
1	Mains	404	366	4	4	10	Long Haul	434	427	4	3
2	Canny Tell	298	293	4	12	11	Randies	479	471	5	7
3	Pear Tree	154	145	3	14	12	Beech Tree	274	265	4	17
4	New Road	395	389	4	2	13	The Holdings	304	293	4	9
5	Houston	283	267	4	16	14	The Dyke	412	409	4	1
6	The Avenue	284	273	4	10	15	The Double	173	152	3	15
7	The Dooket	148	144	3	18	16	The Bum	134	95	3	13
8	Elbow	360	351	4	8	17	The Thorns	251	240	4	11
9	Stankards	418	410	4	6	18	Binnie Craig	383	376	4	5

No. of holes: 18	Yardage: 5592	SSS: 67	**UPHALL GOLF CLUB**
GREEN FEES	Weekdays		Uphall, West Lothian EH52 6JT
Individual round	On application	Gaz ref: Page 132	Clubhouse (01506) 656404
Daily rates	On application	Map ref: Page 156, E2	Pro Shop (01506) 855553
Are visitors free to play?		Yes	Annual closure No
			Weekly closure No
Nearest Airport: Edinburgh, 9.4 miles		Nearest Rail Station: Uphall, 0.9 miles	

TO LOCATE THIS GOLF COURSE ON THE MAPS (p155-159) LOOK FOR THE FLAG WITH THIS PAGE NUMBER.

King's Course, Gleneagles

Still adored by countless thousands of golfers from near and far, James Braid's wondrous creation in the Perthshire countryside continues to enthrall. Now more easily tamed by the pros, it yet offers an unmatched golfing challenge to all who play the game purely for fun – and plenty of that is available at every single hole. It is impossible to pick a fault; with the appearance of the course becoming more and more impressive, it easily retains its place at the top of Scottish golf.

3rd green, King's Course, Gleneagles.

HOLE	NAME	WHITE YARDS	YELLOW YARDS	PAR	STROKE INDEX	HOLE	NAME	WHITE YARDS	YELLOW YARDS	PAR	STROKE INDEX
1	Dun Whinny	362	352	4	6	10	Canty Lye	447	429	4	1
2	East Neuk	405	386	4	14	11	Deil's Creel	230	221	3	10
3	Silver Tassie	374	360	4	9	12	Tappit Hen	395	352	4	13
4	Broomy Law	466	443	4	2	13	Braid's Brawest	448	423	4	7
5	Het Girdle	161	149	3	16	14	Denty Den	260	249	4	15
6	Blink Bonnie	476	455	5	8	15	Howe o' Hope	459	438	4	3
7	Kittle Kink	439	430	4	4	16	Wee Bogle	135	128	3	18
8	Whaup's Nest	158	155	3	17	17	Warslin' Lea	377	367	4	11
9	Heich o' Fash	354	335	4	12	18	King's Hame	525	453	5	5

No. of holes: 18	Yardage: 6790	SSS: 73
GREEN FEES	Weekdays	
Individual round	On application	Gaz ref: Page 134
Daily rates	On application	Map ref: Page 156, E1
Are visitors free to play?		Yes

Nearest Airport: Edinburgh, 40.7 miles   Nearest Rail Station: Gleneagles, 2 miles

KING'S COURSE, GLENEAGLES

Gleneagles Hotel, Auchterarder
PH3 1NF

Clubhouse   (01764) 694469
Pro Shop   -
Annual closure   No
Weekly closure   No

TO LOCATE THIS GOLF COURSE ON THE MAPS (p155-159) LOOK FOR THE FLAG WITH THIS PAGE NUMBER.

King James VI

This is a course we have never featured in "Home of Golf", so its inclusion this time around is overdue. It lies on Moncrieffe Island, which splits the Tay in two as it prepares to leave Perth and head for Dundee. Its situation obviously causes the odd days of heaviness, particularly if the Tay has been swollen by rain upstream but, conversely, lush fairway lies and beautiful greens are the order of the day. A lovely, tree-studded backdrop completes the picture of a course that merits a visit.

King James VI, Perth.

HOLE	NAME	WHITE YARDS	YELLOW YARDS	PAR	STROKE INDEX	HOLE	NAME	WHITE YARDS	YELLOW YARDS	PAR	STROKE INDEX
1	Willie McKay	362	346	4	17	10	Stephens Pride	342	331	10	10
2	Rampart	348	338	4	11	11	Peter Campbell	372	362	2	2
3	Hay Robertson	196	186	3	13	12	Shelter	270	266	12	12
4	White House	474	463	4	1	13	Short Hole	171	159	16	16
5	Willowgate	179	157	3	17	14	Corner	358	308	4	4
6	Spectacles	325	317	4	9	15	Farm	270	238	14	14
7	Dunsie	312	300	4	15	16	Tayside	494	393	6	6
8	Long Hole	529	519	5	5	17	Hawthorn	173	158	18	18
9	Rashes	433	420	4	3	18	Ramsay	430	423	8	8

No. of holes: 18	Yardage: 5684	SSS: 68	
GREEN FEES	Weekdays		
Individual round	£18	Gaz ref: Page 136	
Daily rates	£25	Map ref: Page 155, A7	
Are visitors free to play?		Yes	
Nearest Airport: Edinburgh, 40.1 miles		Nearest Rail Station: Perth, 1.2 miles	

KING JAMES VI GOLF CLUB

Montcreiffe Island, Perth PH2 8NR

Clubhouse   (01738) 445132
Pro Shop   (01738) 632460
Annual closure No
Weekly closure No

TO LOCATE THIS GOLF COURSE ON THE MAPS (p155-159) LOOK FOR THE FLAG WITH THIS PAGE NUMBER.

Downfield

Like many others, I can never leave this superb course out of our annual review as it deserves all the plaudits available. Fabulous holes, always in perfect condition, challenges to get you thinking all the way round and a fabulous arboreal setting for it all. Restored last year as an Open Qualifying course – and not before time – Downfield is rightly in the top ten Scottish inland venues.

11th green, Downfield.

HOLE	NAME	WHITE YARDS	YELLOW YARDS	PAR	STROKE INDEX
1	Outward Bound	425	385	4	1
2	Scotch Corner	408	398	4	7
3	Lucky Slap	228	210	3	15
4	Lost Horizon	538	507	5	11
5	Sleepy Hollow	393	361	4	5
6	The Lang Spane	177	151	3	17
7	Templeton Trail	491	438	5/4	13
8	Double Trouble	407	363	4	3
9	Elysian Fields	414	389	4	9

HOLE	NAME	WHITE YARDS	YELLOW YARDS	PAR	STROKE INDEX
10	Westward Ho	434	382	4	2
11	Paddler's Joy	498	434	5/4	8
12	Davy Jones' Locker	182	148	3	16
13	Devil's Elbow	480	446	5/4	6
14	Witches' Brew	515	481	5	10
15	Rest & Be Thankful	326	322	4	14
16	Round The Bend	352	326	4	12
17	Kidney Punch	151	140	3	18
18	Journey's End	384	366	4	4

No. of holes: 18	Yardage: 6803	SSS: 73
GREEN FEES	Weekdays	
Individual round	£31	Gaz ref: Page 107
Daily rates	£44	Map ref: Page 155, B7
Are visitors free to play?		Yes
Nearest Airport: Edinburgh, 58.2 miles		Nearest Rail Station: Dundee, 3.9 miles

DOWNFIELD GOLF CLUB

Turnberry Av., Dundee DD2 3QP

Clubhouse	(01382) 825595
Pro Shop	(01382) 889246
Annual closure	No
Weekly closure	No

TO LOCATE THIS GOLF COURSE ON THE MAPS (p155-159) LOOK FOR THE FLAG WITH THIS PAGE NUMBER.

Panmure

Many who visit this Open Qualifying course for the first time must wonder, after two or three holes, what all the rave revues were about. Then they reach the sixth tee! It is a flat start and finish, not without difficulty, it must be said, but it's the central twelve or thirteen holes where all the drama awaits. Brilliant design, tough rough if you're awry, devilish greens, bunkers and burns; superb!

hidden **gem**

6th green, Panmure.

HOLE	NAME	WHITE YARDS	YELLOW YARDS	PAR	STROKE INDEX	HOLE	NAME	WHITE YARDS	YELLOW YARDS	PAR	STROKE INDEX
1	–	289	280	4	9	10	–	416	406	4	4
2	–	488	476	5	15	11	–	171	163	3	18
3	–	398	377	4	3	12	–	363	343	4	8
4	–	348	340	4	7	13	–	398	384	4	14
5	–	147	144	3	17	14	–	535	521	5	2
6	–	387	365	4	1	15	–	234	226	3	10
7	–	418	408	4	11	16	–	382	364	4	16
8	–	360	335	4	5	17	–	401	391	4	6
9	–	174	167	3	13	18	–	408	395	4	12

No. of holes: 18	Yardage: 6317	SSS: 71
GREEN FEES	Weekdays	
Individual round	On application	Gaz ref: Page 106
Daily rates	On application	Map ref: Page 155, C7
Are visitors free to play?		Yes (except Saturdays)
Nearest Airport: Edinburgh, 64.1 miles		Nearest Rail Station: Barry Links, 0.2 miles

PANMURE GOLF CLUB

Burnside Road, Barry,
by Carnoustie, DD7 7RT

Clubhouse   (01241) 853120
Pro Shop   (01241) 852460
Annual closure No
Weekly closure No

TO LOCATE THIS GOLF COURSE ON THE MAPS (p155-159) LOOK FOR THE FLAG WITH THIS PAGE NUMBER.

Carnoustie

Like St.Andrews and Muirfield, there are no superlatives left to properly describe the best links in the world. It did not need poor Jean Van de Velde's Open nightmare to publicise it further, but this unbelievably stern test of golf will no doubt pull thousands more golfers to the first tee as a result. Those who are making their first visit will find it awesome; it has no peer across the world.

3rd green 'Jockie's Burn', Carnoustie.

HOLE	NAME	WHITE YARDS	YELLOW YARDS	PAR	STROKE INDEX
1	Cup	401	391	4	7
2	Gulley	435	412	4	3
3	Jockie's Burn	337	316	4	15
4	Hillocks	375	374	4	11
5	Brae	387	375	4	13
6	Long	520	500	5	1
7	Plantation	394	373	4	9
8	Short	167	157	3	17
9	Railway	413	420	4	5

HOLE	NAME	WHITE YARDS	YELLOW YARDS	PAR	STROKE INDEX
10	South America	446	425	4	8
11	Dyke	362	352	4	14
12	Southward Ho	479	462	4	4
13	Whins	161	141	3	18
14	Spectacles	483	468	4	2
15	Lucky Slap	459	442	4	12
16	Barry Burn	245	235	3	16
17	Island	433	421	4	6
18	Home	444	428	4	10

No. of holes: 18	Yardage: 6941	SSS: 72
GREEN FEES	Weekdays	
Individual round	On application	Gaz ref: Page 106
Daily rates	On application	Map ref: Page 155, B7
Are visitors free to play?	Yes	
Nearest Airport: Aberdeen, 65.6 miles	Nearest Rail Station: Carnoustie, 5.1 miles	

CARNOUSTIE GOLF CLUB

3 Links Parade, Carnoustie DD7 7SE

Clubhouse   (01241) 852480
Pro Shop   -
Annual closure No
Weekly closure No

TO LOCATE THIS GOLF COURSE ON THE MAPS (p155-159) LOOK FOR THE FLAG WITH THIS PAGE NUMBER.

Edzell lies a fair distance from any main population centre, yet consistently enjoys huge numbers of annual visitors and outings. It is a particular favourite of those from the Dundee area who are happy to go that wee bit further for a high quality encounter with a class golf course. Quality it most certainly exudes; the glorious setting at the foot of the southern Grampians and amidst a backdrop of firs, beeches and birches is perfection. The presentation of the eighteen holes is ever immaculate.

15th green, Edzell.

HOLE	NAME	WHITE YARDS	YELLOW YARDS	PAR	STROKE INDEX
1	Jim Webster	312	304	4	17
2	The Road	446	436	4	1
3	The Ridge	310	300	4	13
4	The Narrows	370	340	4	9
5	The Shelter	429	425	4	3
6	The Redoubt	178	166	3	11
7	The Howe	385	375	4	5
8	The River	354	342	4	7
9	The Deep End	478	452	5	15

HOLE	NAME	WHITE YARDS	YELLOW YARDS	PAR	STROKE INDEX
10	Hamewith	369	316	4	12
11	The Lang Straucht	433	424	4	2
12	The White Hut	361	336	4	14
13	The Rashie Bog	415	405	4	4
14	Majuba	155	145	3	16
15	The De'il's Neuk	338	300	4	8
16	Spion Kop	316	302	4	10
17	The Corrie	191	178	3	6
18	Home	508	496	5	18

No. of holes: 18	Yardage: 6348	SSS: 71
GREEN FEES	Weekdays	
Individual round	£23	Gaz ref: Page 107
Daily rates	£33	Map ref: Page 155, C5
Are visitors free to play?		Yes

Nearest Airport: Aberdeen, 43 miles   Nearest Rail Station: Montrose, 13.5 miles

THE EDZELL GOLF CLUB

High St. Edzell DD9 7TF

Clubhouse   (01356) 648235
Pro Shop   (01356) 648462
Annual closure   No
Weekly closure   No

TO LOCATE THIS GOLF COURSE ON THE MAPS (p155-159) LOOK FOR THE FLAG WITH THIS PAGE NUMBER.

A secluded, comfortable and well equipped country house, situated on the edge of **Edzell Golf Course** overlooking a sheltered garden with fine views to the Grampian Mountains to the north and west.
Many championship golf courses within easy reach, historic houses, castles and gardens.
Ideal for golfing groups or family holidays.

7 bedrooms, sleeping up to 12 + 2 cots
- staffed and with full board
-short stay and self-catering
-rates on application

Dalhousie Lodge

Dalhousie Lodge
Edzell, by Brechin, Angus

Tel: 01356 624566   Fax: 01356 623725
email: Dalhousieestate@btinternet.com

The essential guide for fishing in Scotland

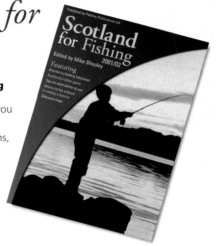

If you enjoy fishing, you'll love **Scotland for Fishing 2001/2002.** Edited by award-winning fisherman and journalist Mike Shepley, Scotland for Fishing will help you get on the water at Scotland's best fishing sites.

If you order your copy direct from Pastime Publications, you can save £1 on the cover price. For just **£5.99** including post and packaging, we'll deliver the guide to your door anywhere in the UK.

Send your cheque, made payable to Pastime Publications, to Pastime Publications, Golf Reader Offer, 5 Dalgety Avenue, Edinburgh EH7 5UF, along with your address details. Then sit back and start planning your Scottish fishing holiday.

Allow 28 days for delivery.

SCOTLAND
HOME OF GOLF
online

www.scotland-for-golf.com

Lynedoch (Murrayshall)

A newcomer to the circuit – but what a corker it may turn out to be. The Murrayshall course is now well known; its shorter sister course is built on the rising ground to the south of it and while that may suggest a fair amount of climbing, it is not a major worry. The clever use of the sloping terrain, trees and other natural features will be, however! Locals confidently predict that the Lynedoch will be a winner. I won't argue.

hidden gem

7th green, Lynedoch (Murrayshall).

HOLE	NAME	WHITE YARDS	YELLOW YARDS	PAR	STROKE INDEX
1	Two Mile	369	359	4	10
2	Burnside	329	319	4	6
3	Heathery Knowe	152	152	3	18
4	Lang Road	374	364	4	2
5	Blackcraig	318	308	4	14
6	Wild Meadow	106	96	3	16
7	Aranbathie	308	298	4	8
8	Birch Lochan	389	379	4	4
9	Scoonie Burn	383	373	4	12

HOLE	NAME	WHITE YARDS	YELLOW YARDS	PAR	STROKE INDEX
10	The Saddle	312	302	4	11
11	Tayview	91	91	3	5
12	Douglas Wynd	456	446	5	17
13	Brae	121	122	3	3
14	MacDuff's Folly	440	428	5	1
15	Lynedoch View	294	294	4	15
16	The Quarry	355	304	4	7
17	Stormont	201	187	3	13
18	Balgarvie	363	363	4	9

No. of holes: 18	Yardage: 5359	SSS: 69
GREEN FEES	Weekdays	
Individual round	£18	Gaz ref: Page 136
Daily rates	£18	Map ref: Page 155, A7
Are visitors free to play?		Yes
Nearest Airport: Edinburgh, 44.4 miles		Nearest Rail Station: Perth, 4.3 miles

CLUB INFORMATION

Murrayshall Country House, Scone, Perthshire PH2 7PH

Clubhouse	(01738) 551171
Pro Shop	-
Annual closure	No
Weekly closure	No

TO LOCATE THIS GOLF COURSE ON THE MAPS (p155-159) LOOK FOR THE FLAG WITH THIS PAGE NUMBER.

Kirriemuir

I hesitate to suggest that a round at Kirriemuir will prove to be more relaxing than others in Tayside for fear of rousing the ire of the locals! It ought to be less taxing, let's put it that way, as the modest length of the course (5500 yards or thereby) offers lots of tempting birdie opportunities. Only one hole of 400 yards-plus means that irons are working over-time while your short game is given a thorough going over. Tight fairways and lots of trees put straightness at the top of the duty roster!

hidden **gem**

11th green, Kirriemuir.

HOLE	NAME	WHITE YARDS	YELLOW YARDS	PAR	STROKE INDEX
1	–	373	–	4	6
2	–	147	–	3	16
3	–	414	–	4	1
4	–	335	–	4	9
5	–	277	–	4	14
6	–	384	–	4	3
7	–	301	–	4	12
8	–	154	–	3	17
9	–	352	–	4	8

HOLE	NAME	WHITE YARDS	YELLOW YARDS	PAR	STROKE INDEX
10	–	330	–	4	13
11	–	325	–	4	10
12	–	388	–	4	4
13	–	391	–	4	2
14	–	352	–	4	7
15	–	285	–	4	15
16	–	119	–	3	18
17	–	195	–	3	11
18	–	388	–	4	5

No. of holes: 18	Yardage: 5510	SSS: 67
GREEN FEES	Weekdays	
Individual round	On application	Gaz ref: Page 107
Daily rates	On application	Map ref: Page 155, B6
Are visitors free to play?		Yes
Nearest Airport: Aberdeen, 62.3 miles		Nearest Rail Station: Dundee, 18.8 miles

KIRRIEMUIR GOLF CLUB

Northmuir, Kirriemuir DD8 4LN

Clubhouse   (01575) 572144
Pro Shop   (01575) 573317
Annual closure No
Weekly closure No

TO LOCATE THIS GOLF COURSE ON THE MAPS (p155-159) LOOK FOR THE FLAG WITH THIS PAGE NUMBER.

Gazeteer of Scotland's Golf Clubs

A guide to using our Gazetteer Section

Scotland has seen many changes in boundaries over the years; we have had County boundaries, District boundaries and Regional boundaries. While our featured courses section is broken down by Regional boundaries, the number of entries in the Gazetteer section makes this rather difficult for the reader to find courses in close proximity when arranging a tour. We have therefore gone back to the old county system to assist you in your search. We have broken Scotland down into nine regions and the Scottish Islands, and listed our twenty-nine counties against them on this page to help you along. Some counties will appear twice if they border two recognised regions. We hope this explanation assists with your search. If you are looking for a specific course, refer to our alphabetical index on page 159.

Borders: Berwickshire, Peebleshire, Roxburghshire, Selkirkshire.

Central: Clackmananshire, Stirlingshire.

Dumfries & Galloway: Dumfriesshire, Kirkudbrightshire, Wigtonshire.

Fife: Fife, Kinross-shire, Perthshire.

Grampian & Moray: Aberdeenshire, Banffshire, Kincardineshire, Morayshire, Nairnshire.

Highlands: Banffshire, Caithness, Inverness-shire, Ross-shire, Sutherland, Islands.

Lothian

Strathclyde: Argyll, Ayrshire, Dunbartonshire, Lanarkshire, Renfrewshire.

Tayside: Angus, Fife.

Islands: Arran, Bute, Cumbrae, Colonsay, Gigha, Islay, Lewis, Mull, Orkney, Skye, Shetland, Tiree.

ABERDEENSHIRE

ABERDEEN
Auchmill Golf Course
Bonnieview Road,
Aberdeen AB16 7FQ.
Tel: (01224) 714577.
18 holes, 5082 yds.
Charges: On application.
Tel: (01224) 714577.

Balnagask Golf Course
St Fitticks Road,
Aberdeen AB11 8TN.
Tel: (01224) 876407.
18 holes, 5472 yds.
Charges: On application.
Starter: (01224) 876407.

Bon Accord Golf Club
19 Golf Road,
Aberdeen AB24 5QB.
Tel: (01224) 633464.
18 holes, 6270 yds, SSS 69.
Charges: On application
Aberdeen Leisure on
(01224) 647647.

Visitors are welcome.
Catering facilities available.
Secretary: F. Shand
Tel: (01224) 633464.

Caledonian Golf Club
20 Golf Road,
Aberdeen AB24 5QB.
Tel: (01224) 632443.
18 holes, 6437 yds, SSS 69.
Charges: £9.50 per round
weekdays, £12 per round
weekends.
For advance reservations
Tel: (01224) 632269.
Driving range nearby plus
6 hole course.
Catering facilities are available.
Entertainment Fri/Sat evenings.
Visitors most welcome.
Secretary: Douglas Esson
Tel: (01224) 632443.

Deeside Golf Club
Bieldside,
Aberdeen AB15 9DL.
Tel: (01224) 869457.
18 holes, 6237 yds, SSS 70.
Charges: £35 per day; £45
weekends/bank holidays.
A practice area, caddy cars and
catering facilities are available.
Visitors are welcome Mon-Fri,Sun.
Professional: Frank Coutts
Tel: (01224) 861041.

Hazlehead Golf Course
Hazlehead,
Aberdeen AB15 8BD.
Tel: (01224) 676474.
2 x 18 hole courses.
Lengths 5673m, 5303m.
9 hole course, length 2531m
Charges: On application.
Starter: (01224) 321830.
Professional: Mr I. Smith
Tel: (01224) 317336.

Kings Links Golf Course

Golf Road,
Aberdeen AB24 1RZ.
Tel: (01224) 632269.
18 holes, 6270 yds, SSS 70
Charges: On application.
Starter: (01224) 632269.
Professional: Mr B. Davidson
Tel: (01224) 641577.

Murcar Golf Club

Bridge of Don,
Aberdeen AB23 8BD.
Tel: (01224) 704354.
E-mail: murcar-golf-club
@LineOne.net
Web Site: www.murcar.co.uk
18 holes, 6287 yds, SSS 71.
Charges: On application.
For advance reservations
Tel: (01224) 704354.
Caddy cars and catering
facilities are available.
Visitors and parties welcome.
Secretary: D. Corstorphine
Tel: (01224) 704354.
FOR MORE INFORMATION, SEE PAGE 62

Northern Golf Club

22 Golf Road,
Aberdeen AB24 3BQ.
Tel/fax: (01224) 622679.
18 holes, 6270 yds, SSS 69
Charges: £11 round (Mon-Fri),
£14 (Sat/Sun).
For advance reservations
Tel: (01224) 522000.
Practice area and catering facilities
are available, please give prior notice.
Visitors are welcome.
Secretary: Alfred W. Gardner -
Tel: (01224) 622679.
Professional: Kings Links Driving
Range Tel: (01224) 641577.

Peterculter Golf Club

Burnside Road,
Peterculter, Aberdeen.
Tel: (01224) 735245.
18 holes, 5601 yds, SSS 69
Charges: £14 round, £18 daily.
For advance reservations
Tel: (01224) 734994.
Practice area, caddy cars and
catering facilities available.
Visitors welcome at all times.
Secretary: K. Anderson
Tel: (01224) 735245.

Professional: D. Vannet
Tel: (01224) 734994.

Royal Aberdeen Golf Club

(2 courses),
Links Road, Bridge of Don,
Aberdeen AB23 8AT.
Tel: (01224) 702571 (clubhouse).
Fax: (01224) 826591
E-mail: reservations@royal-
aberdeen.demon.co.uk
Balgownie Links – 18 holes, 6403
yds. Medal SSS 73, SSS 71, Par 70.
Silverburn Links – 18 holes, 4021
yds. Par 60.
Charges: Balgownie – Weekdays
£60 per round, £85 daily. Weekends
£70 per round.
Silverburn – Weekdays £30
per round, £42.50 daily. Weekends
£35 per round.
Juniors (18 and under) 50% discount.
For advance reservations
Tel: (01224) 702221.
A practice area and full catering
facilities are available.
Times for visitors: Mon-Fri: 10am
-11.30am and 2.30pm - 3.30pm.
Weekends: after 3.30pm. First
Tuesday and third Thursday of
month: after 10.30am. Times are
available outwith the above on
application.
All players must hold handicap
certificate.
Caddies available, but cannot be
guaranteed.
Secretary: Mr Fraser Webster
Tel: (01224) 702571.
Professional: Mr Ronnie MacAskill
Tel: (01224) 702221.
FOR MORE INFORMATION, SEE PAGE 61

Rosehearty Golf Club

Masons Arms Hotel,
Rosehearty AB43 7JJ.
Tel: (01346) 571250.
9 holes, 4018m/4397 yds, SSS 62.
Charges: £8 Mon-Fri round,
£10 weekend round.
For advance reservations
Tel: (01346) 571250.
Visitors welcome all week and
catering facilities available.
Secretary: A. Watt

Westhill Golf Club (1977)

Westhill Heights,
Westhill,
Aberdeenshire AB32 6RY.
Tel: (01224) 742567.
18 holes, 5849 yds, SSS 69
Charges: rounds from £12.
For advance reservations
Tel: (01224) 740159.
Caddy cars, practice area and
catering facilities are available.
Visitors are welcome all
week except Sat.
Administrator: Amelia Burt
Tel: (01224) 742567.
Professional: G. Bruce
Tel: (01224) 740159.

ABOYNE

Aboyne Golf Club

Golf Road, Aboyne
AB34 5HP
Tel: (01339) 886328.
18 holes, 5910 yds, SSS 69
Charges: Mon-Fri £19 per round,
£25 per day; Sat/Sun £23 per
round, £30 per day.
For advance reservations
Tel: (01339) 887078 (Sec).
A practice area, caddy cars and
catering facilities are available.
Visitors are welcome all week.
Secretary: Mrs Mairi MacLean
Tel: (01339) 887078.
Professional: I. Wright

ALFORD

Alford Golf Club

Montgarrie Road,
Alford, AB33 8AE.
Tel: (019755) 62178.
E-mail: golf@alford.co.uk
Web site: http://golf.alford.co.uk
18 holes, 5483 yds, SSS 65
Charges: Mon-Fri £13, weekend
£21 per round.
Mon-Fri £19, weekend £27 daily.
For advance reservations
Tel: (019755) 62178.
A practice area and catering facilities
are available. Visitors are welcome
all week. Please check for weekends.
Club Secretary: Bob Fiddes
Tel: (019755) 62178.

Aberdeenshire

BALLATER
Ballater Golf Club
Victoria Road,
Ballater AB35 5QX.
Tel: (01339) 755567
E-mail: sec@ballatergolfclub.co.uk
Web site: www.ballatergolfclub.co.uk
18 holes, 5638 yds, Par 67.
Charges: On application.
For advance reservations
Tel: (01339) 755567/755658.
A practice area, caddy cars, buggies
and catering facilities are available.
Visitors are welcome.
Secretary: A. Barclay
Tel: (01339) 755567.
Professional: W. Yule
Tel: (01339) 755658.

BANCHORY
Banchory Golf Club
Kinneskie Road,
Banchory, AB31 5TA.
Tel: (01330) 822365,
Fax: (01330) 822491.
18 holes, 5775yds, SSS 68.
Charges: £18 per round,
£25 daily (Mon-Fri), £21 per
round (weekend).
For advance reservations
Tel: (01330) 822447.
A practice area, caddy cars and
catering facilities are available.
Visitors are welcome all week,
restricted at weekends.
Secretary: Mrs Anne Smith
Tel: (01330) 822365.
Professional: David Naylor
Tel: (01330) 822447.

BRAEMAR
Braemar Golf Course
Cluniebank Road,
Braemar AB35 5XX.
Tel: (013397) 41618.
18 holes, 4916 yds, SSS 64
Charges: Weekend - daily £23, per
round £18; mid-week - daily £20,
per round £15.
Caddy cars and catering facilities
are available.
Visitors are welcome all week.
Secretary: John Pennet
Tel: (01224) 704471.

CRUDEN BAY
Cruden Bay Golf Club
Aulton Road,
Cruden Bay.
Tel: (01779) 812285.
18 and 9 holes, 5848m/6395 yds.
SSS 72 (18), 65 (9).
Charges: On application.
For advance reservations
Tel: (01779) 812285.
A practice area, caddy cars and
catering facilities are available.
Visitors are welcome all week
but restricted at weekends.
No society bookings at
weekends. Administration: R.
Pittendrigh
Tel: (01779) 812285.
Professional: Robbie Stewart
Tel: (01779) 812414.

ELLON
McDonald Golf Club
Hospital Road, Ellon.
Tel: (01358) 720576.
18 holes, 5651 yds, SSS 69.
Charges: On application.
Catering facilities available
on request.
Secretary: George Ironside
Tel: (01358) 720576.
Professional: Ronnie Urquhart
Tel: (01358) 722891.
Fax: (01358) 720001.

FRASERBURGH
Fraserburgh Golf Club
Fraserburgh.
Tel: (01346) 518287.
18 holes, 6279 yds, SSS 70.
9 holes, 3400 yds.
Charges: £20 daily (Mon-Fri),
£25 (Sat/Sun). £50 weekly.
A practice area and catering
facilities are available.
Secretary: Mr J. Mollison
Tel: (01346) 516616.
FOR MORE INFORMATION, SEE PAGE 70

HUNTLY
Huntly Golf Club
Cooper Park,
Huntly AB54 4SH.
Tel: (01466) 792643.
18 holes, 5899 yds, SSS 66
Charges: £13 (weekdays),
£20 (weekends) daily.
Catering facilities are available.

INSCH
Insch Golf Club
Golf Terrace,
Insch AB52 6JY
Tel: (01464) 820363
18 holes, 5395 yds, SSS 66 men, SSS
68 ladies.
Charges: On application.
For advance reservations
Tel: (01464) 820363.
Tees reserved Mon., Tues. & Wed.
Visitors welcome at any other time.
Secretarial Assistant: Mrs Sheena
Smith Tel: (01464) 820363.

INVERALLOCHY
Inverallochy Golf Course
Whitelink, Inverallochy, Fraserburgh,
AB43 8XY
Tel: (01346) 582000.
18 holes, 5244 yds, Par 66.
(Further details on application).

INVERURIE
Inverurie Golf Club
Blackhall Road,
Inverurie AB51 5JB.
Tel: (01467) 620207/620193.
18 holes, 5711 yds, SSS 68.
Charges: Round (Mon-Fri) £14,
Daily (Mon-Fri) £18,
Round (Sat/Sun) £18,
Daily (Sat/Sun) £24.
Catering facilities are available.
Wide wheeled caddy cars only.

KEMNAY
Kemnay Golf Club
Monymusk Road, Kemnay.
Tel: (01467) 642060
E-mail: administrator@kemnaygolf-
club.co.uk
Web site: www.kemnaygolfclub.co.uk
18 holes, 6342 yds, SSS 71
Charges: Weekdays – Round £18,
Day £24. Weekends – Round £22,
Day £28.
For advance reservations
Tel: (01467) 642225.
Full catering and bar facilities avail-
able. Visitors welcome: Telephone
for starting times. Administrator:
George Berstan
Tel: (01467) 643746.
Professional: Ronnie McDonald
Tel: (01467) 642225.

KINTORE
Kintore Golf Club
Balbithan Road, Kintore.
Tel: (01467) 632681.
18 holes, 5997 yds, SSS 69.
Charges: £11 midweek per round,
£16 weekends.
For advance reservations
Tel: (01467) 632631.
Visitors are welcome all week
except between 4pm-7pm
Mon, Wed and Fri Apr-Sept.
Secretary: Mrs Vicki Graham.

LONGSIDE
Longside Golf Club
Westend, Longside AB42 7XJ.
Tel: (01779) 821558.
18 holes, 5215yds, SSS 66, Par 66.
Charges: £10 per round, £14 daily
(Mon-Fri), £12 per round, £16 daily
(Sat), £16 per round, £20 daily (Sun).
For advance reservations
Tel: (01779) 821558.
Caddies and caddy cars available.
Visitors are welcome all week, not
before 10.30am Sundays.
Secretary: Mr S. Silcock
Tel: (01779) 821558

NEWBURGH-ON-YTHAN
Newburgh-on-Ythan Golf Club
Beach Road, Newburgh,
AB41 6BE.
Tel: (01358) 789058.
E-mail: secretary@newburgh-on-
ythan.co.uk
Web site: www.newburgh-on-
ythan.co.uk
18 holes, 6162 yds, SSS 70.
Charges: per round £16 (weekdays),
£21 (weekends);
per day £21 (weekdays), £26
(weekends).
For advance reservations
Tel: (01358) 789058 (clubhouse).
A practice area is available. Visitors
are welcome all week but club com-
petitions every Tuesday evening.
Catering available by arrangement.
Secretary: Mrs V. Geoghegan
Tel: (01358) 789084.
FOR MORE INFORMATION, SEE PAGE 63

NEWMACHAR
Newmachar Golf Club
Swailend,
Newmachar, AB21 7UU.
Tel: (01651) 863002.
Fax: (01651) 863055.
Hawkshill Course - 18 holes, 6628
yds, SSS 74.
Charges: £30 round, £45 day (Mon-
Fri), £40 round (Sat/Sun).
Swailend Course - 18 holes, 6388
yds, SSS 71.
Charges: £15 round, £25 day
(Mon-Fri). £20 round, £30 day
(Sat/Sun).
One round on each course £35
(Mon-Fri) £45 (Sat/Sun).
For advance reservations
Tel: (01651) 863002.
Driving Range, practice bunker and
chipping area, putting green.
Powered buggies and caddy cars
for hire.
Fully licensed clubhouse with
catering available 7 days.
Visitors welcome
(advance booking recommended).
Secretary/Manager:
George A. McIntosh.
Tel: (01651) 863002.
Director of Golf: GordonSimpson.
Tel/Fax: (01651) 863222.

OLD MELDRUM
Old Meldrum Golf Club
Kirk Brae, Old Meldrum
Inverurie AB51 0DJ.
Tel: (01651) 872648.
18 holes, 5988 yrds.
SSS 69 (Par 70) Medal Tees,
SSS 66 (Par 68) Forward Tees
Charges: Per round- £14 Mon-Fri,
Sat/Sun £20, weekly (Mon-Fri) £50.
For reservations
Tel: Pro shop - (01651) 873555.
Visitors and visiting parties welcome.
A practice area and bar and full cater-
ing facilities are available.
Secretary: Mr J. Page
Tel: (01651) 872726.
Professional: Hamish Love.

PETERHEAD
Peterhead Golf Club
Riverside Drive, Peterhead AB42 1LT.
Tel: (01779) 472149/480725,
Fax: (01779) 480725.
Old Course: 18 hole links, 6173 yds.
SSS 71 (Par 70) Medal tees,
SSS 68 (Par 69) Forward tees.
Charges: £16 round/£22 daily week-
days. £20 round/£27 daily weekends.
New Course: 9 holes, 2237 yds.
Charges: £9 round/daily. Juniors £4.
Bar and catering – new clubhouse.
Visitors welcome – restricted
Saturdays. Practice area, clubs and
trolleys available.
PGA Professional coaching available.
For advance reservations,
contact Secretary
Tel: (01779) 480725/472149.

PORTLETHEN
Portlethen Golf Club
Badentoy Road,
Portlethen AB12 4YA.
Tel: (01224) 781090.
Fax: (01224) 781090.
18 holes, 6707 yds, SSS 72
Charges: £14 weekdays, £21 week-
end/Bank holidays per round. £21
weekdays (only) daily.
For advance reservations
Tel: (01224) 781090.
Caddy cars, practice area and
catering facilities are available.
Visitors are welcome Mon-Fri;
weekend with member.
Administration Department,
Tel: (01224) 781090.
Professional: Muriel Thomson
Tel/Fax: (01224) 782571.

TARLAND
Tarland Golf Club
Aberdeen Road, Tarland,
Aboyne AB34 4TB.
Tel: (013398) 81413
9 holes, 5386m/5888 yds,
SSS 68 (18 holes).
Charges: £14 Mon-Fri. £18 Sat/Sun
Juniors half price.
For advance reservations
Tel: (01339) 881000.
Trolleys and practice area available.
Visitors are welcome all week, but
phone for weekends.
Secretary: Mrs L.O. Ward.

Aberdeenshire

TURRIFF
Turriff Golf Club
Rosehall, Turriff, AB3 4HD.
Tel: (01888) 562982
Fax: (01888) 568050
E-mail:
secretary@turriffgolf.sol.co.uk
www.turriffgolfclub.free-online.co.uk
18 holes, 6107 yds, SSS 69
Charges: On application.
For advance reservations
Tel: (01888) 563025.
Practice area, clubs, trolleys, catering/bar facilities available.
Visitors are welcome all week
and after 10am Sat/Sun.
Secretary, Tel: (01888) 562982.
Professional: Mr R. Smith
Tel: (01888) 563025.

ANGUS
ARBROATH
Arbroath Golf Course
Arbroath Artisan Golf Club
(Playing over above)
Elliot, by Arbroath, DD11 2PE.
Tel: (01241) 872069.
18 holes, 6185 yds, SSS 70.
Charges: £16 round (Mon-Fri),
£20 round (Sat/Sun). £23 daily
(Mon-Fri), £30 daily (Sat/Sun).
For advance reservations
Tel: (01241) 875837.
A practice area, caddy cars, hire clubs
and catering facilities are available.
Visitors are welcome all week.
Secretary: J. Knox
Tel: (01241) 872069.
Professional: J. Lindsay Ewart
Tel: (01241) 875837.

Letham Grange Golf Club
Colliston,
by Arbroath DD11 4RL.
Tel: (01241) 890373.
Old Course – 18 holes, Blue 6968
yds; White 6632 yds; Yellow 6348
yds; Red 5774 yds. SSS 73.
Charges: £35 round, £45 daily (Mon-
Fri). £40 round, £55 daily (Sat/Sun).
Glens Course – 18 holes, White 5528
yds; Yellow 5276 yds; Red 4687 yds.
SSS 68.
Charges: £18 per round, £25 daily.
One round on each course £40
weekdays; £45 weekends. Practice
areas (putting/chipping/bunker),

powered buggies and catering
facilities available.
Visitors are welcome all week.
Golf Administrator: Ewan Wilson
Tel: (01241) 890377.
Professional: Steven Moir
Tel: (01241) 890377.

BARRY
Panmure Golf Club
Burnside Road, Barry,
by Carnoustie DD7 7RT.
Tel: (01241) 853120
Fax: (01241) 859737
E-mail: secretary@panmuregolf-
club.co.uk
18 holes, 6317 yds, SSS 71.
Charges: On application.
For advance reservations
Tel: (01241) 855120.
A practice area, caddy cars and catering facilities are available. Visitors are
welcome all week, except Saturdays.
Secretary; Major (ret'd) G.W. Paton
Tel: (01241) 855120.
Professional: Neil Mackintosh
Tel: (01241) 852460.
FOR MORE INFORMATION, SEE PAGE 96

BRECHIN
Brechin Golf and
Squash Club
Trinity, by Brechin DD9 7PD.
Tel: (01356) 622383.
18 holes, 6096 yds, SSS 70.
Charges: Mon-Fri £17 round, £25
day. Sat-Sun £22 round, £30 day.
Catering facilities available.Visitors
are welcome without reservation.
Discounted 'Midweek Package' for
groups of 8 or more.
Professional: S. Rennie
Tel: (01356) 625270.

CARNOUSTIE
Carnoustie Golf Links
Buddon Links Course
Links Parade,
Carnoustie DD7 7SE.
18 holes, 5420 yds, SSS 66.
Charges: £20 round,
Juvenile (under 14) round £1.
For advance reservations
Tel: (01241) 853789.
E-mail: carnoustiegolf@aol.com
Caddies, caddy cars and
catering facilities are available.
Visitors are welcome all week.
Secretary: Mr J.M. Martin.
FOR MORE INFORMATION, SEE PAGE 97

Carnoustie Golf Links
Burnside Course
Links Parade,
Carnoustie DD7 7JB.
18 holes, 6020 yds, SSS 69.
Charges: £25 round,
Juvenile round (under 14) £4.
For advance reservations
Tel: (01241) 853789.
E-mail: carnoustiegolf@aol.com
Caddies, caddy cars (no caddy cars
Nov-Apr inc.)and catering facilities
are available.
Visitors are welcome all week.
Secretary: Mr J.M. Martin.

Carnoustie Golf
Links Championship
Course
Links Parade,
Carnoustie DD7 7SE.
18 holes, 6936 yds, SSS 75.
Charges: £70 per round.
For advance reservations
Tel: (01241) 853789.
E-mail: carnoustiegolf@aol.com
Caddies, caddy cars (no caddy cars
Nov-Apr inc.) and catering facilities
are available.
Visitors are welcome all week,
except Saturday morning
and before 11.30am Sunday.
Secretary: Mr J.M. Martin.

DUNDEE

Camperdown Golf Course
Camperdown Park, Dundee.
Tel: (01382) 623398.
18 holes, 6561 yds, SSS 72.
Visitors contact: Art &
Recreation Division,
Tayside House, Dundee.
Tel: (01382) 434000 (ext. 2872).
Secretary: Mrs J. Lettice
Tel: (01382) 623398.
(Further details on application).

Downfield Golf Club
Turnberry Avenue,
Dundee DD2 3QP.
Tel: (01382) 825595.
Fax: (01382) 813111.
18 holes, 6803 yds, SSS 73.
Charges: April and October dis-
counted rates. May - Sept £31 per
round, £44 per day, £34 per day
Sunday (2.00pm onwards).
Caddies, caddy cars, practice area and
catering facilities available.
Visitors are welcome weekdays and
Sunday pm - parties welcome with
pre-booking essential. Other times
Saturday and Sunday call starter on
day of play after 8.00am.
Secretary: Mrs Margaret Stewart
Tel: (01382) 825595,
Fax: (01382) 813111.
Professional/Starter:
Kenny Hutton
Tel: (01382) 889246.
FOR MORE INFORMATION, SEE PAGE 95

EDZELL

The Edzell Golf Club
High Street,
Edzell DD9 7TF.
Tel: (01356) 648235 (clubhouse).
18 holes, 6348 yds, SSS 71.
Charges: Weekday £23 round,
weekend £29 round. Weekday £33
daily, weekend £43 daily.
£90 weekly – excluding Sat & Sun.
For advance reservations
Tel: (01356) 647283.
Golf academy, practice facilities.
Caddy cars and catering facilities are
available.
Visitors are welcome all week.
Secretary: Ian Farquhar
Tel: (01356) 647283
Fax: (01356) 648094
E-mail: secretary@

edzellgolfclub.demon.co.uk
Professional: Alistair J. Webster
Tel: (01356) 648462
Fax: (01356) 648884
E-mail: alistair@webster.virgin.net
FOR MORE INFORMATION, SEE PAGE 98

FORFAR

Forfar Golf Club
Cunninghill, Arbroath Road,
Forfar DD8 2RL.
Tel: (01307) 462120.
18 holes, 6052 yds, SSS 70.
Charges: £20 round (Mon-Fri),
£25 daily, Sat/Sun £30 daily,
£25 per round.
For advance reservations
Tel: (01307) 463773.
Fax: (01307) 468495.
A practice area, caddy cars
and catering facilities are available.
Visitors are welcome all week.
Managing Secretary: W. Baird
Tel: (01307) 463773.
Professional: Mr P. McNiven
Tel: (01307) 465683.

KIRRIEMUIR

Kirriemuir Golf Club
Northmuir, Kirriemuir DD8 4LN.
Tel: (01575) 572144.
18 holes, 5553 yds, SSS 67.
Charges: On application.
Practice area, caddy cars and catering
facilities are available.
Visitors are welcome weekdays.
Professional: Mrs Karyn Dallas
Tel: (01575) 573317.
Fax: (01575) 574608.
FOR MORE INFORMATION, SEE PAGE 101

MONIFIETH

Broughty Golf Club
6 Princes Street, Monifieth, Dundee.
Tel: (01382) 532147.
For advance reservations
Tel: (01382) 532767.
A practice area, caddy cars and cater-
ing facilities are available.
Visitors are welcome all week and
after 2pm on Saturdays.
Secretary: A. Allardice
Tel: (01382) 532147.
Professional: Ian McLeod
Tel: (01382) 532945.

Monifieth Golf Links
Princes Street,
Monifieth DD5 4AW.
Tel/fax: (01382) 535553.
36 holes, Ashludie Course 5123 yds,
SSS 66.
Medal Course 6655 yds, SSS 72.
Charges: Ashludie Course - £15
round (Mon-Fri), £16 round
(Sat/Sun).
Medal Course - £30 round (Mon-
Fri), £14 junior (Mon-Fri), £36
round (Sat/Sun).
Package available: 1 round on each
course plus catering £47 (Mon-Fri
only).
Ashludie Starter: (01382) 532767
Medal Starter: (01382) 532967.
For advance reservations
Tel: (01382) 535553.
Caddies available with prior arrange-
ment. Practice area, caddy cars and
catering facilities are available.
Visitors welcome: Monday to Friday
after 9.32 am. Saturday after 2.15pm
and Sundays after 10am.
Secretary: H.R. Nicoll
Tel: (01382) 585553.
Professional: Ian McLeod
Tel: (01382) 532945.

Angus

Montrose Links Trust
Traill Drive,
Montrose DD10 8SW.
Tel: (01674) 672932.
Fax: (01674) 671800
E-mail:
secretary@montroselinks.co.uk
Web site: www.montroselinks.co.uk
Medal - 18 holes, 6533 yds, SSS 72.
Broomfield - 18 holes, 4800 yds,
SSS 63.
Charges: Medal - Mon-Fri £38 daily,
£48 Sat & Sun. Mon-Fri £28 round,
£32 Sat & Sun.
Broomfield - Mon-Sun £12 round.
Reductions for juniors, members'
guests and unemployed.
For advance reservations
Tel: (01674) 672932.
Caddy cars, practice area and catering
facilities are available. Visitors are
welcome all week. Visitors allowed
Saturdays after 2.30pm & Sundays
after 10am on Medal Course.
Secretary: Mrs Margaret Stewart
Tel: (01674) 672932.
Professional: Kevin Stables
Tel: (01674) 672634.

ARGYLL

BLAIRMORE
**Blairmore & Strone
Golf Club**
High Road, Blairmore,
by Dunoon PA23 8JJ.
Tel: (01369) 840676.
9 (18) holes, 1933m/2112 yds.
Charges: On application.
Vistors are welcome all week,
except Saturday afternoon.
Parties by prior arrangement.
Secretary: J.C. Fleming
Tel: (01369) 860307.

CAMPBELTOWN
The Machrihanish Golf Club
Machrihanish, by Campbeltown.
Tel: (01586) 810213.
18 and 9 holes, 6225 yds, SSS 71.
Charges: Sun-Fri £30 (18),
£6 (9) round, £50 (18) £12 (9) daily.
Saturday round £40, daily £60, £12
(9). Children 14 years and under,
half price on 9 hole course.
For advance reservations
Tel: (01586) 810277.
A practice area, caddy cars

and catering facilities are available.
Visitors are welcome all week
Secretary: Mrs A. Anderson
Tel: (01586) 810213.
Professional: Mr K. Campbell
Tel: (01586) 810277.

CARRADALE
Carradale Golf Course
Carradale,
Kintyre PA28 6Qt
Tel: (01583) 431378.
9 holes, 2387 yds, SSS 64.
Charges: £8 daily, £40 weekly.
For advance reservations
Tel: (01583) 431643.
Visitors welcome all week.
Secretary: Position vacant
Tel: (01583) 431643.

DALMALLY
Dalmally Golf Club
Orchy Bank, Dalmally PA33 1AS.
9 holes, 2264 yds, SSS 63.
Charges: £10 daily.
Visitors are welcome.
Secretary: A.J. Burke.
Tel: (01838) 200370.

DUNOON
Cowal Golf Club
22 Ardenslate Road,
Dunoon PA23 8NN.
Tel/Fax: (01369) 705673.
18 holes, 6063 yds, SSS 70.
Charges: £20 round (Mon-Fri); £30
round (Sat/Sun), £100 week ticket
(weekdays).
For advance reservations
Tel/Fax: (01369) 705673.
Caddy cars and catering facilities
are available.
Secretary: Wilma Fraser
TeilFax: (01369) 705673
Professional Russell .D. Weir.

INNELLAN
Innellan Golf Club
Knockamillie Road,
Innellan PA23 7SG
Tel: (01369) 703242.
9 holes, 18 holes 2342 yds, SSS 64.
Charges: £12 day/£8 for 9 holes.
Catering facilities are available.
Visitors are welcome all week, except
Mon, from 5pm.
Secretary: A. Wilson
Tel: (01369) 702573.

INVERARAY
Inveraray Golf Club
Lochgilphead Road, North Cromalt,
Inveraray PA32 8XT.
Tel: (01499) 302079
9 holes, 2753 yds, SSS 68.
Charges: Adults weekdays and
weekends - £15 per day
(after 5pm £10)
Visitors very welcome.
Various facilities nearby.
Captain: Calum Morrison.

LOCHGILPHEAD
Lochgilphead Golf Club
Blarbuie Road, Lochgilphead.
Tel: (01546) 602340.
9 holes, 4484 yds, SSS 63.
Visitors welcome. Licensed.
Clubhouse available. Open competi-
tions in summer.
Secretary: N. McKay
Tel: (01546) 603840 (after 6pm).

LOCHGOILHEAD
Drimsynie Golf Course
Lochgoilhead PA24 8AD.
Tel: (01301) 703247,
Fax: (01301) 703538.
9 holes, 1817 yds, SSS 60.
Charges: £8 per round. £8 daily.
For advance reservations
Tel: (01301) 703247.
Catering facilities are available.
Visitors welcome.
Secretary: Leonard Gow
Tel: (01301) 703247.

OBAN
Glencruitten Golf Course
Glencruitten Road, Oban.
Tel: (01631) 562868.
18 holes, 4452 yds, SSS 63.
Charges: On application.
For advance reservations
Tel: (01631) 562868.
A practice area and catering
facilities are available. Visitors are
welcome Tues, Wed, Fri and Sun.
Secretary: A.G. Brown
Tel: (01631) 564604 (after 6 pm).

SOUTHEND
Dunaverty Golf Club
Southend,
by Campbeltown PA28 6RX.
Tel: (01586) 830677.
18 holes, 4799 yds, SSS 63.
Charges: On application.
For advance reservations
Tel: (01586) 830677.
Visitors are welcome all week with-
out reservation, but check for club
competitions.
Secretary: David Macbrayne
Tel: (01586) 830619.

TARBET
Tarbert Golf Club
Kilberry Road, Tarbert.
Tel: (01880) 820565.
9 holes, 4744 yds, SSS 64.
Charges: On application.
Licensed clubhouse available.
Visitors are welcome.

TAYNUILT
Taynuilt Golf Club
Laroch, Taynuilt PA35 1JE.
9 holes, 4302 yds.
SSS gents 61, ladies 64.
Charges: On application.
Visitors are welcome all week.
Secretary: Murray Sim
Tel: (01866) 822429.

TIGHNABRUAICH
Kyles of Bute Golf Club
The Moss, Kames,
Tighnabunaich PA21 2EE.
9 holes, 4778 yds, SSS 64.
Charges: £8 per week day.
£10 Saturday and Sunday.
Secretary: Dr. J. Thomson -
Tel: (01700) 811603.

AYRSHIRE

AYR
Belleisle Golf Club
Bellisle Course,
Belleisle Park, Ayr KA7 4DU.
Tel: (01292) 441258.
18 holes, 6431 yds, SSS 64.
Charges: £19 round, £27 daily,
£85 weekly (Mon-Fri).
£21 round, £31 daily (weekend).
For advance reservations
Tel: (01292) 441258.
A practice area, caddy cars and
catering facilities are available.
Visitors are welcome all week.
Starters Office
Tel: (01292) 441258.
Professional: Mr D. Gemmell
Tel: (01292) 441314.

Seafield Course
18 holes, 5481yds, SSS 67.
Charges: £13 round, £20 daily,
£85 weekly (Mon-Fri).
£13.50 round, £25 daily (weekend).

Dalmilling Municipal Golf Club
Westwood Avenue, Ayr.
c/o South Ayrshire Council,
Burns House, Burns Statue Square,
Ayr KA7 1UT.
Tel: (01292) 263893.
18 holes, 5724 yds, SSS 68.
Charges: £13 round, £20 daily,
£85 weekly (Mon-Fri).
£13.50 round, £25 daily (weekend).
For advance reservations
Tel: (01292) 263893.
Caddy cars, practice area and
catering facilities are available.
Visitors are welcome all week.
Starters Office
Tel: (01292) 263893.
Professional: Philip Cheyney
Tel: (01292) 263893
Fax: (01292) 610543.

BARASSIE
Kilmarnock (Barassie) Golf Club
29 Hillhouse Road,
Barassie, Troon KA10 6SY.
Tel: (01292) 313920
E-mail: secretarykbgc@lineone.net
Web Site: www.kbgc.co.uk
18 holes 6817 yds, SSS 74.
9 holes, 2756 yds,
Charges:18 holes £40,
27 holes £50, 36 holes £60.
For advance reservations
Tel: (01292) 313920.
A practice area, caddy cars and
catering facilities are available.
Visitors are welcome Mon-
Tues/Thur/Fri pm.
Secretary/Manager: D.D. Wilson
Tel: (01292) 313920
Professional: Gregor Howie
Tel: (01292) 311322.

BEITH
Beith Golf Club
Bigholm Road,
Beith KA15 2JR.
Tel: (01505) 503166.
18 holes 5641 yds, SSS 68.
Club Secretary's office
Tel: (01505) 506814.
(Further details on application).

GAILES
Glasgow Golf Club
Gailes, Irvine.
Tel: (01294) 311258.
18 holes, 5954 m/6513 yds, SSS 72.
Charges: £42 round Mon-Fri,
£52 daily.
Sat & Sun pm only £47 (1998)
Deposit £10 per person required.
For advance reservations
Tel: 0141 - 942 2011
Fax: 0141 - 942 0770.
A practice area, caddy cars and cater-
ing facilities are available. Caddies
available by prior
arrangement.
Professional: Mr J. Steven
Tel: (01294) 311561.

Western Gailes Golf Club

Gailes, Irvine KA11 5AE.
Tel: (01294) 311649
E-mail: enquiries@westerngailes.com
Web site: www.westerngailes.com.
18 holes, 6639 yds, SSS 73.
Charges: £75 round incl lunch, £100
daily incl lunch.
For advance reservations
Tel: (01294) 311649.
Caddies, caddy cars and catering
facilities available.
Visitors welcome Mon, Wed and Fri.
Secretary: Andrew McBean
Tel: (01294) 311649.

GALSTON
Loudoun Gowf Club

Edinburgh Road,
Galston KA4 8PA.
Tel: (01563) 821993.
18 holes, 6061 yds, SSS 69.
Charges: £20 round, £30 daily.

GIRVAN
Brunston Castle Golf Club,

Dailly, by Girvan KA26 9GD
Tel: (01465) 811471.
18 holes, 6681 yds, SSS 72.
Charges: 9 holes - Mon-Fri £15 per
round, Sat/Sun £16 per round.
18 holes - Mon-Fri £26 per round,
Sat/Sun £30 per round.
36 holes - Mon-Fri £40 per round,
Sat/Sun £45 per round.
Group discounts available for
parties of 12 and over.
For advance reservations
Tel: (01465) 811471.
Caddy cars/motor buggies, driving
range and catering facilities are
available.
Visitors are welcome all week.
Secretary: Jenny Brady.

Girvan Golf Club

Golf Course Road, Girvan.
c/o South Ayrshire Council,
Burns House,
Burns Statue Square,
Ayr KA7 1UT.
Tel: (01465) 714346.
18 holes, 5064 yds, SSS 64.
Charges: £13 round, £20 daily,
£85 weekly (Mon-Fri).
£13.50 round, £25 daily (weekend).
Trolleys are available.
Practice area, caddy cars and

catering facilities available.
Visitors welcome all week.
Starters Office
Tel: (01465) 714346.
Professional: David Gemmell
Tel: (01292) 441314.

IRVINE
The Irvine Golf Club

Bogside, Irvine.
Tel: (01294) 275979.
18 holes, 5858m/6408 yds, SSS 71.
Charges: On application.
For advance reservations
Tel: (01294) 275979.
A practice area, caddy cars and
catering facilities are available
(caddies by arrangement).
Visitors are welcome by
arrangement.
Secretary: Mr W.J. McMahon
Tel: (01294) 278209.
Professional: Mr Keith Erskine
Tel: (01294) 275626.
FOR MORE INFORMATION, SEE PAGE 39

Ravenspark Golf Course

13 Kidsneuk, Irvine.
Tel: (01294) 271293.
18 holes, 6543 yds, SSS 71.
Charges: £8.40 round Mon-Fri,
£14.10 day Mon-Fri, £12.50 round
Sat-Sun, £19 day Sat-Sun.
Visitors welcome except before
2.30pm on Sat. from March-Oct.
Full catering and bar
facilities.
Secretary: G. Robertson
Tel: (01294) 554617.
Professional: P. Bond
Tel: (01294) 276467.

KILBIRNIE
Kilbirnie Place Golf Club

Largs Road, Kilbirnie.
Tel: (01505) 683398.
18 holes, 5500 yds, SSS 67.
Charges: £10 round, £31 day ticket.
Catering facilities are available.
Visitors welcome, except Saturdays.
Secretary: J.C. Walker
Tel: (01505) 683283.

KILMARNOCK
Annanhill Golf Club

Irvine Road,
Kilmarnock KA1 2RT.
Tel: (01563) 521644.
18 holes, 6269 yds, SSS 70.
Charges: £9.50 Mon-Fri. £18 Daily.
Saturday, Sundays and
Bank Holidays £18 Daily.
For advance reservations
Tel: (01563) 521644.
Practice area available and catering
facilities by arrangement.
Visitors welcome all week except
Saturdays.
Secretary: Mr Thomas Denham
Tel: (01563) 521644.

Caprington Golf Club

Ayr Road, Kilmarnock KA1 4UW.
Tel: (01563) 521915.
18 holes, 5718 yds, SSS 68.
Charges: £9.50 round.

LARGS
Largs Golf Club

Irvine Road,
Largs KA30 8EU.
Tel: (01475) 673594.
18 holes, 6155 yds, SSS 71.
Charges: £25 round, £35 daily.
For advance reservations
Tel/fax: (01475) 673594.
Caddy cars and catering facilities
are available.
Visitors are welcome all week.
Parties - Tues & Thurs.
Secretary: D. McGillivray
Tel/fax: (01475) 673594.
Professional: K. Docherty
Tel: (01475) 686192.

Routenburn Golf Club

Routenburn Road, Largs.
Tel: (01475) 673230.
18 holes, 5604 yds, SSS 68.
Charges: £9.10 Mon-Fri,
£18.20 Sat/Sun round.
£13 Mon-Fri, £21 Sat/Sun daily.
For advance reservations
Tel: (01475) 687240.
Practice area, caddy cars and catering
facilities are available.
Visitors welcome.
Secretary: Mr Joe Thomson
Tel: (01475) 675755.
Professional: Mr G. McQueen
Tel: (01475) 687240.

MAUCHLINE
Ballochmyle Golf Club
Mauchline KA5 6LE.
Tel: (01290) 550469
18 holes, 5990 yds, SSS 69.
Charges: On application.
Catering facilities are available.
Visitors are welcome with
reservation.
Secretary: A. Williams
Tel: (01290) 550469

MAYBOLE
Maybole Golf Course
Memorial Park, Maybole.
c/o South Ayrshire Council,
Burns House, Burns Statue Square,
Ayr KA7 1UT.
Tel: (01292) 612000.
9 holes, 2652 yds, SSS 33.
Charges: £8.80 round, £13 daily, £85
weekly (Mon-Fri).
For advance reservations
Tel: (01292) 263893.
Caddy cars available.
Visitors are
welcome all week..
Booking Officer:
Tel: (01292) 612000.
Secretary: Phillip Cheyney
Tel: (01292) 263893.

MUIRKIRK
Muirkirk Golf Club
Furnace Road, Muirkirk.
9 holes, 2690 yds, SSS 66.
Charges: On application.
For advance reservations
Tel: (01290) 661257.
Practice area and catering facilities
are available.
Visitors are welcome all week.
Secretary: Mrs M. Cassagranda
Tel: (01290) 661556.

NEW CUMNOCK
New Cumnock Golf Club
Lochill, Cumnock Road
New Cumnock KA18 4BQ.
Tel: (01290) 338848.
9 holes, 5350 yds (18), SSS 66.
Charges: £8 daily.
Catering facilities weekends only.
Visitors are welcome all times except
Sunday mornings and afternoons
(competition times).
Secretary: Dickson Scott.

PATNA
Doon Valley Golf Club
1 Hillside, Patna KA6 7JT.
Tel: (01292) 531607.
9 holes, 5858 yds. SSS Medal 70,
Yellow Tees 68.
Charges: £10 round, £15 daily.
For advance reservations
Tel: (01292) 531607.
Visitors welcome weekdays, week-
ends by arrangement.
Secretary: H.F. Johnstone MBE.
Tel: (01292) 550411.

PRESTWICK
Prestwick Golf Club
2 Links Road, Prestwick KA9 1QG.
Tel: (01292) 477404
E-mail: bookings@prestwickgc.co.uk
www.prestwickgc.co.uk
18 holes, 6544 yds, SSS 73.
Charges: On application.
Caddies, caddy cars, practice area and
catering facilities are available.
Visitors are welcome Mon, Wed &
Fri 8.00-8.50 am, 10.10-12.30 pm
and 2.40-4.00 pm. Thursday 8.00-
11.30am. No visitors at weekends or
on a Thursday afternoon.
Secretary: I.T. Bunch.
Professional: F.C. Rennie.

Prestwick St. Cuthbert
Golf Club
East Road, Prestwick KA9 2SX.
Tel: (01292) 477101
18 holes, 6470 yds, SSS 71.
Charges: £24 round, £32 daily.
For advance reservations
Tel: (01292) 477101.
Catering facilities are available.
Visitors are welcome Monday to
Friday (not on weekends or
public holidays).
Secretary: J.C. Rutherford
Tel: (01292) 477101.

Prestwick St. Nicholas
Golf Club
Grangemuir Road,
Prestwick KA9 1SN.
Tel: (01292) 477608
Fax: (01292) 473900.
18 holes, 5441m/5952 yds, SSS 69.
Charges: Weekday round £30, £50
day. Weekend round £35
(Sunday pm only)

For advance reservations
Tel: (01292) 477608.
Caddy cars and catering
facilities are available.
Visitors are welcome Monday to
Friday & Sunday pm.
Secretary: C.B.S. Thomson
Tel: (01292) 477608.
Starter's Shop
Tel: (01292) 473904.
FOR MORE INFORMATION, SEE PAGE 40

SKELMORLIE
Skelmorlie Golf Course
Belthglass Road, Upper Skelmorlie
Tel: (01475) 520152.
18 holes, 5030 yds, SSS 65.
Charges: Prices subject to review.
Catering facilities are available
for visitors and parties.
Visitors are welcome all week,
except Saturdays.
Secretary: Mrs A. Fahey
Tel: (01475) 520774.

STEVENSTON
Ardeer Golf Club
Greenhead, Stevenston.
Tel: (01294) 464542.
18 holes, 6409 yds, SSS 71.
Charges: On application.
For advance reservations
Tel: (01294) 465316 (secretary).
Caddy cars, practice area and
catering facilities are available.
Visitors are welcome all week,
except Saturdays.
Secretary: P. Watson
Tel: (01294) 465316.
Starter/Shop: R. Summerfield
Tel: (01294) 601327.

Auchenharvie Golf Complex
Moorpark Road, West Stevenston
KA20 3HU.
Tel: (01294) 603103.
9 holes, 5203 yds/ 4758m, SSS 66
Charges: £5.75 per round (Mon-Fri),
£7.30 per round (Sat/Sun).
For advance reservations
Tel: (01294) 603103.
Driving Range, caddy cars and
catering facilities available.
Visitors are welcome Mon-Fri.
Restricted tee times available during
weekends – Contact Proshop.
Professional: Bob Rodgers,
Tel: (01294) 603103.

TROON
Darley Golf Course
Harling Drive, Troon KA10 6NF.
c/o South Ayrshire Council,
Burns House, Burns Statue Square,
Ayr KA7 1UT.
Tel: (01292) 312464.
18 holes, 6501 yds.
SSS 72
Charges: £15 round, £25 daily;
£25 round, £29 daily weekend;
5 day tickets £85.
For advance reservations
Tel: (01292) 312464.
A practice area, caddy cars and cater-
ing facilities are available.
Visitors are welcome all week.
Starters Office -
Tel: (01292) 312464.
Professional: Gordon McKinley
Tel: (01292) 315566.

Fullarton Golf Course
Harling Drive, Troon KA10 6NF.
c/o South Ayrshire Council,
Burns House, Burns Statue Square,
Ayr KA7 1UT.
Tel: (01292) 312464.
18 holes, 4870 yds.
SSS 63
Charges: £13 round, £20 daily;
£13.50 round, £25 daily weekend; 5
day tickets £85.
For advance reservations
Tel: (01292) 312464.
A practice area, caddy cars and cater-
ing facilities are available.
Visitors are welcome all week.
Starters Office -
Tel: (01292) 312464.
Professional: Gordon McKinlay
Tel: (01292) 315566.

Lochgreen Golf Course
Harling Drive, Troon KA10 6NF.
c/o South Ayrshire Council,
Burns House, Burns Statue Square,
Ayr KA7 1UT.
Tel: (01292) 312464.
18 holes, 6822 yds.
SSS 73
Charges: £19 round, £27 daily;
£21 round, £31 daily weekend;
5 day tickets £85.
For advance reservations
Tel: (01292) 312464.
A practice area, caddy cars
and catering facilities.

Visitors are welcome all week.
Starters Office
Tel: (01292) 312464.
Professional: Gordon McKinley
Tel: (01292) 315566.

Royal Troon Golf Club
Old Course (Championship Course)
Craigend Road, Troon KA10 6EP.
Tel: (01292) 311555.
Fax: (01292) 318204.
E-mail: bookings@royaltroon.com
Old Course: Medal Tees
6641 yds. SSS 73
Portland: Medal Tees 6289 yds.
SSS 71
Charges: Championship Package★
£135 per person.
Portland Package★★ £95 per person.
★One round on the Old Course and
one round on the Portland Course
including morning coffee and
buffet lunch.
★★Two rounds on the Portland
Course including morning coffee
and buffet lunch.
Ladies and under-18s can play
the Portland Course.
Maximum handicap allowed: male
20, female 30 (certificate required).
Visitors are advised to book in
advance and are welcome Mondays,
Tuesdays and Thursdays from May
to October (inclusive).
Secretary: J.W. Chandler.
Professional: R.B. Anderson.

TURNBERRY
Ailsa & Arran
Turnberry Hotel & Golf Courses
KA26 9LT.
Tel: (01655) 331000.
2 x 18 holes, Ailsa 6976 yds, par 70;
Arran currently under reconstruction
opening 2001.
Colin Montgomerie Links Golf
Academy, caddies, dining facilities are
available.
Director of Golf: Brian Gunson.
Golf Sales Manager: Ewen Bowman.
SEE A ROUND AT TURNBERRY, PAGE 6

WEST KILBRIDE
West Kilbride Golf Club
Fullerton Drive,
West Kilbride KA23 9HT.
Tel: (01294) 823911.
18 holes, 6247 yds, SSS 71.
Charges: On application.
For advance reservations
Tel: (01294) 823042.
A practice area, caddy cars and
catering facilities are available.
Visitors welcome Monday to Friday.
For parties Tel: (01294) 823911
Secretary: H.Armour
Tel: (01294) 823911.
Professional: G. Ross
Tel: (01294) 823042.

BANFFSHIRE

BANFF
Duff House Royal Golf Club
The Barnyards, Banff AB45 3SX.
Tel: (01261) 812062.
Fax: (01261) 812224.
18 holes, 6161 yds, SSS 70.
Charges: On application.
For advance reservations
Tel: (01261) 812062/812075.
A practice area, caddy cars and
catering facilities are available.
Visitors are welcome all week
(but within restricted times, as
shown on Tee Booking sheets.
Handicap Certificate preferred).
Secretary: J. Corbett
Tel: (01261) 812062.
Professional: R.S. Strachan
Tel: (01261) 812075.

BUCKIE
Buckpool Golf Club
Barhill Road, Buckie, AB56 1DU.
Tel/Fax: (01542) 832236.
18 holes, 6257 yds, SSS 70.
Charges: Per round - £13 Mon-Fri;
£16 Sat/Sun. Daily tickets - £16
Mon-Fri; £22 Sat/Sun. £55 weekly
(Mon-Fri). £10 for senior citizens,
Juniors under 16 receive 50%
reduction.
For advance reservations
Tel: (01542) 832236.
Catering facilities are available.
Visitors are welcome daily. Visiting
parties are welcome by prior
arrangement.
Club Administrator: Miss M. Coull.

Strathlene Golf Club
Portessie, Buckie AB56 2DJ.
Tel: (01542) 831798.
18 holes, 5977 yds, SSS 69.
Charges: £14 per round, £20 per day.
Tee booking for weekend is
advisable. Discounted golf parties
welcome through prior
arrangement.
Trolleys for hire.
Secretary: George Jappy.

CULLEN
Cullen Golf Club
The Links, Cullen,
Buckie AB56 2UU.
Tel: (01542) 840685
Fax: (01542) 841977
E-mail:
cullengolfclub@btinternet.com.
18 holes, 4610 yds, SSS 62.
Charges: Mon-Fri £12 round.
Sat/Sun £16. Daily Tickets Mon-Fri
£16, Sat/Sun £22. (All fees subject to
review each November). Juniors (2
sections) - under 16 and 16-18 years.
For advance reservations
Tel: (01542) 840685.
A practice area, trolley carts, and
practice putting green, catering
facilities are available. Visitors wel-
come all week (but within restricted
tee times as stated on Starter's Board
for Club Competitions).
Visiting parties/ golfing societies are
welcome by prior arrangement.
Handicap Certificate preferred
but not essential.
Secretary: Ian Findlay
Tel: (01542) 840174
Fax: (01592) 841977.

DUFFTOWN
Dufftown Golf Club
Methercluny, Tomintoul Road,
Dufftown AB55 4BS.
Tel/Fax: (01340) 820325.
18 holes, 5308 yds, SSS 67.
Charges: £10 per round, £15 per day.
Bar evenings: catering by
arrangement.
Visitors are welcome all week.
Administrator: Marion Swann.
Web site:
http://www.speyside.moray.org/Dufft
own/Golfclub/index.html

KEITH
Keith Golf Course
Fife Park, Keith AB55 5DF.
Tel: (01542) 882469.
Fax: (01542) 888176.
18 holes, 5802 yds, SSS 68, Par 69.
Charges: Weekdays £12 per round,
£15 per day. Weekends £15 per
round, £20 per day. Trolley hire £2
per day.
Visitors welcome, catering available.
Parties by arrangement, advisable to
telephone in advance weekends.
Hon. Secretary: N. Gray.

MACDUFF
Royal Tarlair Golf Club
Buchan Street,
Macduff, AB44 1TA.
Tel: (01261) 832897.
Fax: (01261) 833455.
18 holes, 5866 yds, SSS 68.
Charges: £10 per round weekdays,
£15 per round Sat/Sun. £15 per day
weekdays, £20 per day Sat/Sun.
Juniors £6 per day. Adult weekly tick-
et £50, Junior weekly ticket £19.
For advance reservations
Tel: (01261) 832897.
Caddy cars and catering facilities are
available.
Visitors are welcome all week.
Secretary: Mrs Caroline Davidson
Tel: (01261) 832897.
FOR MORE INFORMATION, SEE PAGE 64

BERWICKSHIRE

COLDSTREAM
Hirsel Golf Club
Kelso Road, Coldstream.
Tel: (01890) 882678.
18 holes, 6092 yds.
SSS 70 men, SSS 72 ladies.
Charges: £18 weekdays, £25 Sat/Sun.
6 golf carts and trolleys,
practice area. Full bar & restaurant
facilities. Visitors are welcome
without reservation. Tee times may
be booked with the starter,
Tel: (01890) 882678.
Parties of 10 or over must book
through the Secretary in advance.
Secretary: Jay A. Petrie
Tel/fax: (01890) 882233.

DUNS
Duns Golf Club
Hardens Road, Duns.
Tel: (01361) 882194.
18 holes, 6209 yds.
SSS 70 men, SSS 73 ladies.
Charges: On application.
Catering facilities: by arrangement.
Visitors welcome all week.
Some restrictions, ring in advance.
Secretary: A. Campbell
Tel: (01361) 882717.
FOR MORE INFORMATION, SEE PAGE 22

EYEMOUTH
Eyemouth Golf Club
Gunsgreenhill,
Eyemouth TD14 5SF.
18 holes, 6520 yds, Par 72, SSS 72.
Charges: £20 per round, £25 per day,
reduced for Juniors. Professional's
shop/Practice area.
Magnificent clubhouse with full bar
and restaurant facilities.
Visitors and parties welcome any day
with special all day packages.
Please book tee-off times at Golf
Shop.
Tel: (01890) 750004 (starter).
Tel: (01890) 750551 (clubhouse).
FOR MORE INFORMATION, SEE PAGE 21

LAUDER
Lauder Golf Club
Lauder.
Tel: (01578) 722526.
9 holes, 6002 yds, (18 holes) SSS 70
Charges: On application.
Practice area is available.
Visitors are welcome all week (some
restrictions before noon on Sundays
and 5pm Wednesdays).
Secretary: David Dickson
Tel: (01578) 722526.

CAITHNESS

LYBSTER
Lybster Golf Club
Main Street, Lybster, Caithness.
Tel: (01593) 721308.
9 holes, 1929 yds, SSS 61.
Charges: On application.
Advance reservations not necessary.
Visitors are welcome all week.
Secretary: Angus D. Mackay.

Caithness

REAY
Reay Golf Club
Reay, Thurso KW14 7RE.
18 holes, 5372m/ 5876 yds, SSS 69
Charges: £15 round/daily,
£45 weekly.
A limited practice area is available.
Secretary: Mr McIntosh
Tel: (01847) 811288.
FOR MORE INFORMATION, SEE PAGE 75

THURSO
Thurso Golf Club
Newlands of Geise,
Thurso, KW14 7LF.
Tel: (01847) 893807.
18 holes, 5828 yds, Par 69.
Men SSS 69 ladies 71.
Heathland Course - most northerly
18 hole course on mainiand - views
of Pentland Firth and Orkney Island.
Bar open all day June, July, August –
sandwiches available. Visitors wel-
come. No booking. £15 per day.
Juniors £8, £60 per week. Free golf at
Pentland Hotel, Thurso, and John
O'Groats Hotel, John O'Groats and
Mackays Hotel, Wick. Country
membership £60 p.a.

WICK
Wick Golf Club
Reiss, Wick, Caithness KW1 4RW.
Tel: (01955) 602726.
18 holes, 5796 yds, SSS 69.
Charges: All week £15 daily;
weekly £60; fortnightly £80.
Juniors £3.
Visitors welcome without
reservations.
Society meetings catered for.
Hon. Secretary: D.D. Shearer
Tel: (01955) 602935.

CLACKMANNANSHIRE

ALLOA
Alloa Golf Club
Schawpark, Sauchie, Alloa FK10 3AX.
Tel: (01259) 722745.
18 holes, 6229 yds, SSS 71.
Charges: On application.
For advance bookings contact the
Professional.
Practice areas, caddy cars and
catering facilities are available.
Visitors and visiting parties are
welcome.

Secretary: T. Crampton
Tel: (01259) 722745.
Secretary: Bill Bennett
Tel: (01259) 724476.
Pro Shop: (01259) 724476

ALVA
Alva Golf Club
Beauclerc Street, Alva FK12 5LH.
Tel: (01259) 760431.
9 holes, 2423 yds, SSS 64.
Charges: On application.
Limited opening for catering
facilities.
Visitors are welcome all week.
Secretary: Mrs A. McGuire
Tel: (01259) 760455.

CAMBUS
Braehead Golf Club
Cambus, by Alloa FK10 2NT.
Tel: (01259) 725766
18 holes, 6086 yds, Par 70, SSS 69.
Charges: On application.
Catering available, Pro Shop.
Secretary: Paul MacMichael
Professional: David Boyce
Tel: (01259) 722078

DOLLAR
Dollar Golf Course
Brewlands House,
Dollar FK14 7EA.
Tel: (01259) 742400
Fax: (01259) 743497
E-mail: www.dollar.g.c@
brewlandshouse
freeserve.co.uk
Web site: dollargolfclub.co.uk
18 holes, 5242 yds, SSS 66.
Charges (Mon-Fri) £13.50 round
and £17.50 day. Sat/Sun £22.
For advance reservations
Tel: (01259) 742400.
Catering facilities are available,
except Tuesdays. Visitors welcome.
Secretary: Mr J.C. Brown
Tel: (01259) 743497.

KINCARDINE ON FORTH
Tulliallan Golf Club
Alloa Road, Kincardine, by Alloa.
Tel: (01259) 730396.
18 holes, length of course
5459m/5965 yds, SSS 69.
Charges: £15 round (Mon-Fri),
£20 (Sat/Sun). £25 daily (Mon-Fri),
£30 (Sat/Sun).

For advance reservations:
Tel: (01259) 730798.
Caddy cars and catering
facilities are available.
Visitors are welcome by prior
arrangement.
Secretary: J.S. McDowall
Tel: (01324) 485420.
Professional: Steve Kelly
Tel: (01259) 730798.

MUCKHART
Muckhart Golf Club
Muckhart, Dollar FK14 7JH.
Tel: (01259) 781423.
18 holes, 6034 yds, SSS 70, Par 71.
9 holes, 3060 yds, Par 35.
Charges: £16 per round (Mon- Fri),
£23 (Sat/Sun). £23 Daily (Mon-Fri),
£32 (Sat/Sun).
Caddy cars, bar and catering
facilities are available.
Secretary: A.B. Robertson.
Professional: Mr K. Salmoni.
FOR MORE INFORMATION, SEE PAGE 29

TILLICOULTRY
Tillicoultry Golf Course
Alva Road, Tillicoultry.
9 holes, 5266 yds (18 holes), SSS 66.
Charges: On application.
For advance reservations
Tel: (01259) 750124.
A practice area and catering
facilities are available.
Visitors are welcome all week until
4pm (except competition days).
Secretary: Piers Brown
Tel: (01259) 750124.

DUMFRIESHIRE

ANNAN
Powfoot Golf Club
Powfoot, Annan DG12 5QE.
Tel/Fax: (01461) 700276.
18 holes, 6010 yds, SSS 70.
Charges: £23 per round, £30 per day.
Telephone for advance reservations.
A practice area, caddy cars and catering
facilities are available.
Visitors are welcome all week except
Sat and before 2pm on Sun.
Manager: B.W. Sutherland MBE
Tel: (01461) 700276.
Professional: Gareth Dick
Tel: (01461) 700327.
FOR MORE INFORMATION, SEE PAGE 50

DUMFRIES
Crichton Golf Club
Bankend Road,
Dumfries DG1 4TH.
Tel/Fax: (01387) 247894.
9 holes, 2,976 yds.
SSS 69 White, SSS 68 Blue
Charges: On application.
For advance reservations
Tel: (01387) 247894.
Catering facilities are available.
Visitors are welcome: Mon,
Wed, Fri & Sun.

Dumfries and County Golf Club
Nunfield, Edinburgh Road,
Dumfries DG1 1JX.
Tel:(01387) 253585.
18 holes, 5928 yds, SSS 69.
Charges: £26 per round or per day.
A practice area, caddy carts and
catering facilities are available.
Visitors are welcome all week,
except Saturdays.
Secretary: W.G. Johnstone
Tel: (01387) 253585.
Professional Shop:
Tel: (01387) 268918.
Clubmaster Tel: (01387) 249921.
FOR MORE INFORMATION, SEE PAGE 46

Dumfries and Galloway Golf Club
2 Laurieston Avenue,
Dumfries DG2 7NY.
Tel: (01387) 253582.
18 holes, 6309 yds, SSS 71.
Charges: (Weekdays) £26 round, £26
daily. (Weekends) £32 round, £32
daily, £75 weekly.
For advance reservations
Tel: (01387) 263848.
Practice area, caddy cars and catering
available. Visitors welcome weekdays
except Tuesday.
Secretary: Tom Ross
Tel: (01387) 263848.
Professional: Joe Ferguson
Tel: (01387) 256902.

Pines Golf Centre
Lockerbie Road,
Dumfries DG1 3PF.
Tel: (01387) 247444
Fax: (01387) 249600
E-mail: admin@pinesgolf.com
Web site: www.pinesgolf.com.
18 holes, 5920 yds, SSS 69.
Professionals: Brian Gemmell,
Jim Davidson.

LANGHOLM
Langholm Golf Course
Whitaside,
Langholm DG13 OJS.
Tel: (01387) 381247.
9 holes, 6180 yds, SSS 70.
Charges: £10 round/daily, £30 weekly.
Practice area is available.
Visitors are welcome all week.
Secretary: W.J. Wilson
Tel: (01387) 380673/181247.
e-mail: golf@langholmgolfclub.co.uk
www.langholmgolf.club.co.uk

LOCHMABEN
Lochmaben Golf Club
Castlehillgate, Lochmaben,
Lockerbie DG11 1NT.
Tel: (01387) 810552.
18 holes, 4863m/5336 yds.
SSS 67 ladies, 66 men.
Charges: On application.
A practice area and catering available.
Visitors are welcome weekdays
before 5pm and weekends by
arrangement.
Hon. Secretary: J.M. Dickie
Tel: (01387) 810713.
FOR MORE INFORMATION, SEE PAGE 43

LOCKERBIE
Hoddom Castle Golf Club
Hoddom Bridge,
Lockerbie DG11 1AS
Tel: (01576) 300251.
9 holes, 2274 yds, SSS 66.
Charges: On application.
For advance reservations
Tel: (01576) 300251.
Catering facilities available and
visitors welcome all week, in summer.

Lockerbie Golf Club
Corrie Road, Lockerbie.
Tel: (01576) 203363.
18 holes, 5614 yds, SSS 67.
Charges: £16 Mon-Fri; £22 Sat daily;
£18 per round Sun.
Practice area and catering
facilities are available.
Visitors are welcome all week.
Secretary: J. Thomson
Tel/Fax: (01576) 203363.
FOR MORE INFORMATION, SEE PAGE 47

MOFFAT
The Moffat Golf Club
Coatshill, Moffat DG10 9SB.
Tel: (01683) 220020.
18 holes, 5218 yds, SSS 67.
Charges: On application.
For advance reservations
Tel: (01683) 220020.
Caddy cars and catering facilities
are available.
Visitors are welcome, except
Wednesday after 12 noon.
Secretary: T. Downer
Tel: (01683) 220020.

SANQUHAR
The Euchan Sanquar Golf Club
Black Addie, Sanquhar DG4 6JR.
Tel: (01659) 50577.
9 holes, 5594 yds (18 holes), SSS 68
Charges: On application.
Catering facilities (advance notice by
parties) are available.
Visitors are welcome all week.
Secretary: Mrs J. Murray
Tel: (01659) 58181.

SOUTHERNESS
Southerness Golf Club
Southerness, Dumfries DG2 8AZ.
Tel: (01387) 880677.
18 holes, 6564 yds, SSS 73.
Charges: £32 (Mon-Fri) daily, £45
(weekend). £128 weekly (Mon-Fri).
For advance reservations
Tel: (01387) 880677.
Fax: (01387) 880644.
A practice area, caddy cars and
catering facilities are available.
Visitors - members of recognised golf
clubs only are welcome all week.
Secretary: I.A. Robin
Tel: (01387) 880677
Fax: (01387) 880644.

Dumfrieshire

THORNHILL
Thornhill Golf Club
Blacknest, Thornhill DG3 5DW
Tel: (01848) 330546.
18 holes, 6085 yds, SSS 70, Par 71.
Charges: £21 weekdays,
£26 weekends.
For advance reservations
Tel: (01848) 330546 (Club Steward).
A practice area and catering available.
Visitors are welcome all week.
Secretary: J.F.K. Crichton.

DUNBARTONSHIRE

ALEXANDRIA
Vale of Leven Golf Club
Northfield Road, Alexandria G83 9AT.
Tel: (01389) 752351.
18 holes, 5165 yds, SSS 66.
Charges: Mon-Fri £18 round, £24
day ticket. Weekends: £20 round, £28
day ticket (2000 prices).
Catering facilities are available.
Visitors are welcome all week.
Open fairways discount.
Secretary: J. Stewart
18 Gallacher Crescent, Balloch G83
8HN. Tel: (01389) 757691.

BEARSDEN
Bearsden Golf Club
Thorn Road, Bearsden, Glasgow.
Tel: 0141-942 2351.
9 holes, 6014 yds, SSS 69.
Charges: On application.
Visitors are welcome, but must be
introduced by a member.
Secretary: Mr J.R. Mercer
Tel: 0141-942 2351.

Douglas Park Golf Club
Hillfoot, Bearsden G61 2TJ.
Tel: 0141-942 2220.
18 holes, 5982 yds, SSS 69.
Charges: £22 round, £30 daily.
For advance reservations
Tel: 0141-942 0985.
Caddy cars and catering facilities are
available.
Visiting parties by prior arrangement
are welcome Wednesdays and
Thursdays.
Secretary: J.G. Fergusson
Tel: 0141-942 0985.
Professional: D. Scott
Tel: 0141-942 1482.
FOR MORE INFORMATION, SEE PAGE 35

Glasgow Golf Club
Killermont, Bearsden, Glasgow.
Tel: 0141-942 2011.
Fax: 0141-942 0770.
18 holes, 5456m/5968 yds, SSS 69
Charges: On application.
Visitors by member's introduction.
Professional: Jack Steven
Tel: 0141-942 8507.

Windyhill Golf Club
Baljaffray Road,
Bearsden G61 4QQ.
Tel: 0141-942 2349.
18 holes, 6254 yds, SSS 70.
Charges: £20 round, £20 daily, £80
weekly.
For advance reservations
Tel: 0141-942 2349.
A practice area, caddies, caddy cars
and catering facilities are available.
Visitors are welcome Mon-Fri.
Secretary: Brian Davidson
Tel: 0141-942 2349.
Fax: 0141-942 5874.
Professional: Gary Collinson
Tel: 0141-942 7157.
FOR MORE INFORMATION, SEE PAGE 36

CLYDEBANK
Clydebank & District Golf Club
Glasgow Road, Hardgate,
Clydebank G81 5QY
Tel: (01389) 383407.
18 holes, 5326m/5825 yds, SSS 68
Charges: £15 round.
For advance reservations
Tel: Professional (01389) 383835.
A practice area and catering
facilities are available.
Visitors are welcome Mon-Fri
Secretary: W. Manson
Tel: (01389) 383407.
Professional: David Pirie
Tel: (01389) 383835.

CUMBERNAULD
Palacerigg Golf Club
Palacerigg Country Park,
Cumbernauld G67 3HU.
Tel: (01236) 734969.
18 holes, 5894m/6444 yds, SSS 71
Charges: On application.
For advance reservations
Tel: (01236) 721461.
A practice area and catering
facilities are available.
Visitors are welcome Mon-Fri.
Secretary: David S.A. Cooper
Tel: (01236) 734969.

Westerwood Hotel, Golf & Country Club
Westerwood, 1 St Andrews Drive,
Cumbernauld G68 0EW
Tel: (01236) 457171.
18 holes, 6139m/6616 yds, SSS 72
Par 72
Charges: On application.
For advance reservations
Tel: (01236) 452772.
Caddy cars, practice area and
catering facilities are available.
Visitors are welcome all week.

DULLATUR
Dullatur Golf Club
Glen Douglas Drive,
Craigmarloch, Cumbernauld.
Tel: (01236) 723230.
Carrickstone Course
18 holes, 6204 yds, SSS 70.
Antonine Course
18 holes, 5940 yds, SSS 70.
Charges: On application.
For advance reservations
Tel: (01236) 723230.
Caddy cars, practice area and catering
facilities are available.
Visitors are welcome Mon-Fri
(except 1st Wed in month & public
holidays).
Secretary: Mrs C. Miller
Tel: (01236) 723230.
Professional: D. Sinclair
Tel: (01236) 723230.

DUMBARTON
Cardross Golf Club
Main Road, Cardross,
Dumbarton G82 5LB.
Tel: (01389) 841213.
18 holes, 6469 yds, SSS 72.
Charges: £25 round, £35 day.
For advance reservations
Tel: (01389) 841350.
Caddy cars, practice area and catering
facilities are available.
Visitors welcome weekdays only.
Secretary: I.T. Waugh
Tel: (01389) 841754.
FOR MORE INFORMATION, SEE PAGE 38

Dumbarton Golf Club
Overburn Av., Broadmeadow,
Dumbarton G82 2BQ.
Tel: (01389) 732830.
18 holes, Par 71.
(Further details on application).

HELENSBURGH
Helensburgh Golf Club
25 East Abercromby Street,
Helensburgh G84 75Q.
Tel: (01436) 674173.
18 holes, 6104 yds, Par 69.
FOR MORE INFORMATION, SEE PAGE 37

KIRKINTILLOCH
Hayston Golf Club
Campsie Road,
Kirkintilloch G66 1RN.
Tel: 0141-776 1244.
18 holes, 5808m/6052 yds, SSS 70
Charges: On application.
For advance reservations
Tel: 0141-775 0723.
A practice area, caddy cars and
catering facilities are available.
Secretary: J.V Carmichael
Tel: 0141-775 0723.
Professional: Mr S. Barnett
Tel: 0141-775 0882.

Kirkintilloch Golf Club
Todhill, Campsie Road,
Kirkintilloch G66 1RN.
Tel: 0141 776 1256.
Secretary: 0141 775 2387.
(Further details on application).

LUSS
Loch Lomond Golf Club
Rossdhu House, Luss
Dunbartonshire G83 8NT
Tel: 01436 655555.
Fax: 01436 655500.
18 holes, 7060 yds from
Championship tees.
Private club for the exclusive use of
its members and their guests
Professional: Colin Campbell
Tel: 01436 655555.

MILNGAVIE
Clober Golf Club
Craigton Road,
Milngavie G62 7HP
Tel: 0141-956 1685.
18 holes, 4963 yds, SSS 65.
Charges: £15 per round.
Caddy cars and catering facilities
are available.
Visitors welcome until 4.00pm.
Secretary: T.S. Arthur
Tel: 0141-956 1685.

Esporta Golf Course
Strathblane Road,
Milngavie G62 8HJ.
Tel: 0141 955 2400.
(Further details on application).
Office Secretary: Maureen Young
Tel: 0141 955 2404.
Professional: Craig Everett.
18 holes, 6057 yds, Par 70.
Charges: Mon-Fri, £20, day £35,
Weekend, £25.

Hilton Park Golf Club
Stockmuir Road,
Milngavie G62 7HB.
Tel: 0141-956 4657.
2 x 18 holes, 6054 and 5487 yds.
SSS 70 and 67.
Charges: On application.
Caddy cars, practice area and catering
facilities are available.
Visitors are welcome by prior
arrangement. Monday-Friday, except
2nd and 4th Tuesdays of each month.
Secretary: Mrs J.A. Dawson
Tel: 0141-956 4657.
Professional: Mr W. McCondichie
Tel: 0141-956 5125.

Milngavie Golf Club
Laighpark, Milngavie,
G62 8EP.
Tel: 0141 956 1619.
18 holes, 5818 yds, SSS 68.
Charges: £22 round, £33 daily.
A practice area and catering facilities
are available.
Visitors are welcome if introduced by
a member.
Secretary: Ms S. McInnes
Tel: 0141-956 1619.

FIFE

ABERDOUR
Aberdour Golf Club
Seaside Place,
Aberdour KY3 OTX.
Tel: (01383) 860080.
18 holes, 5460 yds, SSS 66.
Charges: £17 round (£12 winter),
£28 day. Weekend no round tickets.
For advance reservations
Tel: (01383) 860080.
Catering facilities are available.
Visitors are welcome all week.
Secretary: J.J. Train
Tel: (01383) 860080.
Professional: G. Macallum
Tel: (01383) 860256.

ANSTRUTHER
Anstruther Golf Club
Marsfield, Shore Road,
Anstruther KY10 3DZ.
Tel: (01333) 310956.
9 holes, 4504m, SSS 63.
Charges: £12 weekdays,
£15 weekend.
For advance reservations
Tel: (01333) 310956.
Catering facilities are available.
Visitors are welcome.
Secretary: J. Boal.

BURNTISLAND
Burntisland Golf
House Club
Dodhead, Burntisland KY3 9LQ.
Tel: (01592) 874093.
18 holes, 5391m/5897 yds, SSS 70
Charges: £15 (weekday) round,
£25 (Sat/Sun) round. £25 (weekday)
daily, £35 (Sat/Sun) daily.
Weekly by arrangement.
For advance reservations

Tel: (01592) 872116/874093.
A practice area, caddy cars and catering facilities are available.
Visitors are welcome all week.
Manager: W. Taylor
Tel: (01592) 874093.
Professional: Mr J. Montgomery
Tel: (01592) 872116.
FOR MORE INFORMATION, SEE PAGE 59

CARDENDEN
Auchterderran Golf Club
Woodend Road,
Cardenden KY5 0NH.
Tel: (01592) 721579 Clubhouse.
9 holes, 5250 yds, SSS 66.
Charges £9 daily, weekdays. £12.50 daily, weekends. Meals available by advance booking.
Bar facilities/snacks Mon, Wed, Fri–Sun. Visitors welcome. Visiting parties exc. Sat.

Charleton Golf Club
Colinsburgh, Fife KY9 1HG
Club House (01333) 340505.

COWDENBEATH
Dora Golf Course
Seco Place, Cowdenbeath.
Tel: (01383) 511918.
2 x 9 holes, 2981m/3261 yds, SSS 70
Charges: Weekdays £7.50 day, £10.50 day weekend.
For advance reservations:
Tel: (01383) 511918 (Clubhouse).
Practice area, caddy cars and catering facilities available.
Visitors welcome all week.
Secretary: Duncan Ferguson
Tel: (01383) 511918 (Clubhouse).

CRAIL
Crail Golfing Society
Balcomie Club House, Fifeness,
Crail KY10 3XN.
Tel: (01333) 450686
E-mail: crailgolfs@aol.com
Web Site:
golfagent.com/clubsites/crail
2x18 holes, 5922 yds/6700 yds,
SSS 69/73
Charges: £25 round, £38 daily, (weekday). £30 round, £48 daily (weekend). Rental carts and clubs, practice area and catering facilities are possible. Visitors are welcome.
Advance bookings for parties is

recommended.
Manager: Jim Horsfield
Tel: (01333) 450686.
Fax: (01333) 450416.
Professional: G. Lennie
Tel: (01333) 450278/450960.
FOR MORE INFORMATION, SEE PAGE 55

CUPAR
Cupar Golf Club
Hilltarvit, Cupar KY15 5JT.
Tel: (01334) 653549.
2 x 9 holes, 5074 yds, SSS 65, Par 68.
Charges: Adult £15 day, £15 Sunday.
Juvenile £5 day. Family Day Ticket £30.Weekly Ticket £50.
Catering facilities are available.
Visitors welcome except Saturdays.
Secretary: J.M. Houston
Tel: (01334) 654101.

DUNFERMLINE
Canmore Golf Club
Venturefair Avenue, Dunfermline,
Fife KY12 0PE
Tel: (01383) 724969.
18 holes, 4914m/5376 yds,
SSS 66, Par 67.
Charges: Weekdays £15 per round, £20 per day.
Weekends £20 per round, £30 per day.
For advance reservations:
Tel (01383) 728416.
Visiting parties write to Secretary.
Full professional and catering services available.
Visitors welcome except Saturdays.
Secretary: Charlie Stuart
Tel: (01383) 513604.
Professional: Jim McKinnon
Tel: (01383) 728416.

Dunfermline Golf Club
Pitfirrane Crossford,
Dunfermline KY12 8QW.
18 holes, 6126 yds, SSS 70.
Charges: £20 round, £30 daily
Mon-Fri. £25 round, £35 daily Sun.
For advance reservations
Professional: S. Craig
Tel:(01383) 729061 (casual visitor);
Societies phone Secretary.
Clubhouse category 'A' listed building.
Trolleys, practice area and catering facilities are available.
Visitors are welcome Sun-Fri,

Societies welcome Mon-Fri.
Secretary: R. De Rose
Tel: (01383) 723534.

Pitreavie (Dunfermline) Golf Club
Queensferry Road,
Dunfermline KY11 8PR.
Tel: (01383) 722591.
18 holes, 5565m/6086 yds, SSS 69.
Charges: Weekdays £19 round, £26 daily.
Weekends £38 daily - no round tickets.
For advance reservations
Casual visitors Tel: (01383) 723151,
Parties, Societies etc.
Tel: (01383) 722591.
A practice area, caddy cars and catering facilities are available.
Visitors are welcome all week.
Secretary: Mr R.T. Mitchell
Tel: (01383) 722591.
Professional:Colin Mitchell
Tel: (01383) 723151.

ELIE
The Golf House Club
Elie, Fife KY9 1AS.
Tel: (01333) 330301.
18 holes, 6273 yds, SSS 70.
Charges: On application.
For advance reservations
Tel: (01333) 330301.
Catering facilities are available.
Visitors are welcome midweek.
Secretary: A. Sneddon
Tel: (01333) 330301.
Professional: Robin Wilson
Tel: (01333) 330955.
FOR MORE INFORMATION, SEE PAGE 54

FALKLAND
Falkland Golf Course
The Myre, Falkland KY15 7AA.
Tel: (01337) 857404.
9 holes, 2384m/2608 yds. SSS 66 (18)
Charges: On application.
Visitors are welcome.
Parties are welcome by prior arrangement.
Secretary: Mrs H.H. Horsburgh
Tel: (01592) 756075.

GLENROTHES
Balbirnie Park Golf Club
Balbirnie Park, Markinch,
by Glenrothes KY7 6NR.
Tel: (01592) 612095.
18 holes, 6210 yds, SSS 70.
Charges: On application.
For advance reservations contact:
Steve Oliver, Club Administrator
Tel: (01592) 752006.
Full catering facilities contact:
Club Stewardess: Melanie McFarlane
Tel: (01592) 612095.
Visitors welcome.
Tee bookings required.
Professional: David Scott
Tel: (01592) 752006.

Glenrothes Golf Club
Golf Course Road,
Glenrothes KY6 2LA.
Tel: (01592) 758686.
Length of course 5984m/
6444 yds, SSS 71.
Charges: £10 round, £16 daily
(weekdays). £14 round, £20 daily
(weekends).
For advance reservations
Tel: (01592) 754561, Min 12 players.
A practice area and catering facilities
are available.
Visitors are welcome all week.
Hon. Secretary: Mrs P.V. Landells
Tel: (01592) 754561.

KINGHORN
Kinghorn Golf Club
Macduff Cresent,
Kinghorn KY3 9RE.
Tel: (01592) 890 345.
18 holes, 4544m/4969 yds, SSS 66
Par 65.
Charges: On application.
Catering facilities through
Clubmistress Tel: (01592) 890345.
Secretary: Iain Gow
Tel: (01592) 265 445.

KIRKCALDY
Dunnikier Park Golf Course
Dunnikier Way, Kirkcaldy KY1 3LP.
Tel: (01592) 261599.
18 holes, 6036m/6601 yds, SSS 72.
Charges: £12 round, £18 daily (Mon-
Fri). £16 round, £22 daily (Sat/Sun).
A practice area, caddy cars and
catering facilities are available.

Professional: G. Whyte
Tel: (01592) 642121.
Secretary: Mr R.A. Waddell
Tel: (01592) 200627.

Kirkcaldy Golf Club
Balwearie Road,
Kirkcaldy KY2 5LT.
Tel: (01592) 205240 (Office)
(01592) 203258 (Pro shop).
18 holes, 6038 yds, SSS 69.
Charges: £22 round (weekdays), £28
(weekends). £28 daily (weekdays),
£36 weekends.
For advance reservations
Tel: (01592) 203258.
A practice area, caddy cars, petrol
carts and bar and full catering facili-
ties are available.
Visitors are welcome all week, except
Saturdays.
Director of Golf: A. Caira
Tel: (01592) 203258.

LADYBANK
Ladybank Golf Club
Annsmuir, Ladybank KY15 7RA.
Tel: (01337) 830814/830725
E-mail: ladybankgc@aol.com
18 holes, 6601 yds, SSS 72.
Charges: Nov/March – £24 per
round, £30 daily. April/Oct – £35 per
round, £45 daily. Weekly £150.
Prices under review.
For advance reservations
Tel: (01337) 830814.
Caddy cars, a practice area and
catering facilities are available.
Visitors welcome all week, except
Saturdays, limited on Sundays.
Secretary: D.R. Allan
Tel: (01337) 830814.
Professional: M. Gray
Tel: (01337) 830725.

LESLIE
Leslie Golf Club
Balsillie Laws, Leslie,
Glenrothes KY6 3EZ.
Tel: (01592) 620040.
9 holes, 4516m/4940 yds, SSS 64.
Charges: On application.
Bar facilities from 5–11.00pm.
Visitors are welcome all week.
Secretary: G. Lewis.

LEUCHARS
Drumoig Golf Club
& Hotel
Drumoig, Leuchars,
St. Andrews KY16 0BE.
Tel: (01382) 541800.
18 holes, 6420m/7006 yds, SSS 73.
Charges: £20-£25 round.
For advance reservations:
Tel: (01382) 541800.
Petrol buggies, trolleys,
practice area, restaurant and bar
facilities available.
Visitors welcome all week.
Secretary: Tel: (01382) 541800.
Professional: Tel: (01382) 541800.

St Michaels Golf Club
Leuchars, Fife, KY16 0DX
Tel: (01334) 839365,
Fax: (01334) 838666
E-mail: stmichaelsgc@BTclick.com
Web site: stmichaelsgc.co.uk.
18 holes, (Blue tees) 5563 yds, SSS
67, Par 70.
Charges: £20 per round, £28 per day
(Mon-Fri); £22 per round, £30 per
day (Sat & Sun).
Under 16's half price.
For Society reservations contact
Golf Club.
Caddy trolleys, bar and catering
facilities are available.
Visitors are welcome all week
but not before 1pm on Sundays.
Secretary: Joseph Strain.

LEVEN
Leven Links Golf Course
The Promenade,
Leven KY8 4HS.
Tel: (01333) 428859.
18 holes, 6436 yds, SSS 70.
Charges: On application.
For advance reservations
Tel: (01333) 428859/421390.
Caddy cars and catering facilities
are available.
Visitors are welcome Sun–Fri.
Secretary: A. Herd Esq
Tel: (01333) 428859.
FOR MORE INFORMATION, SEE PAGE 52

Fife

Scoonie Golf Club
North Links, Leven KY8 4SP.
Tel: (01333) 307007.
Fax: (01333) 307008.
18 holes, 4967m, SSS 65.
Charges: £11.50 round, £18.50 day.
Caddy cars and full catering facilities
are available.
Visitors welcome. Visiting parties not
accepted on Saturdays. Secretary: Mr
S. Kuczerepa
Tel: (01333) 301986.

LOCHGELLY
Lochgelly Golf Course
Lochgelly Golf Club
Cartmore Road,
Lochgelly KY5 9PB.
Tel: (01592) 780174.
(Further details on application).

LUNDIN LINKS
Lundin Golf Club
Golf Road, Lundin Links,
KY8 6BA.
Tel: (01333) 320202.
18 holes, 6394 yds, SSS 71.
Charges: £32 per round, £40 per day.
Other charges on application.
For advance reservations
Tel: (01333) 320202.
Golf trolleys, practice area and cater-
ing facilities are available.
Visitors: Weekdays between
9am-3.30pm (3pm Fri). After 2.30
Sat (£40 per round). No visitors Sun.
Secretary: D.R. Thomson
Tel: (01333) 320202.
Fax: (01333) 329743.
Professional: D.K. Webster
Tel: (01333) 320051.
FOR MORE INFORMATION, SEE PAGE 53

Lundin Ladies Golf Club
Woodlielea Road, Lundin Links,
Leven KY8 6AR.
9 holes, 2365 yds, SSS 67.
Charges: £10 weekdays, £12 week-
ends daily.
For advance reservations
Tel: (01333) 320832 (Clubhouse)
or write to secretary.
A few caddy cars are available.
Visitors are welcome all week except
Weds. April-Aug. (competitions).
Secretary: Mrs Marion Mitchell.

ST. ANDREWS
St. Andrews Links Trust
Pilmour House,
St Andrews KY16 9SF.
Links Clubhouse open to everyone
with changing facilities, shop and
restaurant.
Eden Clubhouse for golfers on Eden,
Strathyrum and Balgove Courses.
Practice centre open every day
8.00am to 9.00pm.
Tel: (01334) 466666
Fax: (01334) 479555.

Balgove Course
9 holes, beginners course.
Charges: £10 for 18 holes High
Season, £7 for 18 holes Low season.
For advance reservations
Tel: (01334) 466666.
Fax: (01334) 479555.

Eden Course
18 holes, 5602m/6162 yds, SSS 70.
Charges: £28 round (1 Apr-31 Oct),
£22 round (1 Nov-31 Mar).
3 day pass £95. Weekly £190.
Children's rate: 3-day pass £47,
weekly pass £95. These tickets are
valid on all courses except the Old.
For advance reservations
Tel: (01334) 466666.
Caddies and trolleys are available.

Jubilee Course
18 holes, 6223m/6805 yds, SSS 73.
Charges: £37 High Season, £28 Low
Season, Weekly £190,
3 day pass £95. Children's rates:
3 day pass £47, weekly pass £95.
These tickets are valid on all courses
except the Old.
For advance reservations
Tel: (01334) 466666.
Caddies and trolleys available.

New Course
18 holes, 6038m/6604 yds, SSS 72.
Charges: £42 High Season, £31 Low
Season. 3 day pass £95, week pass
£190. Children's rates: 3 Day pass
£47, weekly pass £95.
These tickets are vailid on all
courses except the Old.
Caddies, trolleys, golf buggies
available.
For advance reservations
Tel: (01334) 466666.

St. Andrews Old Course
18 holes, 6004m/6566 yds, SSS 72.
Charges: £85 High Season, £60 in
Nov, £42 Dec – March (mats). Low
season (1 Nov - March 31). (Closed
Sunday).
Caddies are available.
A handicap certificate is required.
Advance booking is essential or
enter daily ballot.
Tel: (01334) 466666.

Strathyrum Course
18 holes, 4658m/ 5094 yds, SSS 64
Charges: £18 per round (1 April – 31
October), £16 per round
(1 Nov – 31 March). 3 day pass £95,
weekly pass £190
(Tickets valid on all courses except
Old Course).
Caddies, trolleys and electric buggies
for over 65s or holders of medical
certificates.
Tel: (01334) 466666.

Duke's Course
Craigton,
St Andrews KY16 8NS
Club House: (01334) 470214
Fax: (01334) 479456
Pro Shop: (01334) 470214
FOR MORE INFORMATION, SEE PAGE 57

Kingsbarns Golf Club
Kingsbarns, St Andrews KY16 8QD.
Tel: (01334) 460860
Fax: (01334) 460877
E-mail: info@kingsbarns.com
www.kingsbarns.com
18 holes, Championship 7126 yards,
regular 6174 yards, Par 72.
Charges: £105 per day, £155 for two.
Visitors welcome 7 days, advanced
reservations advised.
Full catering and bar. Driving range,
caddies by prior request.
Professional: David Scott
Tel: (01334) 460864.
FOR MORE INFORMATION, SEE PAGE 56

SALINE
Saline Golf Club
Kinneddar Hill, Saline KY12 9LT.
Tel: (01383) 852591.
9 holes, 5302 yds, SSS 66.
Charges: £9 per day Mon-Fri.
£11 per day Sun.
For advance reservations

Tel: (01383) 852591 Clubhouse.
Practice area, catering facilities are available.
Visitors are welcome all week, except Saturdays.
Secretary: R. Hutchison
Tel: (01383) 852344.

TAYPORT
Scotscraig Golf Club
Golf Road, Tayport DD6 9DZ.
Tel: (01382) 552515.
18 holes, 6550 yds, SSS 72.
Charges: On application.
Caddies by arrangement, caddy cars, practice area and catering facilities are available.
Visitors are welcome on weekdays, or on weekends by prior arrangement.
Secretary: B.D. Liddle.
FOR MORE INFORMATION, SEE PAGE 58

THORNTON
Thornton Golf Club
Station Road, Thornton KY1 4DW.
Tel: (01592) 771111.
Fax: (01592) 774955.
18 holes, 5560m/6177 yds, SSS 69.
Charges: £15 weekdays, £22 weekends round, £25 weekdays, £35 weekends daily.
Juniors 50% off adult rate.
For advance reservations
Tel: (01592) 771111.
Practice area and catering facilities are available. Visitors are welcome all week.
Secretary: B.S.L. Main
Tel: (01592) 771111.

INVERNESS-SHIRE
AIGAS
Aigas Golf Course
Aigas, by Beauly,
Inverness-shire IV4 7AD
Tel: (01463) 782942.
9 holes, 2439 yds,
Medal tees SSS 64.
Charges: £7 (9 holes) weekdays,
£11 daily weekends, weekdays,
£42 weekly. Daily ticket £15.
Caddy cars and catering facilities are available.
For advance reservations
Tel: (01463) 782942/782423.
Secretary: P. Masheter
Tel: (01463) 782423.

ARISAIG
Traigh Golf Course
Traigh, Arisaig PH39 4NT.
Tel: (01687) 450337.
9 holes, 2456 yds, SSS 65.
Charges: £12 daily, £40 weekly.
Clubs for hire.
Visitors are welcome all week.
Manager: Bill Henderson
Tel: (01687) 450645.
FOR MORE INFORMATION, SEE PAGE 77

BOAT OF GARTEN
Boat of Garten Golf Club
Boat of Garten PH24 3BQ.
Tel: (01479) 831282.
Fax: (01479) 831523.
E-mail: boatgolf@enterprise.net
18 holes, 5866 yds, SSS 69.
Charges: Mon-Fri £23 per round,
£28 daily, Sat/Sun £28 per round,
£33 daily.
Weekly tickets £110.
For advance reservations
Tel: (01479) 831282
(Starting sheet used every day).
Caddies, caddy cars and catering facilities are available.
Visitors are welcome.
Secretary: Paddy Smyth.

CARRBRIDGE
Carrbridge Golf Club
Inverness Road,
Carrbridge PH23 3AU.
Tel: (01479) 841623.
Web site: www.carrbridgegolf.com
9 holes, 5400 yds, SSS 68.
Charges: £12 Mon-Fri (except July,
Aug, Sept). £13 Mon-Fri (July, Aug,
Sept), £15 Sat/Sun.
For advance reservations
Tel: Clubhouse (01479) 841623.
Caddy cars and light catering facilities available.
Visitors welcome all week except
Wed. after 5pm.
Restrictions most Suns.
Secretary: Mrs A.T. Baird
Tel: (01479) 841506.

FORT AUGUSTUS
Fort Augustus Golf Club
Markethill,
Fort Augustus PH32 4DP.
9 holes (18 tees), 5454 yds, SSS 67.
Charges: £10 daily.
For advance reservations

Tel: (01320) 366309/366660.
Clubs for hire. Caddy cars available.
Visitors are welcome all week, except
Saturday afternoons. Lounge bar.
Secretary: H. Fraser
Tel: (01320) 366309.

FORT WILLIAM
Fort William Golf Club
North Road, Torlundy, Fort William
PH33 6SN.
Tel: (01397) 704464.
18 holes, 6217 yds, SSS 71.
Charges: £15 daily.
Visitors are welcome all week.
Secretary: Mr G. Bales.

INVERNESS
Loch Ness Golf Course
Castle Heather, Inverness IV1 6AA.
Tel: (01463) 713335.
18 holes, 6772m, SSS 72, Par 73.
Charges: £20/£25 Daily.
For advance reservations
Tel: (01463) 713335
20 Bay Driving Range (covered and floodlit). Buggies available for hire along with power trolleys and pull trolleys. Caddies by arrangement.
Visitors welcome all week.
Secretary: Neil D. Hampton
Tel: (01463) 713335.
Professional: Martin Piggott
Tel: (01463) 713334.

Inverness Golf Club
Culcabock Road,
Inverness IV2 3XQ.
Tel: (01463) 239882
E-mail: igc@freeuk.com
Web site:
www.invernessgolfclub.co.uk.
18 holes, 5694m/6226yds, SSS 70.
Charges: £29 per round, £39 day ticket (weekdays, weekends and public holidays). Weekly ticket by arrangement.
For advance reservations
Tel: (01463) 239882/231989
A practice area, caddy cars, caddies, by arrangement with professional, and catering facilities available.
Visitors welcome all week (restrictions on Saturdays).
Club Manager: J.S. Thomson
Tel: (01463) 239882.
Professional: A.P. Thomson
Tel: (01463) 231989.

Torvean Golf Club
Glenurquhart Road,
Inverness IV3 8JN.
Tel: (01463) 225651
Club E-mail: torveangolfclub
@btinternet.com.
18 holes, 5784 yds, SSS 68, Par 69.
Charges: £13 (weekdays), £15 (week-ends) per round, £17.50 (weekdays),
£20 (weekends) daily.
For advance reservations
Tel: (01463) 711434
Visitors welcome all week but
booking is advisable.
Secretary: Mrs K. M. Gray
Tel: (01463) 225651.

KINGUSSIE
Kingussie Golf Club
Gynack Road, Kingussie PH21 1LR.
Tel: (01540) 661374 Clubhouse.
Tel: (01540) 661600 Sec. Office.
18 holes, 5079m/5555yds, SSS 68.
Charges: On application.
For advance reservations
Tel: (01540) 661600/661374.
Caddy cars and catering facilities
are available.
Visitors are welcome all week.
Secretary: N.D. MacWilliam
Tel: (01540) 661600.

NETHY BRIDGE
Abernethy Golf Club
Nethy Bridge, Inverness-shire
PH25 3EB.
Tel: (01479) 821305
E-mail:
bob_robbie@compuserve.com
Web site: www.nethybridge.com/
golfclub.htm
Visitors are always welcome.
Tee reservation is often unnecessary
(check at weekends in case of Club
competition).
Green fees: £13/day Mon-Fri,
£16/day Sat/Sun, Weekly £70.
Clubhouse (unlicensed) serving
refreshments and snacks is open
from April to October.
No credit cards. Practice facilities,
trolleys and club hire available.
Secretary: Mr R.H. Robbie.

NEWTONMORE
Newtonmore Golf Club
Newtonmore, PH20 1AT.
Tel: (01540) 673328 Clubhouse.
Tel/Fax: (01540) 673878.
18 holes, 6029 yds, SSS 69.
Charges: On application.
For advance reservations & group
bookings contact tel: (01540) 673878.
Caddy cars and buggies available.
Catering everyday except Tuesdays.
Visitors most welcome.
Professional: R. Henderson
Tel: (01540) 673611.

SPEAN BRIDGE
Spean Bridge Golf Club
2 Aonachan Gardens,
Spean Bridge PH34 4ET.
Tel: (01397) 703379.
9 holes, 2203yds, SSS 62.
Charges: On application.
Visitors welcome all week (except
Tuesdays after 5pm).
Secretary: G.B. Thomson
Tel: (01463) 239882.
Professional: John Lennan
Tel: (01397) 703379.

KINCARDINESHIRE
AUCHENBLAE
Auchenblae Golf Club
Auchenblae,
Laurencekirk AB30 1AA.
Tel: (01561) 320002.
9 holes, 2226 yds, SSS 30, Par 33.
Charges: On application.
OAP's and juniors half price.
Visitors welcome all week
(except Wed & Fri evenings
5.30-9pm).
Secretary: J. McNicoll
Tel: (01561) 330678.

STONEHAVEN
Stonehaven Golf Club
Cowie, Stonehaven AB39 3RH.
Tel: (01569) 762124.
18 holes, 5103yds, SSS 65.
Charges: On application.
For advance reservations
Tel: (01569) 762124.
A practice area. catering & full
icensing facilities are available.
Visitors are welcome Mon-Fri.
Late afternoon and evening on
Saturday and all day Sunday.

Secretary: Mr W.A. Donald
Tel: (01569) 762124.
Fax: (01569) 765973.

Torphins Golf Club
Torphins, Aberdeenshire AB31 4JU.
Tel: (01339) 882115.
9 holes, 4738 yds, SSS 64.
Charges: On application.
Members evening from 5pm Tues.
Secretary: Mr S. MacGregor
Tel: (01339) 882402.

KINROSS-SHIRE

Kinnesswood
Bishopshire Golf Course
Kinnesswood.
Tel: (01592) 780203.
(Further details on application).

KINROSS
Green Hotel Golf Courses
Green Hotel, Kinross KY13 8AS.
Tel: (01577) 863407.
Red Course 18 holes, 5717m/6256
yds, SSS 73.
Blue Course 18 holes, 5888m/6438
yds, SSS 71.
Charges: Visitors, Weekday round
ticket £17, day ticket £27. Weekend
round ticket £27, day ticket £37.
Hotel residents, Weekday round
ticket £10, day ticket £15. Weekend
round ticket £15, day ticket £25.
For advance reservation
Tel: Green Hotel, 01577 863467
Caddy cars and catering facilities
are available.
Co-ordinator: Booking office.

MILNATHORT
Milnathort Golf Club Ltd
South Street,
Milnathort KY13 9XA.
Tel: (01577) 864069.
9 holes, 5702 yds, SSS 69.
Charges: £12 per round, £18 daily
(weekdays), £14 per round,
£20 daily (weekends).
For advance reservations
Tel: (01577) 864069.
A practice area is available.
Catering available.
Visitors are welcome all week.
Hon. Secretary: A. Jones
Tel: (01577) 864069.

KIRKCUDBRIGHTSHIRE

CASTLE DOUGLAS
Castle Douglas Golf Course
Abercromby Road,
Castle Douglas DG7 1BA.
Tel: (01556) 502801.
9 holes, 5408 yds, SSS 66.
Charges: On application.
No reservation for visitors.
Secretary: A.D. Millar
Tel: (01556) 502099.

DALBEATTIE
Colvend Golf Club
Sandyhills, Colvend,
by Dalbeattie DG5 4PY.
Tel: (01556) 630398.
18 holes, 4716 yds, SSS 67.
Charges: £20 daily, juniors £10.
Catering facilities are available.
Visitors are welcome - (Apr-Sept
course closed: Tues. from 4pm.
Thurs from 5.30pm).
Secretary: Mr J.B. Henderson,
9 Glenshalloch Road, Dalbeattie.
Tel: (01556) 610878.
FOR MORE INFORMATION, SEE PAGE 44

Dalbeattie Golf Club
Dalbeattie.
Tel: (01556) 611421.
(Further details on application).

GATEHOUSE OF FLEET
Cally Palace Hotel Golf Club
Gatehouse of Fleet DG7 2DL
Tel: (01557) 814522.
www.callypalace.co.uk
18 holes, 5802 yds, Par 70.
Exclusive to hotel guests.

Gatehouse Golf Club
Laurieston, Castle Douglas DG7 2PW
Tel: (01557) 814766.
9 holes, 2521 yds, SSS 66, Par 66.
Visitors welcome all week.
Restrictions Sunday mornings.
Charges: £10 round. £10 day.
Administrator: Mr K. Cooper
Tel: (01644) 450260.

KIRKCUDBRIGHT
Kirkcudbright Golf Club
Stirling Crescent,
Kirkcudbright DG6 4EZ.
Tel: (01557) 330314.
18 holes, 5121m/5739 yds, SSS 69.
Charges: On application.

Phone for advance reservations.
Visitors are welcome all week.
Secretary: N. Russell
Tel: (01557) 330314.
FOR MORE INFORMATION, SEE PAGE 49

NEW GALLOWAY
New Galloway Golf Club
New Galloway DG7 3RN.
9 holes, 2313m/2529 yds, SSS 65.
Charges: On application.
Visitors are welcome all week.
Secretary: Mr Nevile White
Tel: (01644) 450685.

LANARKSHIRE

ABINGTON
Arbory Brae Hickery Golf Links
Abington
Tel: 01555 664634
E-mail: whgl@morrissnr.freeserve.
co.uk
www.sabres.demon.co.uk/golf
9 holes, 1885 yds, Par 34.

AIRDRIE
Airdrie Golf Club
Glenmavis Road, Airdrie ML6 0PQ.
Tel: (01236) 762195.
(Further details on application).

Easter Moffat Golf Club
Mansion House, Plains ML6 8NP.
Tel: (01236) 842878.
18 holes, 5690m/6222 yds, SSS 70.
Charges: £15 round, £20 daily.
For advance reservations
Tel: (01236) 842878.
A practice area is available.
Visitors are welcome Mon to Fri
Secretary: Mr G. Miller
Tel: (01236) 761440.
Professional: Mr G. King

BELLSHILL
Bellshill Golf Club
Orbiston, Bellshill ML4 2RZ.
Tel: (01698) 745124.
18 holes, 5900 yds, SSS 69.
Charges: £18 weekdays £25
(Sundays and Public Holidays).
For advance reservations
Tel: (01698) 745124.
Catering facilities available.
Visitors welcome except Saturdays.
Secretary: R. Baird
Tel: (01698) 745124.

BIGGAR
Biggar Golf Club
The Park, Broughton Road,
Biggar ML12 6HA.
Tel: (01899) 220618.
18 holes, 5416 yds, SSS 66, Par 67.
Charges: Weekday £7.25 per round,
weekend £8.50, Juniors & OAP's
weekdays £3.60, weekends £4.25
round. Daily: Weekdays day ticket
£11, weekends and Bank holidays
£14. Juniors & OAP's £4.50 and £8
Single round tickets available after
4pm daily.
For advance reservations
Tel: (01899) 220319.
Caddy cars and catering facilities
are available.
Visitors are welcome all week.
Secretary: W.S. Turnbull
Tel: (01899) 220566.

BOTHWELL
Bothwell Castle Golf Club
Blantyre Road, Bothwell,
Glasgow G71 8PJ.
Tel: (01698) 853177.
18 holes, 5705m/6240 yds, SSS 70.
Charges: On application.
For advance reservations
Tel: (01698) 852052.
A practice area, caddy cars and cater-
ing facilities are available.
Visitors are welcome Mon-Fri.
Secretary: D.A. McNaught
Tel: (01698) 854052.
Professional: Mr A. McCloskey
Tel: (01698) 852052.

CAMBUSLANG
Cambuslang Golf Club
Westburn, Cambuslang G72 7NA.
Tel: 0141-641 3130.
9 holes, 6146 yds, SSS 69.
Visitors welcome when
accompanied by member.
Secretary: R.M. Dunlop
Tel: 0141-641 3767.

Kirkhill Golf Club
Greenlees Road, Cambuslang,
Glasgow G72 8YN.
Tel/fax: (0141) 641 8499.
18 holes, 6030 yds, SSS 68.
Charges: £15 per round, £22 daily
(weekdays).
For advance reservations.
Tel: (0141) 641 8499.

Caddy cars, practice area and catering facilities are available. Visitors are welcome weekdays only.
Secretary: J. Young
Tel: (0141) 641 8499.
Professional: D. Williamson
Tel: (0141) 641 7972.

CARLUKE
Carluke Golf Club
Mauldslie Road, Hallcraig,
Carluke ML8 5HG.
Tel: (01555) 771070.
18 holes, 5308m/5805 yds, SSS 68.
Charges: On application.
Advance reservations must be made in writing to secretary.
A practice area and catering facilities are available. Visitors are welcome all week until 4pm, except Sat/Sun & public holidays.
Secretary: D. Black
Tel: (01555) 770574.
Professional: R. Forrest
Tel: (01555) 751053.

CARNWATH
Carnwath Golf Course
Main Street, Carnwath ML11 8JX.
Tel: (01555) 840251
Fax: (01555) 841070.
18 holes, 5953 yds, SSS 69.
Charges: £25 weekday (£15 per round), £30 Sunday (£20 per round).
Visitors are welcome until 4.00pm, except Saturdays. Prior booking required on Sunday.
Caddy cars and catering available.
Secretary: Mrs Linda McPate
Tel: 01555 841 070.

COATBRIDGE
Coatbridge Golf Centre
Townhead Road,
Coatbridge ML5 2HX
Tel: (01236) 421475.
18 holes, 5877 yds, SSS 68.
Charges: On application.
For advance reservations
Tel: (01236) 421492.
A practice area, caddy cars and catering facilities are available.
19 bay elevated driving range.
Visitors are welcome at all times, except 1st Saturday of month.
Secretary: G. McCoombs
Tel: (01236) 421492.

Drumpellier Golf Club
Drumpellier Avenue,
Coatbridge ML5 1RX.
Tel: (01236) 424139.
Fax: (01236) 428723.
18 holes, 6227 yds.
Charges: £25.50 round, £35.50 daily.
A practice area, caddy cars and catering facilities are available.
Visitors are welcome Mon, Tues, Wed, Thur, Fri.
Secretary: Mr William Brownlie
Tel: (01236) 423065.
Professional: Mr D. Ross
Tel: (01236) 432971.

EAST KILBRIDE
East Kilbride Golf Club
Nerston, East Kilbride G74 4PF.
Tel: (01355) 247728.
18 holes, 6419 yds, SSS 71.
Charges: £20 round, £30 daily.
Visiting parties welcome weekdays on application to the Secretary.
Weekends, no visitors unless accompanied by a member.
Secretary: W.G. Gray.
Professional: Willie Walker, Playfair Golf Ltd.

Torrance House Golf Club
Strathaven Road,
East Kilbride G75 0QZ.
Tel: (013552) 49720.
18 holes, 6415 yds, SSS 71.
Charges: On application.
For advance reservations
Tel: (013552) 49720.
Caddy cars, practice area and catering facilities are available. Visitors are welcome all week by arrangement with: Recreation Manager (Golf), Leisure Services Department, South Lanarkshire Council.
Tel: (01355) 806000.
Professional: J. Dunlop
Tel: (01355) 806000.

GLASGOW
Alexandra Golf Course
Alexandra Park, Sannox Gardens,
Dennistoun, Glasgow G31 3BS.
Tel: 0141-556 1294.
9 holes, 2008 yds.
Charges: On application. Advance bookings welcome. A practice and catering area are available.
Visitors are welcome at all times.

Bishopbriggs Golf Club
Brackenbrae Road,
Bishopbriggs, Glasgow G64 2DX.
Tel: 0141-772 1810.
18 holes, 6041 yds, SSS 69.
Charges: On application.
Catering facilities are available.
Parties are welcome with reservation, Tues, Wed & Thurs only (apply to secretary at least one month in advance).
Secretary: James J. Quin
Tel: 0141-772 8938.

Cawder Golf Club
Cadder Road, Bishopbriggs.
2 x 18 holes, length of courses:
Cawder 5711m/6244 yds,
Keir 5373m/5885 yds.
SSS 71 & 68
Charges: £26 per round, £31 daily.
For advance reservations
Tel: 0141-772 5167.
A practice area, caddy cars and catering facilities are available.
Visitors are welcome Mon–Fri.
Secretary: G.T. Stoddart
Tel: 0141-772 5167.
Professional: K. Stevely
Tel: 0141-772 7102.
FOR MORE INFORMATION, SEE PAGE 34

Cowglen Golf Club
301 Barrhead Road,
Glasgow G43 1AU.
Tel: 0141-632 0556.
18 holes, 6079 yds, SSS 70.
Charges: £25 per round, £35 daily.
Practice driving area, pitching green and putting green.
Full catering facilities available.
Visitors welcome through arrangement with secretary.
No visitors at weekends.
Professional: Simon Payne
Tel: (0141) 649 9401.
Secretary: Ronald Jamieson
Tel: (01505) 503000.

Crow Wood Golf Club
Garnkirk Estate, Muirhead,
Chryston G69 9JF.
Tel: (0141) 779 2011.
18 hole, 6261 yds, SSS 71, Par 71.
Visitors Mon-Fri. (Prior notice
required). Charges: £20 round.
£28 two rounds. Packages to
include food.
Secretary: I. McInnes
Tel: 0141-779 4954.
Professional: B. Moffat
Tel: 0141-779 1943.

Deaconsbank Golf Course
Rouken Glen Golf Centre,
Stewarton Road, (Junction A726)
Thornliebank, Giffnock G46 7UZ.
Tel: 0141-638 7044 or 620 0826.
18 holes, 4800 yds, SSS 63, Par 64.
Charges: Mon-Fri £9.50, Sat/Sun £11
per round. Day tickets £16 & £20
until 3.30pm.
Catering facilities are available.
15 bay floodlit driving range, shop
facilities and hiring of clubs, etc.
Visitors are welcome.
Secretary: Christine Cosh.

Dougalston Golf Club
Strathblane Road, Milngavie,
Glasgow G62 8HJ.
Tel: 0141 955 2400.
18 holes, BT 6354 - FT 5959 yds.
SSS BT 72 FT 70.
Charges: £12 round. Advance
reservations Tel: 0141-956 5750.
Practice area. caddy cars and catering
facilities available.
Visitors welcome Mon-Eri.
Secretary: Ian Glen Muir
Tel: 0141-956 5750.

Whitecraigs Golf Club
72 Ayr Road, Giffnock G46 6SW.
Tel: (0141) 639 4530 (Office)
(0141) 639 1681 (Clubhouse)
18 holes, 6013 yds, Par 70, SSS 70.
Charges: £37 round including roll
and bacon before golf and high tea
after, £50 day including roll and
bacon, lunch and high tea.
Visiting parties on Wednesdays only.
Secretary: Mr A. Keith
Professional: Alastair Forrow
Tel: (0141) 639 2140

Haggs Castle Golf Club
70 Dumbreck Road,
Glasgow G41 4SN.
Tel: (0141) 427 1157.
18 holes, 6426 yds, SSS 71.
Charges: £35 round, £45 daily.
For advance reservations
Tel: 0141-427 1157.
A practice area, caddy cars and
catering facilities are available.
Visitors must be introduced by a
member. Parties only on Wed.
Secretary: Alan Williams
Tel: 0141-427 1157.
Professional: J. McAlister
Tel: 0141-427 3355.

Knightswood Golf Course
Lincoln Avenue,
Glasgow G13 3DN.
Tel: 0141-959 6358
9 holes, 2703 yds, SSS 68.
Charges: £3.70 round.
(Further details on application).
Secretary: J. Dean
Tel: 0141-954 6495.

Lethamhill Golf Course
Hogganfield Loch,
Cumbernauld Road,
Glasgow G33 1AH.
Tel: 0141-770 6220.
18 holes. Charges: On application.
(Further details on application).

Linn Park Golf Course
Simshill Road, Glasgow G44 5TA.
Tel: 0141-637 5871.
18 holes.
Charges: On application.
For advance reservations
Tel: 0141-637 5871.

Littlehill Golf Course
Auchinairn Road,
Glasgow G64 1UT.
Tel: 0141-772 1916.
18 holes. Charges: On application.

Mount Ellen Golf Club
Johnstone House,
Johnstone Road, Gartcosh G69 8EY.
Tel: (01236) 872277.
18 holes, 5525 yds, SSS 67.
Charges: £14 round, £22 daily.
Package deal: £32.
Visitors welcome on weekdays only.
For advance reservations
Tel: (01236) 872277.
Catering facilities are available.
Secretary: J. Docherty.

Pollok Golf Club
90 Barrhead Road,
Glasgow G43 1BG.
18 holes, 6257 yds, SSS 70.
Secretary: Tel: 0141-632 4351
Fax: 0141-649 1398.
Clubmaster: 0141-632 1080.
(Further details on application).

The Williamwood
Golf Club
690 Clarkston Road,
Glasgow G44 3YR.
Tel: 0141-637 1783.
18 holes, 5878 yds, SSS 69.
Charges: On application.
Visitors are welcome by
arrangement and when introduced
by, and playing with members.
Secretary: T.D.M. Hepburn
Tel: 0141-637 1783.
Professional: S. Marshall
Tel: 0141-637 2715.

HAMILTON
Hamilton Golf Club
Riccarton, Ferniegair,
by Hamilton ML3 7UE.
Tel: (01698) 282872.
FOR MORE INFORMATION, SEE PAGE 33

Strathclyde Park
Golf Club
Motehill, Hamilton ML3 6BY
Tel: (01698) 429350.
9 holes, 3147 yds, SSS 70.
Charges: On application.
For advance reservations: same day
booking only - lines open 8.45am -
Tel: (01698) 429350.
A practice area is available.
Visitors are welcome all week.
Professional: W. Walker
Tel: (01698) 281155.

Lanarkshire

LANARK
Lanark Golf Club
The Moor, Whitelees Road,
Lanark ML11 7RX.
Tel: (01555) 663219.
18 hole and 9 hole, 6306 yds, SSS 71
(18 hole)
Charges: £26 per round, £40 per day.
For advance reservations
Tel: (01555) 662349.
A practice area, caddy cars and cater-
ing facilities are available (Caddies if
requested).
Visitors are welcome Monday to
Friday.
Secretary: G.H. Cuthill
Tel: (01555) 663219.
Professional: A. White
Tel: (01555) 661456.
FOR MORE INFORMATION, SEE PAGE 32

LARKHALL
Larkhall Golf Course
Burnhead Road, Larkhall ML9 3AB.
Tel: (01698) 889597.
(Further details on application).

LENZIE
Lenzie Golf Club
19 Crosshill Road, Lenzie G66 5DA.
Tel: 0141 776 1535
Web site: www.lenziegolfclub.com
18 holes, 5984 yds, SSS 69.
Charges: On application.
For advance reservations
Tel: 0141-776 6020.
Practice area, caddy cars and catering
facilities available.
Visitors welcome except weekends.
Secretary: Scott M. Davidson
Tel: 0141 812 3018.
Professional: Jim McCallum
Tel: 0141 777 7748.

LESMAHAGOW
Hollandbush Golf Club
Acretophead,
Lesmahagow ML11 OJS
Tel: (01555) 893484.
18 holes, 6218 yds, SSS 70, Par 71.
Practice area and catering facilities
available. Visitors welcome.
Secretary: J. Hamilton.
Professional: I. Rae
Tel: (01555) 893643.

MOTHERWELL
Colville Park Golf Club
Jerviston Estate, Merry Street,
Motherwell ML1 4UG.
Tel: (01698) 263017.
18 holes, 5724m/6265 yds, SSS 70,
Par 71.
Charges: On application.
For advance reservations
Tel: (01698) 263017.
Practice area and catering available.
Visitors are welcome by prior
arrangement Monday to Friday.
Secretary: Leslie Innes
Tel: (01698) 262808 (after 5pm).

Dalziel Park Golf & Country Club
100 Hagan Drive,
Motherwell ML1 5RZ.
Tel: (01698) 862862.
18 holes (opening June 2000), 6200
yds, SSS 70.
Charges: Mon - Fri £20, juniors
half price. Practice areas (putting,
chipping & bunker).
Visitors welcome Mon–Fri.
Admin Dept: Michelle Creasey
Tel: (01698) 862444.

RIGSIDE
Douglas Water Golf Club
Ayr Road, Rigside ML11 9NP..
Tel: (01555) 880361.
9 holes, 2945m, SSS 69.
Charges: £6 (Mon-Fri) day ticket, £8
Sun day ticket.
Please write for advance reservations.
A practice area is available, light
refreshments are available at the
weekend. Visitors are welcome all
week. No visitors on Saturdays due
to competition.
Secretary: Mr D. Hogg.

RUTHERGLEN
Blairbeth Golf Club
Fernbrae Avenue,
Ruthergien G73 4SF.
Tel: 0141-634 3355.
(Further details on application).

Cathkin Braes Golf Club
Cathkin Road, Rutherglen,
Glasgow G73 4SE.
Tel: 0141-634 6605.
Fax: 0141-630 9186

e-mail: golf@cathkinbraes.
freeserve.co.uk
18 holes, 6208 yds, SSS 71.
Charges: On application.
For advance reservations
Tel: 0141-634 6605.
Golf carts, caddy cars, practice
area and catering facilities available.
Visitors are welcome Mon to Fri.
Secretary: H. Millar
Tel: 0141-634 6605.
Professional: S. Bree
Tel: 0141-634 0650.

SHOTTS
Blairhead Golf Course
Shotts Golf Club Blairhead, Shotts
ML7 5BJ.
Tel: (01501) 820431.
Charges: On application.
Visitors are welcome weekdays.
(Further details on application).

STRATHAVEN
Strathaven Golf Club
Overton Avenue,
Glasgow Road,
Strathaven ML10 6NL.
Fax: (01357) 520539.
18 holes, 5770m/6250 yds, SSS 70.
Charges: £25 round, £35 daily (1999).
For advance reservations
Tel: (01357) 520421
A practice area, caddy cars and
catering facilities are available.
Secretary: Mr A.W. Wallace
Tel: (01357) 520421.
Professional: Mr M. McCrorie
Tel: (01357) 521812.

UDDINGSTON
Calderbraes Golf Club
57 Roundknowe Road,
Uddingston, Glasgow G71 6NG.
Tel: (01698) 813425.
9 holes,

WISHAW
Wishaw Golf Club
55 Cleland Road, Wishaw ML2 7PH.
Tel: (01698) 372869.
18 holes, 6073 yds, SSS 69.
Charges: On application.
A practice area, caddy cars and
catering facilities are available.
Secretary: Ronald Hutchison.
Professional: Stuart Adair.

LOTHIANS

ABERLADY
Luffness New Golf Club
The Clubhouse,
Aberlady EH32 0QA.
Tel: (01620) 843336.
18 holes, 6122 yds, SSS 70.
Charges: On application.
For advance reservations
Tel: (01620) 843336.
A practice area and catering
facilities are available.
Visitors are welcome weekdays
by arrangement.
Secretary: D.A. Leckie
Tel: (01620) 843336.
Clubmaster tel: (01620) 843376.

Kilspindie Golf Club
Aberlady, EH32 0QD.
Tel & Fax: (01875) 870358
18 holes, Traditional Scottish Links,
5480 yds, SSS 66.
Visitors are welcome.
Charges: £25 round (Mon-Fri), £30
(Sat/Sun). £40 daily (Mon-Fri), £50
(Sat/Sun).
Some practice facilities, caddy cars.
Fully licensed restaurant, bar and
snacks available.
General Manager: P.B. Casely
Tel: (01875) 870216
Professional: G.J. Sked
Tel: (01875) 870216

BATHGATE
Bathgate Golf Course
Edinburgh Road,
Bathgate EH48 1BA.
Tel: (01506) 652232.
18 holes, 6325 yds, SSS 70.
Charges: £21 daily (Mon-Fri),
£32 (Sat/Sun).
For advance reservations
Tel: (01506) 630505 (8.00-3pm).
A practice area, caddy cars, buggies
and catering facilities are available.
Secretary: Allan Osborne
Tel: (01506) 630505.
Professional: Sandy Strachan
Tel: (01506) 630553.

BO'NESS
West Lothian Golf Club
Airngath Hill,
by Linlithgow EH49 7RH.
Tel: (01506) 826030.
18 holes, 6578 yds, SSS 71.

Charges: £19 round, £25 daily, Mon-
Fri, £25 round, £30 daily, Weekends.
For advance reservations
contact Ian Taylor
Tel: (01506) 825060.
Caddy cars, practice area and
catering facilities are available.
Visitors are welcome mid-week
at all times. Weekend by
arrangement.
Secretary: Ian Osborough
Tel: (01506) 326030.
Professional: Ian Taylor
Tel: 01506 825060

BONNYRIGG
Broomieknowe Golf Club
36 Golf Course Road,
Bonnyrigg EH19 2HZ.
Tel: 0131-663 9317.
Fax: 0131-663 2152 (Club).
18 holes, 6150 yds, SSS 69.
Charges: £17 round, £25 daily.
Sat/Sun £20 round 1 round only.
For advance reservations
Tel: 0131-663 9317.
A practice area, caddy cars and
catering facilities are available.
Visiting parties are welcome
Mon-Fri
Secretary: J. G. White
Tel: 0131-663 9317.
Professional: Mr M. Patchett
Tel: 0131-660 2035.
FOR MORE INFORMATION, SEE PAGE 79

BROXBURN
Niddry Castle Golf Club
Castle Road, Winchburgh,
Broxburn EH52 6RQ.
Tel: (01506) 891097.
9 holes, 5514 yds, SSS 67.
Charges: £12 round, £17 weekend.
For advance reservations
Tel: (01506) 891097.
Catering facilities available.
Visitors welcome Mon-Fri,
weekend by arrangement.
Secretary: J. Thomson
Tel: (01506) 844983.

DALKEITH
Newbattle Golf Club Ltd
Abbey Road,
Dalkeith, Midlothian.
Tel: 0131-663 2123.
18 holes, 5498m/6012 yds, SSS 70.
Charges: £18 round, £27 daily.

For advance reservations
Tel: 0131-660 1631 or secretary.
A practice area, caddy cars and
catering facilities are available.
Visitors welcome all week, except
weekends and public holidays.
Secretary: Mr H.G. Stanners
Tel: 0131-663 1819.
Fax: 0131-654 1810.

DUNBAR
Dunbar Golf Club
East Links, Dunbar EH42 1LL.
Tel: (01368) 862317.
18 holes, 5854m/6404 yds, SSS 71.
Charges: £35 daily, £28 per round,
weekdays. £45 daily, £35 per round,
weekends.
For advance reservations
Tel: (01368) 862317.
A practice area, caddies (if reserved)
and catering facilities are available.
Visitors are welcome all week, after
9.30 am (except Thurs).
Secretary: Liz Thom
Tel: (01368) 862317.
Professional: Jacky Montgomery
Tel: (01368) 862086.
FOR MORE INFORMATION, SEE PAGE 86

Winterfield Golf Club
North Road, Dunbar.
Tel: (01368) 862280.
18 holes, 5155 yds, SSS 65.
Charges: On application.
For advance reservations
Tel: (01368) 863562.
Caddy cars and catering facilities
are available.
Secretary: Mr M. O'Donnell
Tel: (01368) 862564.
Professional: Mr K. Phillips
Tel: (01368) 863562.
FOR MORE INFORMATION, SEE PAGE 87

EDINBURGH
Baberton Golf Club
50 Baberton Avenue,
Juniper Green, EH14 5DU.
Tel: 0131 453 4911.
18 holes, 6129 yds, SSS 70.
Charges: £22 round, £32 daily,
Weekend round £30.
Visitors are welcome. Catering
facilities available by arrangement.
Professional: K. Kelly
Tel: 0131 453 3555.

Braid Hills Golf Courses
Braid Hills Approach,
Edinburgh EH10 6JZ.
Tel: 0131-447 6666.
(Further details on application).
FOR MORE INFORMATION, SEE PAGE 81

The Bruntsfield Links Golfing Society
32 Barnton Avenue,
Davidsons Mains EH4 6JH.
Tel: 0131-336 2006.
18 holes, 6407 yds, SSS 71.
Charges: £38 per round, £50 per day.
For advance reservations
Tel: 0131-336 1479/4050.
Lunch time carvery facilities are
available.
Secretary: CDR. D.M. Sandford
Tel: 0131-336 1479,
Fax: 0131-336 5538.
Professional: Brian MacKenzie
Tel: 0131-336 4050.

Carrickknowe Golf Club
27 Glendevon Park, Edinburgh
EH12 5XA.
Tel: 0131-337 2217.
18 holes, 6500 yds, SSS 68.
Charges: £12.50 per day.

Craigentinny Golf Course
Craigentinny Avenue, Edinburgh
EH7 6RG.
Tel: 0131-554 7501.
(Further details on application).

Craigmillar Park Golf Club
1 Observatory Road,
Edinburgh EH9 3HG.
Tel: 0131-667 0047.
18 holes, 5851 yds, SSS 69.
Charges: £17.50 round, £25.50 daily.
For advance reservations
Tel: 0131-667 0047.
Caddy cars, practice area and catering
facilities are available.
Visitors welcome on weekdays before
3.30pm (not weekends).
Secretary: T. Lawson
Tel: 0131-667 0047.
Professional: B. McGhee
Tel: 0131-667 2850

Duddingston Golf Club
137-139 Duddingston Road West,
Edinburgh EH15 3QD.
Tel: 0131 661 7688.
18 holes, 6420 yds, SSS 71.
Charges: Visitors (Mon-Fri) £27
round, £34 daily. Societies £23 round,
£30 daily (Tues & Thurs only).
For advance reservations
Tel: 0131-661 7688.
A practice area, caddy cars and cater-
ing facilities are available.
Secretary/General Manager:
Mr M.G. Corsar
Tel: 0131-661 7688.
Professional: Mr A. McLean
Tel: 0131-661 4301.

Kingsknowe Golf Club Ltd
326 Lanark Road,
Edinburgh EH14 2JD.
Tel: 0131-441 1144.
18 holes, 5469m/5979 yds.,SSS 69.
Charges: On application.
For advance reservations
Tel: 0131-441 4030.
A practice area, caddy cars and
catering facilities are available,
buggies for hire.
Visitors are welcome.
Secretary: R. Wallace
Tel: 0131-441 1145.
Professional: A. Marshall
Tel: 0131-441 4030.

Liberton Golf Club
297 Gilmerton Road,
Edinburgh EH16 5UJ.
Tel: 0131-664 3009.
18 holes, 5299 yds, SSS 66.
Charges: On application.
For advance reservations
Tel: 0131-664 1056.
A practice area and catering facilities
are available.
Visitors are welcome all week
- Sat & Sun after 1.30pm only.
Secretary: T.J. Watson
Tel: 0131-664 3009.
Professional: Iain Seath
Tel: 0131-664 1056.

Lothianburn Golf Club
106a Biggar Road,
Edinburgh EH10 7DU.
Tel: 0131-445 2206.
18 holes, 5662 yds, SSS 68.
Charges: £16.50 round, £22.50 daily,

Mon-Fri, £22.50 round, £27.50 daily,
Weekends.
Visitors welcome.
Secretary/Treasurer:
W.F.A. Jardine Tel: 0131-445 5067.
Professional: Kurt Mungall
Tel: 0131-445 2288.

Marriott Dalmahoy Hotel and Country Club
Kirknewton, Midlothian,
EH27 5EB.
Tel: 0131 333 1845.
Fax: 0131 335 3203.
East (Championship) Course:18
Holes, 6677 yards, Par 72, SSS 72.
West Course: 18 Holes, 5185 yards,
Par 68, SSS 66.
Visitor Green Fees: East – Mon-Fri
£65, hotel resident £45, Weekend
£80, hotel resident £60. West – Mon-
Fri £45, hotel resident £35, Weekend
£55, hotel resident £45. Weekday day
ticket (one round on each course)
£90, hotel resident £80, Weekend day
ticket (one round on each course)
£120, hotel resident £105.
Excellent catering facilities
available. Trolley, buggy and club &
shoe hire. Family Fun Putting
Green, 12 bay all weather floodlit
driving range.
PGA Golf Academy.
Company/Society Golf Packages
available weekdays. (Members and
residents weekends).
Director of Golf: Brian Anderson.
Secretary: Mrs Jennifer Bryans.
Pro: Neal Graham.

Merchants of Edinburgh Golf Club
10 Craighill Gardens,
Edinburgh EH10 5PY.
Tel: 0131-447 1219.
18 holes, 4889 yds, SSS 64.
Charges:On application.
For advance reservations
Tel: 0131-447 1219.
Catering facilities are available by
arrangement.
Visiting clubs welcome Monday to
Friday by request to the Secretary.
Secretary: I.L. Crichton
Tel: 0131-447 2814.
Professional: Neil M. Colquhoun
Tel: 0131-447 8709.

Mortonhall Golf Club
231 Braid Road, EH10 6PB.
Tel: 0131-447 2411.
18 holes, 5987m/6548 yds, SSS 72.
Charges: On application.
Catering facilities available.
Visitors are welcome with
introduction.
Secretary: Mrs C.D. Morrison
Tel: 0131-447 6974.
Professional: D. Horn
Tel: 0131-447 5185.

Murrayfield Golf Club
43 Murrayfield Road,
Edinburgh EH12 6EU.
Tel: 0131 337 0721
Fax: 0131 313 0271.
18 holes, 5765 yards, SSS 69.
Manager: Mrs MK Thomson.
Green fees on application.
Full catering facilities. Visitors
weekdays only. Trolley and club hire.
FOR MORE INFORMATION, SEE PAGE 80

Portobello Golf Club
Stanley Street,
Edinburgh EH15 1JJ.
Tel: 0131-669 4361.
9 holes, 2167m/2400 yds, SSS 32.
Charges: On application.
For advance reservations
Tel: 0131-669 4361.
Visitors are welcome all week.
Secretary: Mr Alistair Cook.

Prestonfield Golf Club
6 Priestfield Road North,
Edinburgh EH16 5HS.
Tel: 0131-667 9665.
18 holes, 5685m/6214 yds, SSS 70.
Charges: On application.
For advance reservations
Tel: 0131-667 8597.
A practice area, caddy cars and cater-
ing facilities are available.
Secretary: Mr A.S. Robertson.
Professional: J. Macfarlane.

Ratho Park Golf Club
Ratho, Newbridge,
Midlothian EH28 8NX.
Tel: 0131-333 2566.
18 holes, 5398m/5900 yds, SSS 68.
Charges: £25 round, £35 daily,
£35 weekend.
For advance reservations
Tel: 0131-333 1752.

A practice area, caddy cars and cater-
ing facilities are available.
Visiting parties are welcome Tues,
Wed and Thur.
Secretary: J.S. Yates
Tel: 0131-333 1752.
Professional: Mr A. Pate
Tel: 0131-333 1406.
FOR MORE INFORMATION, SEE PAGE 91

Ravelston Golf Club
24 Ravelston Dykes Road,
Edinburgh EH4 3NZ.
Tel: 0131-343 2177.
9 holes, 4754m/5200 yds, SSS 65
(men), SSS 69 (ladies).
Charges: On application.
Visitors are welcome (Mon-Fri).
Secretary: Mr Jim Lowrie
Tel/Fax: 0131-315 2486.

The Royal Burgess Golfing Society of Edinburgh
181 Whitehouse Road,
Edinburgh EH4 6BY.
Tel: 0131-339 2075.
E-mail: secretary@
royalburgess.co.uk
Web site:
www.royalburgess.demon.co.uk
18 holes, 6494 yds, SSS 71.
Charges: On application
For advance reservations
Tel: 0131-339 2075.
Trolley and catering facilities
are available.
Visitors/parties welcome Mon-Fri.
Secretary: John P. Audis
Tel: 0131-339 2075.
Professional: George Yuille
Tel: 0131-339 6474.

Silverknowes Golf Club
Silverknowes Parkway,
Edinburgh EH4 5ET.
Tel: 0131 336 5359
(further details on application).

Swanston Golf Club
111 Swanston Road,
Edinburgh EH10 7DS.
Tel: 0131 445 2239.
18 holes, 5024 yds, SSS 66.
Charges: On application.
For advance reservations
Tel: 0131-445 4002 (Prof.).
Catering facilities are available.
Visitors are welcome 9am-4pm

Mon-Fri.
Secretary: John Allan
Tel: 0131-445 2239.
Professional: I. Taylor
Tel: 0131-445 4002.

Torphin Hill Golf Club
Torphin Road, Edinburgh
EH13 0PL.
Tel: 0131-441 1100,
18 holes, 4597m/5020 yds, SSS 66.
Charges: On application.
For advance reservations
Tel: 0131-441 1100.
Practice area and catering facilities
are available.
Visitors are welcome all week,
except competition days (phone
for details).
Secretary: Andrew Hepburn
Tel: 0131-441 1100.
Professional: Jamie Browne
Tel: 0131-441 4061.

Turnhouse Golf Club Ltd.
154 Turnhouse Road,
Edinburgh EH12 0AD.
Tel: 0131 339 1014.
18 holes, 6153 yds, SSS 70.
Charges: £25 per round, £33 daily.
For advance reservations
Tel: 0131-539 5937.
Caddy cars, practice area and
catering facilities are available.
Visitors are welcome (only as
a society) Mon-Fri, except on
competition days - usually Wed
and Fri.
Secretary: A.B. Hay
Tel: 0131-539 5937.
Professional: J. Murray
Tel: 0131-339 7701.

FAULDHOUSE
Greenburn Golf Club
60 Greenburn Gardens, Whitburn,
Bathgate EH47 8NL.
Tel: (01501) 770292.
18 holes, 6000 yds, SSS 69
Charges: £17 round, £20 daily, Mon-
Fri, £25 round, £30 daily, Weekends.
Professional Tel: 01501 771187.
FOR MORE INFORMATION, SEE PAGE 88

GIFFORD
Castle Park Golf Club
Gifford, Haddington, East Lothian
EH41 4PL.
Tel: (01620) 810733
Fax: (01620) 810723
E-mail: stuartfortune@aol.com
Web site: www.castleparkgolfclub.co.uk
9 holes, 5266 yds, SSS 68.
Charges: £12 round, £14 daily, Mon-
Fri, £18 round, £22 daily, Weekends.
Secretary: Stuart Gifford
Professional: Derek Small
Tel: (01368) 862872.

Gifford Golf Club
Edinburgh Road, EH41 4QN.
Tel: (01620) 810267.
9 and 11 Tees, 6243 yds, SSS 70.
Charges: £12 round (Mon-Sun).
A small practice area is available.
Visitors welcome. Course closed all
day first Sunday of April to October.
Secretary: G.P. MacColl
Tel: (01620) 810267.

GULLANE
Gullane No.1 Golf Course
East Lothian EH31 2BB.
Tel: (01620) 842255.
18 holes, 6466 yds, SSS 72.
Charges: £58 (Mon-Fri), £72
(Sat/Sun) round. £87 daily (Mon-
Fri). (2000 rates).
Reservations, Tel:(01620) 842255.
Caddy cars, caddies and catering
facilities are available.
Secretary: S.C. Owram
Tel: (01620) 842255.
Professional: J. Hume
Tel: (01620) 843111.
FOR MORE INFORMATION, SEE PAGE 82

Gullane No.2 Golf Course
East Lothian EH31 2BB.
Tel: (01620) 842255.
18 holes, 6244 yds, SSS 70.
Charges: £26 round (Mon-Fri), £32
(Sat/Sun). £40 daily (Mon-Fri), £49
(Sat/Sun) (2000 rates).
For advance reservations
Tel: (01620) 842255.
Caddy cars, caddies and catering
facilities are available.
Secretary: S.C. Owram
Tel: (01620) 842255.
Professional: J. Hume
Tel: (01620) 843111.

Gullane No.3 Golf Course
East Lothian EH31 2BB.
Tel: (01620) 842255.
18 holes, 5252 yds, SSS 66.
Charges: £16 round (Mon-Fri), £21
(Sat/Sun). £25 daily (Mon-Fri), £32
(Sat/Sun) (2000 rates).
For advance reservations
Tel: (01620) 842255.
Caddy cars, caddies and catering
facilities are available.
Secretary: S.C. Owram
Tel: (01620) 842255.
Professional: J. Hume
Tel: (01620) 843111.

The Honourable Company of Edinburgh Golfers, Muirfield
Gullane, East Lothian EH31 2EG.
Tel: (01620) 842123.
18 holes, 6601 yds, SSS 73.
Charges: £80 round, £105 daily
(2000).
For advance reservations
Tel: (01620) 842123.
Caddies and catering facilities available.
Visitors are welcome on Tues and
Thurs only, but check with club.
Secretary: Group Captain
J.A. Prideaux
Tel: (01620) 842123.

HADDINGTON
Haddington Golf Club
Amisfield Park,
Haddington EH41 4PT.
Tel: (01620) 823727/823627
E-mail: Hadd.Golf1@tesco.net
Web site: www.haddingtongolf.co.uk
18 holes, 5764m/6317 yds, SSS 70.
Charges: £18 round (Mon- Fri), £23
(weekends). £26 daily (Mon-Fri),
£32 – 32 holes (weekends).
For advance reservations
Tel: (01620) 822727 or 823627.
Practice area, trolley and buggy hire
and catering facilities are available.
Visitors are very welcome all week.
Tel: (01620) 823627.
Fax: (01620) 826580.
Professional: John Sandilands
Tel: (01620) 822727.

LASSWADE
Melville Golf Course
Melville Golf Centre, Lasswade,
Midlothian EH18 1AN.
Tel: 0131-663 8038/654 0224.
Fax: 0131-654 0814.
9 hole Pay and Play SSS 62.
18 holes 2140m/4580 yds.
Charges: £7-9 holes, £12-18 holes,
Weekday & Concessions. £9, 9 holes,
£16, 18 holes Weekend.
24 hour advance bookings
Tel: 0131-654 0224. Large groups
well in advance. Otherwise Play &
Play. 22 Bay Floodlit Range. Practice
area and Putting Green.
Golf Shop. P.G.A. tuition.
Equipment Hire - clubs, shoes, bags,
trolleys etc. Vended drinks - crisps,
rolls etc. Changing room & toilets.
Visitors welcome 7 days all year.
Usual Golf Etiquette applies.
Large car park, easy access. 8 mins off
Edinburgh City Bypass on A7.
Contact: Mr & Mrs MacFarlane.
Tel: 0131-663 8038.
Professional: Garry Carter - Range/
hop/Tuition -Tel: 0131-663 8038.

Kings Acre Golf Course
Lasswade, Midlothian EH18 1AU.
Tel: 0131 663 3456.
18 holes, 5935 yards, SSS 70.
Charges: £16 weekdays (ex-public
holidays) £22 weekends. Visitors
welcome.
Full service catering and bar.
Motorised buggies, practice area,
driving range, trolley and club hire.
Professional: Alan Murdoch
PGA Coach: Adam Hunter.
FOR MORE INFORMATION, SEE PAGE 89

LINLITHGOW
Linlithgow Golf Club
Braehead, Linlithgow EH49 6EL.
Tel: (01506) 842585.
18 holes, 5239m/5729 yds, SSS 68.
Charges: £20 per round, £30 daily
(Mon-Fri); £30 per round, £37 daily
(weekend). Large discounts available
for visiting parties.
For advance reservations
(Contact the Professional)
Tel: (01506) 844356.
A practice area, caddy cars and
catering facilities are available.
Visitors are welcome all week except

Sat and Tues by special arrangement.
General Manager: Mr David Roy
Tel: (01506) 842585.
Professional: Mr Steven Rosie
Tel: (01506) 844356.

LIVINGSTON
Deer Park Golf & Country Club
Golf Course Road,
Knightsridge West,
Livingston EH54 8AB.
Tel: (01506) 431037.
18 holes, 6688 yds, SSS 72.
Charges: £24 round, £36 daily (Mon-Fri), £36 round, £48 daily weekend.
For advance reservations:
Tel: (01506) 431037.
Practice area, caddy cars and catering facilities available.
Visitors welcome 7 days.
Professional: B. Dunbar
Tel: (01506) 431037.

LONGNIDDRY
Longniddry Golf Club
Links Road,
Longniddry EH32 0NL.
Tel: (01875) 852141.
Fax: (01875) 853371.
18 holes, 6260 yds, SSS 70.
Charges: £32 per round weekdays, £45 per day. £42 per round weekends.
For advance reservations (more than 7 days) contact the secretary
Tel: (01875) 852141.
To reserve the tee within 7 days, contact the ProShop/Starters
Tel: (01875) 852228.
Practice area, practice putting green and net available. Well stocked ProShop, with clubs and trolleys for hire. Catering available seven days.
Secretary: N. Robertson
Tel: (01875) 852141.
Professional: J. Gray
Tel: (01875) 852228.

The Musselburgh Golf Club
Monktonhall, Musselburgh.
Tel: 0131-665 2005/7055.
18 holes, 6725 yds, SSS 73.
Charges: On application.
Catering facilities are available.
Visitors welcome with reservation.
Secretary: G. Finlay
Professional: Mr F. Mann

Musselburgh Links, The Old Golf Course
The Starter's Hut,
10 Balcarres Road,
Musselburgh EH21 7SB
Tel & Fax: 0131 665 5438
Web Site: www.musselburgholdlinks.co.uk
9 holes, 2808 yds, SSS 34.
Charges: £8 Adults (9 holes), £5.50 OAP/Juv (9 holes).
For advance reservations
Tel: 0131-665 6981.
Practice area available. Catering available by prior arrangement.
Visitors always welcome.
Resident Club: Musselburgh Old Course Golf Club.
Secretary: Mr Lionel Freeman
Tel: (0131) 665 6981
The World's Oldest Playing Golf Course.

NORTH BERWICK
Glen Golf Club
East Links, Tantallon Terrace,
North Berwick EH39 4LE.
Tel: (01620) 892221.
18 holes, 6079 yds, SSS 69.
Charges: On application.
Advance booking recommended.
Catering facilities available throughout the year.
Secretary: D.R. Montgomery
Tel: Starter's box (01620) 892726.
Professional: (shop only): R. Affleck
Tel: (01620) 894596.

The North Berwick Golf Club
Beach Road, North Berwick.
Tel: (01620) 895040.
18 holes, 6420 yds, SSS 71.
Charges: £40 per round, £60 daily.
For advance reservations
Tel: (01620) 892135.
Caddies, practice area, trolley caddy cars and catering facilities are available.
Visitors welcome all week.
Secretary: N.A. Wilson
Tel: (01620) 895040.
Professional: D. Huish
Tel: (01620) 893233.
FOR MORE INFORMATION, SEE PAGE 85

Whitekirk Golf Course
Whitekirk, nr. North Berwick,
East Lothian EH39 5PR.
For advance reservations
Tel: (01620) 870300,
Fax: (01620) 870330.
e-mail: golf@whitekirk.u-net.com
18 holes, 6526 yds, SSS 72, Par 72.
Charges: £18 per round, £30 day, Mon-Fri. £25 per round, £40 day, Sat & Sun.
Buggies, practice area, caddy cars and catering facilities available.
Visitors Welcome.

PENICUIK
Glencorse Golf Club
Milton Bridge,
Penicuik EH26 0RD.
Tel: (01968) 677177.
18 holes, 5205 yds, SSS 66.
Charges: On application.
For advance reservations tel: (01968) 677189.
(Clubs/Societies only).
Caddy cars and catering available.
Visitors welcome on Mon–Thurs.
Secretary: W. Oliver
Tel: (01968) 677189.
Professional: Mr C. Jones
Tel: (01968) 676481.

PRESTONPANS
Royal Musselburgh Golf Club
Preston Grange House,
Prestonpans EH32 9RP.
Tel: (01875) 810276.
18 holes, 6237 yds, SSS 70.
Charges: £20 (round), £35 (daily) weekdays. £35 (round) weekends (1996).
Advance reservations in writing preferable.
Caddy cars, practice area and catering facilities are available.
Visitors are welcome weekdays, except Friday afternoons.
Management Secretary: T.H. Hardie
Tel: (01875) 810276.
Professional: J. Henderson
Tel: (01875) 810139.
FOR MORE INFORMATION, SEE PAGE 90

PUMPHERSTON
Pumpherston Golf Club
Drumshoreland Road,
Pumpherston,
Livingston EH53 0LF
Tol: (01506) 432869.
9 holes, 4950 yds/4526 m.
Par 66, SSS 64.
Catering and bar facilities are available. Societies welcome Mon–Fri.
Visitors only with a member.
Secretary: I. McArthur
Tel: (01506) 854584.

SOUTH QUEENSFERRY
Dundas Parks Golf Club
South Queensferry,
West Lothian EH30 9SS.
Tel: 0131-331 3179
9 holes, 6024 yds, SSS 70.
Charges £10 per round/daily.
For advance reservations
Tel: 0131-331 3179.
A practice area is available.
Visitors are welcome (not weekends)
by prior arrangement with secretary.
Secretary: Christine Wood
Tel: 0131-319 1347.

UPHALL
Uphall Golf Club
Houston Mains, Uphall EH52 6JT.
7 miles west of Edinburgh Airport.
Tel: (01506) 856404.
18 holes, White Tees 5592 yds, SSS
67, Par 69.
Yellow Tees 5272 yds, SSS 66, Par 69.
Charges: On application.
Societies welcome by prior arrangement. Visitors welcome 7 days, competitions permitting.
For advance reservations
Tel: (01506) 855553.
Excellent Clubhouse facilities. Bar
snacks and meals served all day.
Secretary: W.A. Crighton
Tel: (01506) 856404.
Professional: G. Law
Tel:(01506) 855553.
FOR MORE INFORMATION, SEE PAGE 92

WEST CALDER
Harburn Golf Club
West Calder EH55 8RS.
Tel: (01506) 871131
Fax: (01506) 870286.
18 holes, 5921 yds, SSS 69.
Charges: £18 (Mon-Thurs), £21 (Fri),

£23 (Sat/Sun) round; £25 (Mon-Thurs), £29 (Fri), £34 (Sat/Sun) daily.
Package deals available for Golf
Societies. For advance reservations
Tel: (01506) 871131.
Caddy cars and golf buggy available
for hire. Practice area and catering
facilities are available.
Visitors are welcome all week.
Secretary: J. McLinden
Tel: (01506) 871131.
Professional: S. Mills
Tel: (01506) 871582.

WHITBURN
**Polkemmet Country Park
Golf Club**
West Lothian Council,
Park Centre,Whitburn EH47 0AD.
Tel: (01501) 743905.
9 holes, 2969m.
Charges: On application.
15-bay floodlit golf driving range
within the park. Caddy cars and
catering facilities are available.
Visitors are welcome all week.

MORAYSHIRE
ELGIN
Elgin Golf Club
Hardhillock, Birnie Road,
Elgin IV30 3SX.
Tel: (01343) 542338.
18 holes, 5853m/6401 yds, SSS 71.
Charges: Weekdays £23 round,
£30 daily. Weekends: £28 round, £35
daily.. For advance reservations:
Tel: (01343) 542338.
Caddies (by arrangement), caddy
cars, practice area, catering facilities
are available.
Visitors are welcome.
Secretary: David F. Black
Tel: (01343) 542338.
Fax: (01343) 542341.
Professional: Ian Rodger
Tel: (01343) 542884.

FOCHABERS
**Garmouth & Kingston
Golf Club**
Garmouth, Fochabers.
Tel: (01343) 870388.
18 holes, 5874 yds, SSS 68.
Charges: Mon-Fri £12 round, £18
daily. Weekends £16 round, £20 daily.
Reduced terms for parties over 10.

For advance reservations
Tel: (01343) 870231.
Catering and bar facilities available.
Visitors are very welcome.
Secretary: A. Robertson
Tel: (01343) 870231.

Spey Bay Golf Club
Spey Bay Hotel, Spey Bay,
Fochabers IV32 7PJ.
Tel: (01343) 820424.
18 holes, 6092 yds, SSS69.
Charges: On application.
Caddy cars, practice area, catering
facilities and Driving Range on site
available.
Visitors and golf outings welcome.
(Enquiries to hotel manager).

FORRES
Forres Golf Club
Muiryshade, Forres IV36 0RD.
Tel: (01309) 672250.
18 holes, 6236 yds, SSS 70.
Charges: £19 round, £27 daily
Weekdays. Discounts for parties.
For advance reservations
Tel: (01309) 672250
Buggies, caddy cars, club hire, practice area and catering facilities are
available.
Visitors are welcome all week.
Professional: Sandy Aird
Tel: (01309) 672250.

GRANTOWN ON SPEY
**Grantown on Spey
Golf Club**
Golf Course Road,
Grantown-on-Spey PH26 3HY
Tel: (01479) 872079
Fax: (01479) 873725
E-mail: secretary@ grantownonspey-golfclub.com.uk
Web Site: www.grantownonspey-golfclub.co.uk
18 holes, 5710 yds, SSS 68.
Charges: Weekdays £20 day ticket,
Weekends £25 day ticket..
For advance reservations
Tel: (01479) 872079.
Caddy cars, practice area, putting
green, shop, bar and catering facilities
are available.
Visitors are welcome all week.
Secretary: James A. Matheson
Tel: (01479) 872079.

HOPEMAN
Hopeman Golf Club
Hopeman, Elgin,
Morayshire IV30 5YA.
Tel: (01343) 830578.
18 holes, 4817m/5590 yds, SSS 67.
Charges: On application.
For advance reservations
Tel: (01343) 830578.
A small practice area and catering
facilities are available.
Visitors are welcome all week.
Secretary: J. Fraser
Tel: (01343) 830578.
FOR MORE INFORMATION, SEE PAGE 66

LOSSIEMOUTH
Moray Golf Club
Stotfield, Lossiemouth IV31 6QS.
Tel: (01343) 812018.
Fax: (01343) 815102.
36 holes.
Charges: On application.
Caddy cars, practice area and
catering facilities are available.
Visitors welcome without
reservation.
Secretary: Boyd Russell
Tel: (01343) 812018.
Professional: A. Thomson
Tel: (01343) 813330.

ROTHES
Rothes Golf Club
Blackhall, Rothes AB38 7AN.
Tel: (01340) 831443.
2 x 9 holes, 4972 yds, SSS 64.
Charges: £10 Mon-Fri, £12
weekends.
Practice nets available, bar open
weekends and summer evenings.
Visitors welcome all week.
Secretary: J.P. Tilley
Tel: (01340) 831277.

NAIRNSHIRE

NAIRN
The Nairn Golf Club
Seabank Road, Nairn IV12 4HB.
Tel:(01667) 453208.
18 holes, 6745 yds, SSS 74, Par 72.
Charges: £70 per round Mon-Sun
inclusive. For advance reservations
Tel: (01667) 453208.
A practice area, caddies, caddy cars
and catering facilities are available.
Visitors are welcome all week.

Hosted 37th Walker Cup in 1999.
Secretary: Mr J.G. Somerville
Tel: (01667) 453208.
Professional: Mr R. Fyfe
Tel: (01667) 452787.
FOR MORE INFORMATION, SEE PAGE 68

Nairn Dunbar Golf Club
Lochloy Road,
Nairn IV12 5AE.
Tel: (01667) 452741.
Fax: (01667) 456897.
18 holes, 6720 yds, SSS 73.
Charges: £25 round, £33 daily (Mon-
Fri). £30 round, £40 daily (Sat/Sun).
A practice area and caddy cars are
available.
Secretary: J. Falconer.
Professional: Brian Mason
Tel: (01667) 453964.
FOR MORE INFORMATION, SEE PAGE 67

PEEBLESHIRE

INNERLEITHEN
Innerleithen Golf Club
Leithen Water EH44 6HZ.
Tel: (01896) 830951.
9 holes, 6066 yds, SSS 69.
Charges: Mon-Fri £11/£16 per day.
Sat/Sun £13/£19 per day.
Secretary: S.C. Wyse
Tel: (01896) 830071.
Practice facilities and bar available.
Visitors welcome.
FOR MORE INFORMATION, SEE PAGE 23

PEEBLES
Peebles Golf Club
Kirkland Street, Peebles EH45 8EU.
Tel: (01721) 720197.
18 holes, 5636m 6160 yds, SSS 70.
Charges: £20 round, £27 daily.
A practice area, caddy cars and
catering facilities are available.
Visitors welcome (subject to tee
availability).
FOR MORE INFORMATION, SEE PAGE 25

WEST LINTON
West Linton Golf Club
West Linton EH46 7HN.
Tel: (01968) 660463.
18 holes, 5607m/6132 yds, SSS 70.
Charges: £19 round (Mon-Fri), £28
(Sat/Sun). £28 daily (Mon-Fri).
For advance reservations
Tel: (01968) 660256.

A practice area and catering facilities
are available.
Visiting parties welcome Mon- Fri,
casual visitors welcome also, at week-
end after 1pm.
New Clubhouse opened 1997.
Secretary: G. Scott
Tel: (01968) 660970 (Office), or
Tel: (01968) 675843 (Home).
FOR MORE INFORMATION, SEE PAGE 24

PERTHSHIRE

ABERFELDY
Aberfeldy Golf Club
Taybridge Road,
Aberfeldy PH15 2BH.
Tel: (01887) 820535.
18 holes, 5100m/5577 yds, SSS 66.
Charges: £22 daily, £14 per round
(Mon-Fri). £25 daily, £16 per round
(Sat/Sun). Caddy cars and catering
facilities are available all day.
Secretary: P. Woolley
13 Farragon Drive, Aberfeldy,
Perthshire PH15 2BQ.
Tel: (01887) 829422
Advance bookings at all times.

ALYTH
Glenisla Golf Centre
Pitcrocknie, Alyth,
Perthshire PH11 8JJ.
Tel: (01828) 632445
Fax: (01828) 633749
E-mail: info@golf-glenisla.co.uk
Web site: www.golf-glenisla.co.uk
18 holes, 6402 yds, SSS 71
Charges: Weekdays £22 round, £26
daily. Weekends £33 round, £39 daily.
Putting green and practice net,
trolleys and buggies available.
Licensed clubhouse, ProShop,
conference and function facilities.
Visitors, corporate and society
outings welcome all year.
On-site B&B and self-catering
accomodation available.

The Alyth Golf Club
Pitcrocknie,
Alyth PH11 8HF.
Tel: (01828) 632268.
18 holes, 5676m/6205 yds, SSS 71
(Boxes 70)
Charges: Weekdays £20 round,
£30 daily. Weekends £25 round, £40
daily.

For advance reservations
Tel: (01828) 632268.
Large practice area, caddy cars and
catering and bar facilities available.
Visitors welcome all week.
Professional: Mr Tom Melville
Tel: (01828) 632411.

Strathmore Golf Centre
Leroch, Alyth PH11 8NZ.
Tel: (01828) 633322.

Rannaleroch Golf Course
18 holes, 5901m/6454 yds, Par 72.
Charges: £19 per round weekdays,
£29 daily, £24 per round weekend,
£36 daily weekend.

Leitfie Links Golf Course
9 holes, 1572m/1719 yds, Par 29.
Charges: £8 per day Mon-Fri,
£10 per day Sat & Sun.
£8 for 18 holes.
For advance reservations
Tel: (01828) 633322.
Driving range, caddy cars and
catering facilities available.
Visitors very welcome all week.
Secretary: Patrick Barron
Tel: (01828) 633322.

AUCHTERARDER
Auchterarder Golf Club
Orchil Road, Auchterarder PH3 IL5
Tel/fax: (01764) 662804.
ProShop: (01764) 663711.
18 holes, 5778 yds, SSS 68.
Charges: £20 round, £30 daily,
weekdays. Saturday/Sunday £25
round, £40 daily.
For advance reservations
Tel: (01764) 662804/663711.
Professional shop and catering
facilities are available.
Secretary: Mr W.M. Campbell
Tel: (01764) 662804
(Office hrs. 9am-5pm).
Professional: Gavin Baxter
Tel: (01764) 663711.

The Gleneagles Hotel
Golf Courses
King's Course
The Gleneagles Hotel,
Auchterarder PH3 1NF.
Tel: (01764) 694469.
Fax: (01764) 664383.
E-mail: visitor.golf@gleneagles.com
Web site: www.gleneagles.com
18 holes, 6790 yds, SSS 73.
Charges: On application.
Caddies are available. Golf Academy
and practice area and full catering
facilities are available.
No restrictions to visitors.
FOR MORE INFORMATION, SEE PAGE 93

The Monarch's Course
Auchterarder PH3 1NF.
Tel: (01764) 694469.
Fax: (01764) 694383.
E-mail: visitor.golf@gleneagles.com
Web site: www.gleneagles.com
18 holes, 5605 yds.
SSS: Blue 74, White 73, Yellow 71,
Green 67 (Ladies 74), Red (Ladies) 71.
Charges: On application
Golf Academy and practice area and
full catering facilities are available.
Carts are available. No restrictions to
visitors.

The Queen's Course
Auchterarder PH3 1NF.
Tel: (01764) 694469.
Fax: (01764) 694383.
E-mail: visitor.golf@gleneagles.com
Web site: www.gleneagles.com
18 holes, 5965 yds, SSS 70.
Charges: On application
Caddies are available. Golf Academy
and practice area and full catering
facilities are available. No restrictions
to visitors.

Wee Course
Auchterarder PH3 1NF.
Tel: (01764) 664469.
Fax: (01764) 694383.
9 holes, 1481 yds, Par 27.
Charges: On application
Golf Academy and practice area and
catering facilities are available. No
restrictions to visitors.

BLAIR ATHOLL
Blair Atholl Golf Club
Invertilt Road,
Blair Atholl PH18 5TG.
Tel: (01796) 481407.
9 holes, SSS 68
Charges: £13 per day Mon-Fri,
£16 per day Sat/Sun, £60 weekly.
Parties welcome. For advance
reservations: Tel: (01796) 481407.
Picturesque Parkland Course. Caddy
cars and catering facilities are
available.
Secretary: P.A. Turner.

BLAIRGOWRIE
Blairgowrie Golf Club
Lansdowne Course, Golf Course
Road, Rosemount PH10 6LG.
Tel: (01250) 872622.
18 holes, 6895 yds, SSS 74.
Charges: On application.
Caddies, caddy cars, practice area and
catering facilities are available.
Visiting societies are welcome: Mon,
Tues & Thurs.
Secretary: J.N. Simpson
Tel: (01250) 872622.
Professional: Charles Dernie
Tel: (01250) 873116.

Rosemount Course
Golf Course Road, Rosemount,
Blairgowrie PH10 6LG.
Tel: (01250) 872622.
18 holes, 6588 yds, SSS 73.
Charges: On application.
For advance reservations
Tel: (01250) 872622.
Caddies, caddy cars, practice area and
catering facilities are available.
Visiting societies are welcome Mon,
Tues, Thurs.
Secretary: J.N. Simpson
Tel: (01250) 872622.
Professional: Charles Dernie
Tel: (01250) 873116.

Wee Course
Golf Course Road, Rosemount,
Blairgowne PH1O 6LG.
Tel: (01250) 872622.
9 holes, 4614 yds, SSS 65.
Charges: On application.
Secretary: J.N. Simpson
Tel: (01250) 872622.
Professional: Charles Dernie
Tel: (01250) 873116.

CALLANDER
Callander Golf Club
Aveland Road, Callander FK17 8EN.
Tel: (01877) 330090
Fax: (01877 330062
E-mail: callandergc@nextcall.net
Web site: www.golfagent-
callander.co.uk
18 holes, 5151 yds, Par 66, SSS 66
Charges: £18 Weekdays, weekends
£26 (round). Weekdays £26,
weekends £31 (daily), Seven day tick-
et £100.
For advance reservations
Tel: Society Bookings (01877)
330090.
Fax: (01877) 330062.
Caddy cars, practice area and catering
facilities are available.
Visitors welcome all days but with
Handicap Certificates on Wed &
Sun.
Manager/Secretary: Sandra Smart
Tel: (01877) 330090.
Professional: Allan Martin
Tel: (01877) 330975.

COMRIE
Comrie Golf Club
Laggan Braes, Comrie,
Perthshire PH6 2LR.
Secretary Tel: (01786) 880727.
9 holes, 6016 yds,SSS 70.
Charges: £12 daily (Mon-Fri), £18
per round weekends and Public
Holidays.
For advance reservations
Tel: (01764) 670055.
A practice area, caddy cars and
catering facilities also available.
Visitors are welcome all week, except
Monday and Tuesday evenings from
4.30pm.
Secretary: S.T. van der Walt.
See page 40 for more information.

CRIEFF
Crieff Golf Club Ltd
Perth Road, Crieff PH7 3LR.
Tel: (01764) 652909.
Ferntower Course
18 holes, 6402 yds, SSS 71.
Charges: On application.
Dornock Course: 9 holes, 2386 yds,
SSS 63. Charges: On application.
For all reservations
Tel: (01764) 652909.
Buggies, caddy cars and catering

facilities are available.
Visitors are welcome all week (it is
advisable to book well in advance).
Secretary: J.S. Miller
Tel: (01764) 652397.
Professional: D. Murchie
Tel: (01764) 652909.

Foulford Inn Golf Course
by Crieff PH7 3LN.
Tel: (01764) 652407.
9 holes, 918 yds, SSS 63.
Charges: £3 round, £5 daily.
For advance reservations
Tel: (01764) 652407.
Catering facilities available.
Visitors welcome all week.

DUNBLANE
Dunblane New
Golf Club
Perth Road, Dunblane
FK15 0LJ.
Tel: (01786) 821521.
18 holes,5536 yds, SSS 67.
Charges: £20 round (Mon-Fri),
£32 day.
(Charges subject to revision).
For advance reservations
Tel: (01786) 821521.
Caddy cars and catering facilities (by
advance order) are available.
Visitors are welcome Mon-Fri.
Secretary: John H. Dunsmore
Tel: (01786) 825281.
Professional: R.M. Jamieson
Tel: (01786) 821521.

DUNKELD
Dunkeld & Birnam
Golf Club
Fungarth, Dunkeld
PH8 0HU.
Tel: (01350) 727524.
18 holes, 5508 yds, SSS 67.
Charges: On application
Caddy cars and catering facilities
are available.
Visitors are welcome all week.
Booking advisable at weekends.
Secretary: Mr T.A. Wain
Tel: (01350) 727524.

DUNNING
Dunning Golf Club
Rollo Park, Dunning.
Tel: (01764) 684747.
9 holes, 4836 yds, SSS 63.
Charges: On application.
For Club/society bookings
Tel: (01764) 684372.
Caddy cars available.
Secretary: Mrs May Ramsey
Tel: (01764) 684237.

Whitemoss Golf Club
Mosshead Farm, Dunning,
Perthshire PH2 OQX.
18 holes, 5968 yds, Par 68, SSS69.
Charges: £20 day, £15 round, £5 junior round. Visiting parties: £26 day
ticket (inc. Breakfast & Lunch), £32
day ticket (inc. Breakfast, Lunch &
High Tea), 10% advance deposit
required. Practice areas and clubhouse catering. Tel: (01738) 730300.
Catering facilities are available.
Visitors are welcome all week.

GLENSHEE (SPITTAL O')
Dalmunzie Golf Course
Glenshee, Blairgowrie PH10 7QG.
Tel: (01250) 885224
9 holes, 2099 yds, SSS 60.
Charges: £10 daily. Under-14's half
price, under-7's free. Weekly
family ticket £75.
Catering and accommodation
available.

KENMORE
Kenmore Golf Course
Mains of Taymouth,
Kenmore PH15 2HN
Tel: (01887) 830226.
e-mail: info@taymouth.co.uk
Web site: www.taymouth.co.uk
9 holes, 2751m/3026 yds.
18 holes, 5502m/6052 yds, SSS 69.
Charges: 9 holes: £8 Mon-Fri,
£9 Sat & Sun.
18 holes: £12 Mon-Fri, £13
Sat & Sun.
For advance reservations
Tel: (01887) 830226.
Practice area, caddy cars and catering
facilities are available.
Parties and visitors welcoms.
Secretary: Robin Menzies
Tel: (01887) 830226.

Perthshire

Taymouth Castle Golf Course
Kenmore, Tayside PH15 2NT.
Tel: (01887) 830228.
Fax: (01887) 830765.
18 holes, 6066 yds.
Mens Medal Tees SSS 69
Yellow Tees SSS 67 Ladies SSS 72
Charges:On application.
For advance reservations
Tel: (01887) 830228.
Caddy cars, a practice area and catering facilities are available.
Visitors are welcome all week with reservations.
Professional: Alex Marshall
Tel: (01887) 830228.

KILLIN
Killin Golf Club
The Golf House, Killin.
Tel: (01567) 820312.
9 holes, 2508 yds, SSS 65.
Charges: On application.
Caddy cars and catering facilities are available.
Visitors are welcome all week.
Secretary: Mr J. Greaves
Tel: (01567) 820705.

MUTHILL
Muthill Golf Club
Peat Road, Muthill,
Crieff PH5 2DA.
Tel: (01764) 681523.
9 holes, 2350 yds
SSS 63 Men SSS 67 Ladies
Charges: Mon-Fri £13/round,
£15/day. Weekends £16/round.
Weekly tickets available on request.
Party bookings taken.
Visitors welcome all week.
Morning coffee, lunches, high teas.
Golf club and trolley available.
For reservations: The Secretary
Tel: (01764) 681523.

PERTH
The Craigie Hill Golf Club
(1982) Ltd. Cherrybank,
Perth PH2 ONE
Tel: (01738) 624377.
18 holes, 5386 yds, SSS.67.
Charges: £18 round, £30 daily
(Mon-Fri). £25 round, £30 daily
(Sun).
For advance reservations

Tel: (01738) 622644.
A practice area and catering facilities are available.
Visitors are welcome all week except Saturdays.
Secretary: Andrew Tunnicliffe
Tel: (01738) 620829.
Professional: Ian Muir
Tel: (01738) 622644.

King James VI Golf Club
Moncreiffe Island, Perth
PH2 8NR.
Tel: (01738) 625170.
18 holes, 5684 yds, SSS 68.
Charges: £18 round, £25 daily (Mon-Fri), £20 round, £30 daily (Sun) (2001).
A practice area, caddy cars and full catering facilities are available.
Secretary: Helen Blair
Tel: (01738) 445132
Professional: tel (01738) 632460.
FOR MORE INFORMATION, SEE PAGE 94

Murrayshall Golf Club
Murrayshall Country House
Hotel & Golf Course, Scone
PH2 7PH.
Tel: (01738) 551171.
18 holes, 6043 yds, SSS 70.
Charges: On application.
For advance reservations
Tel: (01738) 551171.
Caddies, caddy cars, buggies, practice area and catering facilities are available.
Visitors are welcome all week.
Professional: Alan Reid
Tel: (01738) 552784.
Teaching professional: Jamie Carver.

Lynedoch Golf Course
Murrayshall Country House
18 holes, 5359 yds, SSS 69.
Charges: £18 round/daily
FOR MORE INFORMATION, SEE PAGE 100

North Inch Golf Club
North Inch (off Hay Street), Perth
PH1 5HT.
18 holes, 4936m, SSS 63.
Charges: On application.
For advance reservations
Tel: (01738) 636481.
Catering facilities are available.
Visitors are welcome all week.

PITLOCHRY
Pitlochry Golf Course Ltd
Golf Course Road,
Pitlochry PH16 5Q7.
Tel: (01796) 472792 (bookings).
18 holes, 5811 yds, SSS 69.
Charges: On application.
Caddy cars, tuition and catering facilities are available.
Visitors are welcome all week.
Secretary: D.M. McKenzie.
Tel: (01796) 472114.
Professional: George Hampton
Tel: (01796) 472792.

ST. FILLANS
St. Fillans Golf Club
South Lochearn Road,
St. Fillans PH6 2NJ.
Tel: (01764) 685312.
9 boles, 4812m/5628 yds, SSS 67.
Charges: £12 day ticket (Mon-Fri); £16 day ticket (Sat/Sun/Bank hols).
Caddy cars are available.
Visitors are welcome all week.
Visiting groups by arrangement.
Secretary: K.W. Foster
Tel: (01764) 685312/679509

STRATHTAY
Strathtay Golf Club
Lorne Cottage, Dalguise,
Dunkeld PH8 0JX.
Tel: (01350) 727797.
9 holes, 4082 yds (18 holes), SSS 63
Charges: On application.
For advance reservations
Tel: (01350) 727797.
Visitors are welcome all week, except
Sun 12-5 and Mon 6-9.
Secretary: T.D. Lind.
All correspondence to:
Lorne Cottage, Dalguise, Dunkeld
PH8 0JX. Tel: (01350) 727797.

RENFREWSHIRE
BARRHEAD
Fereneze Golf Club
Fereneze Avenue, Barrhead.
Tel: 0141-881 1519
18 holes, 5908 yds, SSS 70.
Visiting parties on application
Monday to Friday. Contact secretary:
A. Johnston, C.A.,
7 Glasgow Road, Paisley PA1 3QS.
Tel: 0141-887 4141
Fax: 0141-887 1103.

BISHOPTON
Erskine Golf Club
Bishopton PA7 5PH.
Tel: (01505) 862302.

BRIDGE OF WEIR
Ranfurly Castle Golf Club Ltd
Golf Road, Bridge of Weir PA11 3HN.
Tel: (01505) 612609.
18 holes, 6284 yds, SSS 71.
Charges: £27 round, £40 daily.
For advance reservations
Tel: (01505) 612609.
Practice area, caddy cars and
catering facilities available.
Visitors welcome weekdays only.
Secretary: J. King
Tel: (01505) 612609.
Professional: T. Eckford
Tel: (01505) 862108.

The Old Course Ranfurly
Golf Club Ltd, Ranfurly Place,
Bridge of Weir PA11 3DE.
Tel: (01505) 613214/613612.
18 holes, 6200 yds, SSS 70.
Charges: £20 round, £30 daily.
For advance reservations
Tel: (01505) 613214.
Catering facilities available.
Visitors welcome Tues–Thurs.
Secretary: K.C. Young
Tel: (01505) 613214.

CALDWELL
Caldwell Golf Club Ltd
Uplawmoor G78 4AU.
18 holes, 6207 yds, SSS 70.
Charges: On application.
For advance reservations
Tel: (01505) 850616.
Caddy cars, practice area and catering
facilities are available.
Visitors are welcome Mon-Fri.
Secretary: H.I.F. Harper
Tel: (01505) 850366.
Professional: Stephen Forbes
Tel: (01505) 850616.

EAGLESHAM
Bonnyton Golf Club
Eaglesham G76 0QA.
Tel: (01355) 302781.
18 holes, 6252 yds, SSS 71.
Charges: £38 daily.
Caddy cars, practice area and catering
facilities are available.
Secretary: A. Hughes

Tel: (01355) 302781.
Professional: K. McWade
Tel: (01355) 302256.

ELDERSLIE
Elderslie Golf Club
63 Main Road, Elderslie PA5 9AZ.
Tel: (01505) 322835/323956.
18 holes, 6175 yds, SSS 70.
Charges: £20 round, £30 daily.
For advance reservations
Tel: (01505) 323956.
A practice area and catering facilities
are available. Plus P.G.A.
professional shop.
Tel: (01505) 320032.
Secretary: A. Anderson
Tel: (01505) 323956.

GOUROCK
Gourock Golf Club
Cowal View, Gourock PA19 1HD.
Tel: (01475) 631001.
18 holes, 5936m 6512 yds, SSS 73.
Charges: On application.
A practice area and catering
facilities are available.
Visitors welcome Mon– Fri.
Secretary: Mr A. D. Taylor
Tel: (01475) 631001.
Professional: Gavin Coyle
Tel: (01475) 636834.

GREENOCK
Greenock Golf Club
Forsyth Street, PA16 8RE.
Tel: (01475) 720793.
27 holes, 5838 yds, SSS 68.
Charges: £20 round, £25 daily.
For advance reservations
Tel: (01475) 787236.
A practice area, caddy cars and cater-
ing facilities are available. Visitors are
welcome except Saturdays.
Secretary: E.J. Black.
Professional: Stewart Russell.

Cochrane Castle Golf Club
Craigston, Johnstone PA5 0HF.
Tel: (01505) 320146.
18 holes, 6226 yds, SSS 71.
Charges: £17 round, £25 daily.
Advance reservations by letter only.
Caddy cars, a practice area and cater-
ing facilities are available.
Visitors are welcome Mon–Fri.
Secretary: J.C. Cowan
Tel: (01505) 320146.

Professional: Jason J. Boyd
Tel/fax: (01505) 328465.

Greenock Whinhill Golf Club
Beith Road, Greenock.
Tel: (01475) 724694.
18 holes, 5504 yds, SSS 68.
Charges: On application.
Visitors welcome all week.
Secretary: Raymond Kirkpatrick
Tel: (01475) 724694.

KILMACOLM
Kilmacolm Golf Club
Porterfield Road,
Kilmacolm PA13 4PD.
Tel: (01505) 872139.
18 holes, 5890 yds, SSS 69.
Charges: On application.
Caddy cars, a practice area and
catering facilities are available.
Visitors are welcome on weekdays.
Secretary: D.W. Tinton.
Professional: D. Stewart
Tel: (01505) 872695.

LANGBANK
The Gleddoch Club
Langbank PA14 6YE.
Tel: (01475) 540711
Fax: (01475) 540201.
18 holes, 6332 yds, SSS 71.
Charges: £30 for visitors (day ticket)
Mon-Fri, £35 (weekends).
For advance reservations
Tel: (01475) 540704.
Buggies,trolleys, practice area, hire of
equipment and catering facilities are
available. Adjacent to course is
Gleddoch House Hotel.
Visitors are welcome Mon–Fri
excluding Bank Holidays. Golf Day
Packages and Golf Breaks available.
Secretary: Tel: (01475) 540304.
Professional: (01475) 540704.

LOCHWINNOCH
Lochwinnoch Golf Club
Burnfoot Road, Lochwinnoch.
Tel: (01505) 842153
E-mail:
admin@lochwinnochgolf.co.uk
18 holes, 6025 yds, SSS 71.
Charges: £20 round/day.
For advance reservations write
to secretary.
A practice area, caddy cars and
catering facilities are available.

Visitors are welcome Monday
to Friday.
Club Administrator:
R.J.G. Jamieson
Secretary: Mrs Wilson
Tel: (01505) 842153.
Professional: Gerry Reilly
Tel: (01505) 843029.

NEWTON MEARNS
Cathcart Castle Golf Club
Mearns Road, Glasgow G76 7YL.
Tel: 0141-638 9449.
18 holes, 5330m/5832 yds.
(Further details on application).

The East Renfrewshire Golf Club
Pilmuir, Newton Mearns,
Glasgow G7 6RT.
Tel: (01355) 500256.
18 holes, 6097 yds, SSS 70.
Charges: £30 daily.
Professional: Stewart Russell
Tel: 01355 500206.

Eastwood Golf Club
Muirshield, Loganswell,
Newton Mearns,
Glasgow G77 6RX.
Tel: (01355) 500261.
18 holes, 5864 yds, SSS 69.
Charges: £24 round, £30 daily
(Subject to application and approval).
For advance reservations
Tel: (01355) 500280.
Caddy cars and catering facilities
are available.
Visitors are welcome all week.
Secretary: V.E. Jones
Tel: (01355) 500280 (mornings).
Professional: A. McGinness
Tel: (01355) 500285.

PAISLEY
Barshaw Golf Club
Barshaw Park, Paisley PA1 3JA.
Tel: 0141-889 2908.
18 holes, 5703 yds, SSS 67.
Charges: £8.20 round.
Visitors are welcome all week.
Secretary: Mr W. Collins
Tel: 0141-884 2533.

The Paisley Golf Club
Braehead, Paisley PA2 8TZ.
Tel: 0141 884 3903.
18 holes, 6466 yds, SSS 72.
Charges: £24 round, £32 daily.
(2001)
Handicap Certificate required.
Practice area and nets. Catering
facilities are available.
Club administrator: John Hillis
Professional: G. Stewart
Tel: 0141 884 4114.

Ralston Golf Club
Strathmore Avenue, Ralston,
Paisley PA1 3DT.
Tel: 0141-882 1349.
18 holes, 6091 yds, SSS 69.
Charges: On application.
For advance reservations
Tel: 0141-882 1503.
Caddy cars and catering facilities
available.
Visitors welcome midweek by
prior arrangement.
Secretary: J. Pearson
Tel: 0141-882 1503.
Professional: Colin Munro
Tel: 0141-810 4925.

PORT GLASGOW
Port Glasgow Golf Club
Devol Road, Port Glasgow PA14 5XE.
Tel: (01475) 704181.
18 holes, 5592m/5712 yds, SSS 68.
Charges: On application.
For advance reservations
Tel: (01475) 704181.
A practice area and catering facilities
are available.
Visitors are welcome uninvited
before 3.55 pm, not on Saturdays and
invited only Sundays.
Secretary: N.L. Mitchell
Tel: (01475) 706273.
Golf Shop Tel: (01475) 705671

RENFREW
Renfrew Golf Club
Blythswood Estate,
Inchinnan Road, Renfrew PA4 9EG.
Tel: 0141-886 6692.
Fax: 0141-886 1808.
18 holes, 6281m/6818 yds, SSS 73.
Charges: £25 round, £45 daily.
Catering services are available.
Secretary: I Murchison
Tel: 0141-886 6692.

ROSS-SHIRE

ALNESS
Alness Golf Club
Ardross Road, Alness IV17 0QA.
Tel: (01349) 883877
E-mail: info@alnessgolfclub.co.uk
18 holes, 4886 yds, SSS 64, Par 67.
Charges: On application.
Parties: special rates (according to
numbers) .
(Advance notice for parties - tel
01349 883877).
Licensed bar and catering facilities
are available, also hiring of clubs and
trolleys.
Visitors are welcome all week (check
for competitions).
Secretary: Mrs Mary Rogers
Tel: (01349) 882833.

FORTROSE
Fortrose & Rosemarkie Golf Club
Ness Road East, Fortrose
IV10 8SE.
Tel: (01381) 620529
Fax: (01381) 621328
E-mail:
secretary@fortrosegolfclub.co.uk
Web Site:
www.fortrosegolfclub.co.uk
18 holes, 5875 yds, SSS 69.
Charges: £21 per round, £32 daily -
Mon-Fri; £26 per round Sat & Sun,
£37 daily. £75 5-day ticket. £105 10-
day ticket.
For advance reservations
Tel: (01381) 620529 (parties only).
Practice area and caddy car available.
Visitors are welcome all week.
Secretary: Margaret Collier
Tel: (01381) 620529.

GAIRLOCH
Gairloch Golf Club
Gairloch IV21 2BQ
Tel: (01445) 712407.
9 holes, 18 holes/4250 yds, SSS 63
Charges: On application.
Caddy cars are available. Club hire.
Visitors are welcome all week.
Secretary: A. Shinkins
FOR MORE INFORMATION, SEE PAGE 76

INVERGORDON
Invergordon Golf Club
King George Street, Invergordon
IV18 OBA..
Tel: (01349) 852715.
18 holes, 6020 yds, SSS 69.
Charges: £15 round, £20 per day,
juniors £5. Weekly/fortnightly
charges on application.
Practice area available. Clubs, caddy
cars for hire. Bar & catering facilities
are available April-September.
October-March weekends only and
by arrangement.
Visitors and visiting parties welcome.

LOCHCARRON
Lochcarron Golf Club
Lochcarron, Wester Ross IV54 8YA.
9 holes, 1789 yds, SSS 60.
Charges: £10 (daily), £40 (weekly).
Clubs for hire.
Visitors are welcome all week.
Booking not necessary.
Secretary: A.G. Beattie
Tel: (01520) 766211.

MUIR OF ORD
Muir of Ord Golf Club
Great North Road,
Muir of Ord IV6 7SX.
Tel: (01463) 870825.
18 holes, 5557 yds, SSS 68.
Charges: On application.
For advance reservations
Tel: (01463) 871311/870825.
A practice area and catering
facilities are available.
Visitors are welcome all week.
Administrator/Manager:
Mrs J. Gibson
Tel: (01463) 870825.

PORTMAHOMACK
Tarbat Golf Club
Portmahomack.
Tel: (01862) 871236.
(Further details on application.)

STRATHPEFFER
Strathpeffer Spa Golf Club
Strathpeffer IV14 9AS.
Tel: (01997) 421219.
18 holes, 4000m/4792 yds, SSS 64.
Charges: £14 round, £20 daily.
Weekly (Mon-Fri) £50. Package deal
with meals. (anyday) £29.(1998).
For advance reservations

Tel: (01997) 421219/421011.
A small practice area, caddy cars and
catering facilities are available.
Visitors are welcome all week.
Secretary: Mr N. Roxburgh
Tel: (01997) 421396.
Shop: Tel/Fax: (01997) 421011.

TAIN
Tain Golf Club
Tain IV19 1JE
Tel: (01862) 892314.
Fax: (01862) 892099.
E-mail: tgc@cali.co.uk
Web site: mywebaddress.net/
taingolfclub
18 holes, 6404 yds, SSS 71.
Charges: Weekdays – 1 round £30, 2
rounds £36. Weekends - 1 round £36,
2 rounds £46. Discounts for parties
of 12 or over.
For advance reservations
Tel: (01862) 892314.
Full catering facilities are available.
Visitors are welcome.
Secretary: Mrs Kathleen D. Ross.

ROXBURGHSHIRE

HAWICK
Hawick Golf Club
Vertish Hill, Hawick TD9 0NY.
Tel: (01450) 372293.
18 holes, 5390m/5929 yds, SSS 69.
Charges: £20 per round, £25 per day
7 days each week.
For advance reservations
Tel: (01450) 372293.
Caddy cars and catering
facilities available.
Visitors welcome all week but
course busy Sat. before 3pm.
Secretary: J. Harley
Tel: (01450) 374947.

Minto Golf Club
Denholm, Hawick TD9 8SH.
Tel: (01450) 870220.
Fax: (01450) 870126.
E-mail: mintogolfclub.
freeserve.co.uk
18 holes, 5542 yds/5069 m, SSS 67.
Charges: Weekdays £18 per round,
£23 daily. Weekends £23 per round,
£28 daily. Telephone for packages
(01450) 870220.
A practice area, caddy cars and catering facilities are available.

Visitors are welcome all week.
Secretary: Peter Brown
Tel: (01450) 375841.

JEDBURGH
Jedburgh Golf Club
Dunion Road, Jedburgh TD8 6TA.
Tel: (01835) 863587.
9 holes, 2746m/5492 yds, SSS 67.
Charges: On application.
For advance reservations
Tel: (01835) 863587 (Evenings).
Catering facilities are available.
Visitors are welcome all week.

KELSO
Kelso Golf Club
Abbot Seat Road, Kelso TD5 7SL.
Tel: (01573) 223009.
(Further details on application).

The Roxburghe Golf Course
Kelso, Rovburghshire, TD5 8JZ
Tel: 01573 450331
Fax: 01573 450611
E-mail: hotel@roxburghe.net
Website: www.roxburghe.net
18 holes, medal 6925 yards, SSS 74.
Visitors require handicap certificates.
(24 men/36 ladies). £35 round, £50
per day weekends.
Full catering and bar.
Trolley/buggy hire, practice facilities,
driving range.
Professional: Gordon Niven.
FOR MORE INFORMATION, SEE PAGE 28

MELROSE
Melrose Golf Club
The Clubhouse, Dingleton Road,
Melrose TD6 9HS.
Tel: (01896) 822855.
9 holes, 5098m/5579yds, SSS 68.
Charges: £16 per round, £20 per day
(7 days). Visitors welcome excluding
Saturdays.
(Further details on application).

NEWCASTLETON
Newcastleton Golf Club
Holm Hill, Newcastleton.
9 holes, 5748m, SSS 68.
Charges: £7 weekdays, £8 weekends.
For advance reservations
Tel:(01387) 375257.
Visitors are welcome all week.
Secretary: F.J. Ewart -
Tel: (01387) 375257.

Roxburghshire

ST. BOSWELLS
St. Boswells Golf Club
Braehead, St Boswells,
Melsose TD6 ODE
Tel: (01835) 823527.
9 holes, 5274 yds, SSS 66.
Charges: Mon-Sun £15 per
round/day
For advance reservations
Tel: (01835) 823527.
Visitors are welcome all week.
Secretary: J.G. Phillips
Tel: (01835) 823527.

SELKIRKSHIRE
GALASHIELS
Galashiels Golf Club
Ladhope Recreation Ground,
Galashiels TD1 2BF.
Tel: (01896) 753724.
18 holes, 5185 yds, SSS 66.
Charges: £13 Mon-Fri, £15 Sat &
Sun per round. £18 Mon-Fri, £20 Sat
& Sun daily. Booking essential for
parties of 8 or more at weekends.
Tel: (01896) 753724.
A practice area and catering
facilities are available. Visitors are
welcome all week but booking
essential for weekends.
Secretary: R. Gass
Tel: (01896) 755307.

Torwoodlee Golf Club
Edinburgh Road, Galashiels
TD1 2NE
Tel: (01896) 752260.
18 holes, 6200 yds.
Charges: £20 round, £27 daily
Mon-Fri. £25 round, £30 daily
weekends. Package deals available
from £27.
A practice area, caddy cars and
catering facilities every day
except Tuesday (Limited).
Visitors welcome.
Secretary: George Donnelly
Tel: (01896) 752260.
FOR MORE INFORMATION, SEE PAGE 26

SELKIRK
Selkirk Golf Club
Selkirk Hills, Selkirk TD7 4NW.
Tel: (01750) 20621.
9 holes, 5636 yds.
Charges: On application.
Visitors are welcome. Parties of 8 or

more should confirm.
Catering and bar available
on request.
Secretary: A. M. Wilson
Tel: (01750) 20907.

STIRLINGSHIRE
ABERFOYLE
Aberfoyle Golf Club
Braeval, Aberfoyle FK8 3UY.
Tel: (01877) 382493.
18 holes, 4760m/5204 yds, SSS 66.
Charges: On application.
For advance reservations
Tel: (01877) 382493.
Visitors are welcome all week,
restrictions at weekends.
Secretary: R.D. Steele
Tel: (01877) 382638.

BALMORE
Balmore Golf Club
Golf Course Road, Balmore,
Torrance G64 4AW.
Tel: 01360 620240
18 holes, 5542 yds, SSS 66.
Charges: £25 round/£35 day.
A practice area, caddy cars and
catering facilities are available.
Visitors are welcome Mon-Fri
with a member.
Secretary: S. Keir
Tel: 01360 620284.

BONNYBRIDGE
Bonnybridge Golf Club
Larbert Road,
Bonnybridge FK4 1NY.
Tel: (01324) 812822.
9 holes, 6058 yds, SSS 69.
Charges: On application.
Practice area and catering facilities
are available.
Visitors welcome by arrangement.
Secretary: J. Mullen
Tel: (01324) 812822.

BRIDGE OF ALLAN
Bridge of Allan Golf Club
Sunnylaw, Bridge of Allan,
Stirling SK9 4LY.
Tel: (01786) 832332.
9 holes, 4508m/4932yds, SSS 65.
Charges: £12 round, £16 Sundays.
A practice area is available.
Visitors are welcome all week except
Sat and during Sun competitions.

DRYMEN
Buchanan Castle
Golf Club
Drymen G63 OHY.
Tel: (01360) 660369/07/30.
18 holes, 6086 yds, SSS 69.
Charges: £30 per round, £140 per day.
For advance reservations
Tel: (01360) 660307.
Visitors welcome by arrangement.
Secretary: R. Kinsella
Tel: (01360) 660307.
Professional: Mr K. Baxter
Tel: (01360) 660330.

Strathendrick Golf Club
Drymen G63.
Tel: (01360) 660695.
9 holes, 5116 yds (gents), 4586 yds
(ladies). SSS 65/64
Charges: £8 per round.
Visitors are welcome Mon-Fri,
May - Sept, must be accompanied
by members at weekends,
restrictions on competition days.
Secretary: Mr Gair
Tel: 0141 772 8043.
Professional: D. Pirie
Tel: 01360 620123.

FALKIRK
Falkirk Golf Club
Carmuirs, 136 Stirling Road,
Falkirk FK2 7YP.
Tel: (01324) 611061/612219.
18 holes, 6267 yds, SSS 70.
Charges: £15 round, £20 daily.
£30 Sunday.
Advance reservations by arrangement
with starter
Tel: (01324) 612219.
A practice area and catering facilities
are available.
Visitors are welcome Monday to
Friday up to 4.00pm, (Parties -
Mon/Tues/Thurs/Fri/Sun).
Secretary: J. Elliott
Tel: (01324) 634118 (home).

Grangemouth Golf Course
Polmont Hill, By Falkirk FK2 OYA.
Tel: (01324) 711500.
18 holes, 6400 yds, SSS 70.
Charges: £12 round.

KILSYTH
Kilsyth Lennox Golf Club
Tak-Ma-Doon Road,
Kilsyth G65 0HX.
Tel: (01236) 824115.
18 holes, 5940 yds, SSS 70, Par 70.
Charges: On application.
Catering facilities are available.
Visitors are welcome all week with
reservation.
Secretary: A.G. Stevenson.

LARBERT
Falkirk Tryst Golf Club
86 Burnhead Road,
Stenhousemuir,
Larbert FK5 4BD.
Tel: (01324) 562415.
18 holes, 5533m 6083 yds, SSS 69.
Charges: £16 round, £25 daily.
For advance reservations
Tel: (01324) 562054.
Golf trolleys, practice area and
catering facilities are available.
No unintroduced visitors on
Saturdays/Sundays.
Secretary: R.D. Wallace
Tel: (01324) 562415/562054.
Professional: Steven Dunsmore
Tel: (01324) 562091.

Glenbervie Golf Club
Stirling Road, Larbert
FK5 4SJ.
Tel: (01324) 562605.
18 holes, 6234 yds, SSS 71.
Charges: £30 round, £40 daily.
For advanced reservations
Tel: (01324) 562605 (visiting parties).
A practice area, caddy cars and
catering facilities are available.
Visitors are welcome Mon–Fri up to
4pm.(Parties Tues & Thurs).
Secretary: Dr S. Hartley
Tel: (01324) 562605.
Professional: Mr J. Chillas
Tel: (01324) 562725.
FOR MORE INFORMATION, SEE PAGE 30

LENNOXTOWN
Campsie Golf Club
Crow Road, G65 7HX.
Tel: (01360) 310244.
18 holes, 5509 yds, SSS 68, Par 70.
Charges: On application.
Catering facilities available.
Visitors welcome any time Mon-Fri,
weekends by arrangement.

Secretary: D. Barbour
Tel: (01360) 310244.
Professional: M. Brennan
Tel: (01360) 310920.

MADDISTON
Polmont Golf Club Ltd.
Manuel Rigg, Maddiston,
Falkirk FK2 0LS.
Tel: (01324) 711277.
9 holes, 6603 yds, SSS 70.
Charges: Daily £8 (Mon-Fri),
£14 Sunday.
Catering facilities are available.
Visitors are welcome all week,
except after 5pm and Saturdays.
Secretary: P. Lees
Tel: (01324) 713811.

STIRLING
Stirling Golf Club
Queen's Road, Stirling FK8 3AA.
Tel: (01786) 473801.
18 holes, 6400 yds.
SSS Medal 71, Front Tee 69.
Charges: £25 round, £35 daily.
A practice area, caddy cars and
catering facilities are available.
Visitors are welcome by
arrangement.
Secretary: Mr Gordon Easson
Tel: (01786) 464098.
Professional: Mr I. Collins
Tel: (01786) 471490.
FOR MORE INFORMATION, SEE PAGE 31

SUTHERLAND
BONAR BRIDGE
Bonar Bridge-Ardgay Golf Club
Migdale Road,Bonar Bridge,
Sutherland IV24 3EJ.
Tel: (01863) 766199
E-mail: secbbagc@aol.com
Web site:
www.bonarbridgegolfclub.co.uk
9 holes, 5284 yds, SSS Men 66,
Ladies 68.
Charges: £12 (adults) £5 (juniors
under 16) daily, £60 (adults) £25
(juniors under 16) weekly. Evening
round after 5.30pm - £8 (adults)
£3 (juniors).
For advance reservations
Tel: (01863) 766375 (groups only).
Visitors are welcome all week.
Secretary: Frank Mussand

Tel: (01863) 766375.
Fax: (01863) 766738.

BRORA
Brora Golf Club
Golf Road, Brora KW9 6QS.
Tel: +44(0) 1408 621417
Fax: +44(0) 1408 622157
E-mail: secretary@broragolf.co.uk
Web site: www.broragolf.co.uk,
www.highlandescape.com
18 holes, 6110 yds, SSS 69.
Charges: Weekdays £25 round, £35
per day (£12 Nov-Apr).
For advance reservations
Tel: +44(0) 1408 621417
Caddy cars, practice area and catering
facilities are available.
Visitors are welcome all week.
Visitors can compete in any of our
open competitions provided they
have a current certificate of handicap
with them.
Secretary: James Fraser
Tel: +44(0) 1408 621417.
FOR MORE INFORMATION, SEE PAGE 74

DORNOCH
Royal Dornoch Golf Club
Golf Road, Dornoch IV25 3LW.
Web Site:
http://www.royaldornoch.com

Championship Course
Tel: (01862) 810219.
18 holes, 5958m/6514 yds
Charges: £60 weekday/Saturday,
£70 Sunday. (Discounted if staying in
local hotel, B&B.)
For advance reservations
Tel: (01862) 810219.
Fax: (01862) 810792.
It is advisable to book.
Handicap certificates required.
Caddies, caddy cars, practice area and
catering facilities are available.
Visitors are welcome all week, but
limited times on Saturdays.
Secretary: John S. Duncan
Tel: (01862) 811220.
Professional: A. Skinner
Tel: (01862) 810902.
FOR MORE INFORMATION, SEE PAGE 73

Sutherland

The Struie Course (Dornoch)
18 holes, 5438 yds, Par 69, SSS 66
Charges: £18 round, £25 daily (2001).
Caddies, caddy cars and
practice facilities.
For advance reservations -
Tel: (01862) 810219.
Fax: (01862) 810792.
Visitors welcome all week.
Secretary: John S. Duncan
Tel: (01862) 811220.
Professional: A. Skinner
Tel: (01862) 810902.

The Carnegie Club
Skibo Castle
Dornoch, Sutherland IV25 3RQ
Tel: 01862 894600
Fax: 01862 894601
E-mail: skibo@carnegieclubs.com
www.carnegie.club.co.uk
18 holes, 6671 yds, Par 71, SSS 72
Charges: £130 round incl. 3-course
lunch.
Professional: David Thomson,
Tel: 01862 894600

DURNESS
Durness Golf Club
Durness IV27 4PN.
9 holes, 5555 yds/5040m, SSS 69.
Charges: On application.
For advance reservations
Tel: (01971) 511364/511351.
Caddy cars, practice area and
catering facilities are available.
Visitors are welcome all week.
Secretary: Mrs Lucy Mackay
Tel: (01971) 511364.

GOLSPIE
Golspie Golf Club
Ferry Road, Golspie KW10 6ST.
Tel: (01408) 633266.
Fax: (01408) 633393.
18 holes, 5337m/5836 yds,
SSS 68 (Gents), SSS 71 (Ladies)
Charges: Weekdays £25 round. £30
day. Weekends & Bank Hols. £25
round, £30 Day. Weekly ticket £85.
Package deals for parties of 10 or
more - contact secretary. Parties
must book in advance. A practice
area, caddy cars and catering
facilities are available.
Secretary: Mrs Marie MacLeod.

HELMSDALE
Helmsdale Golf Club
Golf Road, Helmsdale KW8 6JA.
Tel: (01431) 821650.
(2 x 9 holes), 3720 yds, SSS 60.
Charges: On application.
Advance reservations not necessary.
Visitors and new members are
welcome all week.
Secretary: D. Bishop

WIGTOWNSHIRE

GLENLUCE
Wigtownshire County Golf Club
Mains of Park, Glenluce,
Newton Stewart DG8 ONN.
Tel: (01581) 300420.
18 holes, 5344m/5847 yds, SSS 68.
Charges: £18.50 per round, £24 daily
(weekdays). £20.50 per round, £26
daily (Sat/Sun & Bank Hols).
For advance reservations
Tel: (01581) 300420.
Catering facilities are available.
Visitors are welcome all week except
Wednesdays after 5.30pm.
Secretary: R. McKnight
Tel: (01581) 300532.
FOR MORE INFORMATION, SEE PAGE 45

NEWTON STEWART
Newton Stewart Golf Club
Kirroughtree Avenue,
Minnigaff,
Newton Stewart DG8 6PF.
Tel: (01671) 402172.
18 holes, 5370m/5900 yds, SSS 70.
Charges: £20 per round, £23 daily
midweek. £23 per round, £27 daily
weekends and public holidays.
£90 per week.
For advance reservations
Tel: (01671) 402172.
Catering facilities are available.
Buggies for hire.
Visitors are welcome all week.
Secretary: M. Large
Tel: (01671) 402172 (Clubhouse)
Tel: (01671) 402177 (Home)

PORTPATRICK
Portpatrick Golf Club
Portpatrick
DG9 8TB.
Tel: (01776) 810273
Fax: (01776) 810811
E-mail: portpatrickgolf1@aol.com
Web site: www.portpatrick.scottish-golf.com
18 holes Dunskey Course, 5408 yds,
SSS 69.
9 holes Dinvin Course.
Charges: Dunskey – £22 round, £33
daily (Mon-Fri). £27 round, £38
daily (Sat/Sun). £110 weekly.
Handicap Certificate required.
Booking advisable.
Dinvin – £9 round (18 holes), £13
daily. No Handicap Certificate or
booking required. Juniors under 18
half stated price.
Secretary: J.A. Horberry
Tel: (01776) 810273.
FOR MORE INFORMATION, SEE PAGE 42

PORT WILLIAM
St. Medan Golf Club
Monreith, Newton Stewart
DG8 8NJ
Tel: (01988) 700358.
9 holes, 2227 yds, SSS 63.
Charges: £12 round/daily, £15 daily,
£45 weekly.
Catering facilities are available.
Visitors are welcome all week.
Secretary: E.C. Richards
Tel: (01988) 500201/326.

STRANRAER
Stranraer Golf Club
Creachmore, Leswalt,
Stranraer DG9 0LF.
Tel: (01776) 870245.
Fax: (01776) 870445.
18 holes, 6308 yds, SSS 72.
Charges: Weekdays £20 per 18 holes,
£26 per 27 holes, £30 per 36 holes.
Weekends £25 per 18 holes, £31 per
27 holes, £35 per 36 holes.
3 day (Mon–Fri) £45,
5 day (Mon–Fri) £75.
Visitors welcom (booking advisable).
Handicap cert may be required.
Juniors under-18 half stated price.
Practice area, cart and trolley hire and
catering facilities available.
Secretary: Bryce C. Kelly.
FOR MORE INFORMATION, SEE PAGE 51

Wigtown & Bladnoch Golf Club
Wigtown,
Newton Stewart DG8 9EF.
Tel: (01988) 403354.
9 holes, 2521m, SSS 67.
Charges: £8 (9 holes), £12 (18 holes),
£17 Day tickets. £6 (18 holes)
pensioners.
Catering facilities are available April
to Sept inc. Visitors are welcome.
Secretary: Barry Kaye
Tel: (01671) 402414.

ISLANDS

ISLE OF ARRAN
Brodick Golf Club
Brodick, Isle of Arran KA27 8DL.
Tel: (01770) 302349.
18 holes, 4736 yds, SSS 64.
Charges: £16 (Sat/Sun). £18 daily,
£25 (Sat/Sun). Weekly £65.
For advance reservations
Tel: (01770) 302513.
A practice area, caddy cars and
catering facilities are available.
Visitors are welcome; parties by
advance reservation with secretary.
Secretary: Mr H.M. MacRae.
Professional: Mr R.S. McCalla
Tel: (01770) 302513.

Corrie Golf Club
Sannox, Isle of Arran KA27 8JD.
Tel: (01770) 810223/600403.
9 holes, 1948 yds, SSS 61.
Charges: On application.
Catering facilities are available
March to October.
Visitors are welcome all week
except Saturdays.
Secretary: G. Welford.
FOR MORE INFORMATION, SEE PAGE 71

Lamlash Golf Club
Tel: (01770) 600296 Clubhouse.
Starter (01770) 600196
Web site: arrangolf.co.uk
18 holes, 4640 yds, SSS 64.
Charges: £10 round Mon-Fri, £12
after 4.00pm. £16 daily (Mon-Fri),
£20 daily Sat/Sun. Weekly £50.
Visitors, no restrictions.
Caddy cars and golf buggies available.
Secretary: J. Henderson
Tel: (01770) 600272.

Lochranza Golf Course
Isle of Arran KA27 8HL.
Tel/Fax: (01770) 830273.
18 holes, 5487 yds, Par 70.
'Play & Pay' 7 days. Open 2nd Sun.
Late April to mid-October.
Green fees: £13 every day.
Visitors always welcome.

Machrie Bay Golf Club
Machrie Bay, by Brodick,
Isle of Arran.
Tel: (01770) 850232.
9 holes, 1957m/2143 yds, SSS 62.
Charges: £7 daily, £28 weekly.
Catering facilities are available -
no bar.
Visitors are welcome all week.
Secretary: John Milesi
Tel: (01770) 850247.

Shiskine Golf and Tennis Club
Blackwaterfoot,
Isle of Arran KA27 8HA.
Tel: (01770) 860226.
12 holes, 3000 yds, SSS 42.
Charges: Weekdays £13 per round,
£18 daily, Weekend £16 round, £22
daily. Weekly ticket £60, fortnightly
£80. Maximum of 2 rounds per day.
Tearoom open April-October,
lunches, high teas. No bar.
Visitors are welcome.
Club Manager:
Mrs Fiona M. Crawford
Tel: (01770) 860226,
Fax: (01770) 860205.

Whiting Bay Golf Club
Golf Course Road, Whiting Bay, Isle
of Arran.
Tel: 01770 700 487.
Charges: On application.
Secretary: Margaret Auld.
Tel: (01738) 636481.

ISLE OF BUTE
Bute Golf Club
Acadamy Road, Sithean, Rothesay
PA20 OBG.
Tel: (01700) 504369.
9 holes, 2284m/2497 yds, SSS 64.
Charges: £8 per day, juniors £4 per
day. Visitors are welcome, except
Saturdays before 11.30 am.
Secretary: I. McDougall.

Port Bannatyne Golf Club
Bannatyne Mains Road,
Port Bannatyne.
Tel: (01700) 504544.
18 holes, 4653m/ 5085 yds. SSS 67
Charges: On application.
For advance reservations
Tel: (01700) 502009.
Visitors are welcome all week.
Secretary: Mr Iain L. MacLeod
Tel: (01700) 502009.

Rothesay Golf Club
Canada Hill, Rothesay.
Tel: (01700) 502244.
18 holes, 5395 yds, SSS 66.
Charges: On application (round and
day tickets available). Pre-booking for
parties essential Saturday/ Sunday.
Full catering available.
All bookings to the professional:
J. Dougal
Tel: (01700) 503554.
FOR MORE INFORMATION, SEE PAGE 78

ISLE OF CUMBRAE
Millport Golf Club
Golf Road, Millport,
Isle of Cumbrae KA28 0HB.
Tel: (01475) 530311.
5828 yds, SSS 69.
Charges: £20 round, £25 daily (Mon-
Fri), £25 round, £31 daily (Weekends).
Full catering facilities are available.
Visitors are welcome all week
without introduction.
Secretary: D. Donnelly
Tel: (01475) 530306.
Starter: Tel: (01475) 530305.
Professional: H. Lee
Tel: (01475) 530305.

ISLE OF GIGHA
Isle of Gigha Golf Club
Isle of Gigha,
PA41 7AA.
Tel: (01583) 505242.
9 holes, 5042 yds, SSS 65.
Charges: £10 per round, £45 weekly.
Catering facilities are available at the
Gigha Hotel.
Visitors welcome.
Secretary: J. Bannatyne
Tel: (01583) 505242.

Islands

Islands

ISLE OF ISLAY
The Islay Golf Club
The Machrie Hotel & Golf Club,
Port Ellen PA42 7AN.
Tel: (01496) 302310.
www.islay.golf.btinternet.co.uk
18 holes, 6225 yds, SSS 70.
Charges: £40 daily, £30 round.

ISLE OF LEWIS
Stornoway Golf Course
Lady Lever Park,
Stornoway HS2 0XP.
Tel: (01851) 702240
E-mail:
admin@stornowaygolfclub.co.uk
Web Site:
www.stornowaygolfclub.co.uk
18 holes, 5252 yds, SSS 67.
Charges: £20 daily, £15 round.

ISLE OF MULL
Craignure Golf Club
Scallastle, Argyll PA65 6AY.
Tel: (01680) 300402.
9 holes - 18 tees, 5233 yds, SSS 66.
Charges: £11 per day, under-15s
half price.
Clubhouse open all day during
summer. Course open all year.
Visitors very welcome.

Tobermory Golf Club
Erray Road, Tobermory PA75 6PS.
Tel: (01688) 302238.
9 holes, 4890 yds, SSS 64.
Charges: £13 daily, £50 week.
A practice area is available.
Visitors are welcome all week.
Secretary: L.F. Howard
Tel: (01856) 874165.

ORKNEY
Orkney Golf Club
Grainbank.
Tel: (01856) 872487.
18 holes, 5406 yds, SSS 67.
Charges: On application.
A practice area is available.
Visitors are welcome all week.
Secretary: Ross Donaldson
Tel: (01856) 877 533.

Stromness Golf Club
Ness, Stromness, Orkney
KW16 3DL
Tel: (01856) 850772
E-mail:
graham.bevan@btinternet.co.uk
www.stromnessgc.co.uk
18 holes, 4762 yds, Par 69, SSS 68.
Charges: On application.
Secretary: Graham A.B. Evan.

ISLE OF SKYE
Isle of Skye Golf Club
Sconser IV48 8TD.
9 holes, 4677 yds, SSS 64.
Charges : £12 per Day including
weekends.
Visitors welcome all week.
Secretary: M. Macdonald
Tel: (01478) 650235.

SKEABOST BRIDGE
Skeabost Golf Club
Skeahost House Hotel,
Skeabost Bridge IV51 9NP.
Tel: (01470) 532215.
9 holes, 3114 yds, SSS 60.
1st 9 holes, 1597 yds, SSS 30.
2nd 9 holes, 1535 yds, SSS 30.
Charges: On application.
For advanced reservations
Tel: (01470) 532215.
Catering facilities are available.
Visitors are welcome all week.
Secretary: D.J. Matheson
Tel: (01470) 532319.

ISLE OF COLONSAY

Isle of Colonsay Golf Club
Machrens Farm,
Isle of Colonsay PA61 7YP
Tel: (01951) 200364.
18 holes, 4475 yds, SSS 72.
Charges: Annual membership £5
Caddie cars available and visitors
welcome at all times.
Secretary: Hugh McNeil
Tel: (01951) 200364.

SHETLAND
The Shetland Golf Club
Dale Golf Course
P.O. Box 18, Lerwick.
Tel: (01595) 840369.
18 holes, 5279m/5776 yds, SSS 68.
Charges: On application.
Visitors are welcome.
Secretary: Mrs Alison Bain.

ISLE OF TIREE
Vaul Golf Club
Scarinish PA77 6XH
9 holes, 2911 yds.
SSS 70 (18 holes).
Secretary: Mr Johnstone -
Tel: (01879) 220319.
(Further details on application).

Accommodation Guide

BORDERS

Abbotsford Arms Hotel
Mrs CW Scott
63 Stirling Street,
Galashiels TD1 1BY
Tel: 01896 752517
Fax: 01896 750744
*Mintole Classic Gold

Type of Accomodation Hotel, STB 4 stars
Number of Rooms 123
Room Facilities Sat. TV, Pay TV, 24hr Room
Service, Tea/Coffee, Trouser Press, all en-suite
Packed Lunch? Yes
Season Dates All year
Prices £90-120

Special Features
Small, friendly family run
hotel. Central situation for
20 golf courses in area,
near town centre. Good
food at reasonable prices

Ashlyn Guest House
7 Abbotsford Road,
Galashiels TD1 3DP
Tel: 01896 752416
Fax: 01896 752416
E-mail: ashlyn7@hotmail.com

Type of Accomodation B&B
Number of Rooms 3
Room Facilities All en-suite, TV, Tea/Coffee, CH
Packed Lunch? No
Season Dates All year
Prices £45 per double room B&B

Special Features
Old Mill House
Totally non-smoking
Special rates for
Torwoodlee Golf Course

Kings Arms Hotel
M & H Dalgety
High Street, Melrose TD6 9PB
Tel: 01896 822143
Fax: 01896 823812

Type of Accomodation Hotel, STB 3 stars
Number of Rooms 24
Room Facilities All en-suite, Phone, TV, Tea/Coffee
Packed Lunch? Yes
Season Dates All year
Prices B&B from £32.50pppn, BBEM from £42pppn

Special Features
Log fires, Real ales,
extensive menus

King's Hotel
56 Market Street,
Galashiels TD1 3AN
Tel: 01896 755497
Fax: 01896 755497
E-mail: kingshotel@talk21.com

Type of Accomodation Hotel
Number of Rooms 7
Room Facilities All en-suite, TV, Tea/Coffee
Packed Lunch? Yes
Season Dates All year
Prices Single £46pn, Twin/Double £36pppn

Special Features
Car park, Restaurant and
Bar all on site

CENTRAL

Radisson SAS
Airth Castle & Hotel
Airth by Falkirk
Stirlingshire FK2 8JF
Tel: +44 1324 831411
Fax: +44 1324 831329
www.radissonsas.com

Type of Accomodation Hotel, STB 3 stars
Number of Rooms 13
Room Facilities All en-suite
Packed Lunch? Ask
Season Dates March to October
Prices £BBEM £60pp

Special Features
2 restaurants, 2 bars, Health
centre (gymnasium, sauna,
steam room, solarium,
whirlpool) 9 conference and
banqueting rooms

DUMFRIES AND GALLOWAY

Balcary Bay Hotel
Auchencairn, Nr. Castle Douglas
Dumfries & Galloway DG7 1QZ
Tel: 01556 640217
Fax: 01556 640272
E-mail: reservations@balcarry-bay-
hotel.co.uk
www.balcarry-bay-hotel.com

Type of Accomodation Hotel
Number of Rooms 20
Room Facilities En-suite
Packed Lunch? Ask
Season Dates All year
Prices £52–£60 DBB, pppn

Special Features
Comfort, personal service.
Many courses nearby

Accomodation Guide

Lochinvar Hotel
3 Main Street, Castle Douglas,
Kirkcudbrightshire DG7 3UP
Tel: 01644 430210
Fax: 01644 430210

Type of Accomodation Hotel
Number of Rooms 15
Facilities 2 bars, restaurant
Packed Lunch? Ask
Season Dates All year
Prices On application

Special Features
9 hole golf course 3 miles
away and many others
within a short drive

Selkirk Arms Hotel
High Street, Kirkcudbright
DG6 4JG
Tel: 01557 330402
www.selkirkarmshotel.co.uk

Type of Accomodation Hotel AA 3 star
Number of Rooms 17
Room Facilities En-suite
Packed Lunch? Ask
Season Dates All year
Prices 2 nights DBB £118

Special Features
2 18-hole golf courses
nearby – £18 per round

LOTHIAN

Craigesk
Miss A R Mitchell
10 Albert Terrace, Musselburgh,
East Lothian EH21 7LR
Tel: 0131 665 3344/3170
Fax: 0131 665 3344
E-mail: craigesk-b-b@faxvia.net

Type of Accomodation STB 5 star
Number of Rooms 20
Room Facilities All en-suite, DD phones,
Tea/Coffee, Trouser Press, CTV
Season Dates 30th Dec - 18th Dec
Prices DB&B from £50pppn

Special Features
Near all East Lothian golf
courses. 20 minutes from
Edinburgh. Private parking.

Fisherman's Hall
Jan & Bill Boggan
The Banks, South Queensferry
EH30 9SL
Tel: 0131 3313878
Fax: 0131 3315867

Type of Accomodation Beach house (4 stars)
Number of Rooms 4 bedrooms + 2
Room Facilities Fully equipped
Packed Lunch? n/a
Season Dates All year
Prices £350 - £750 per week

Special Features
Spectacular views of the
Bass Rock, Forth Islands
and sunsets – only 30
minutes from Edinburgh.
Beside quiet harbour.

Golf Hotel
34 Dirleton Avenue, North Berwick
Tel: 01620 892202
Fax: 01620 892290
E-mail: simon@thegolfhotel.net
www.thegolfhotel.net

Type of Accomodation Family-run hotel
Number of Rooms 13
Room Facilities 10 with en-suite
Packed Lunch? Ask
Season Dates All year
Prices Rates on application, Special winter rates

Special Features
Ideally situated for all 16
of East Lothian's golf
courses. Only 30 minutes
from Edinburgh.

Harbour House Hotel
North Berwick
Tel: 01620 892529
E-mail:
sheila@harbourhousehotel.com
www.harbourhousehotel.com

Type of Accomodation Hotel
Number of Rooms 11
Room Facilities All en-suite, TV, phone,
internet connection
Packed Lunch? Ask
Season Dates All year
Prices £35pppn B&B

Special Features
Good old-fashioned
Scottish hospitality.

The Monks' Muir
Haddington, East Lothian
EH41 3SB
Tel: 01620 860340
Fax: 01620 861770
E-mail: d@monksmuir.com
www.monksmuir.co.uk

Type of Accomodation Caravan park
Number of Rooms 35 static plus touring
Room Facilities TV, toilets, 1-3 bed
Packed Lunch? n/a
Season Dates all year
Prices £130 - £440 per week

Special Features
On-site shop and cafe.
Childrens' play area.
2 shower blocks.

FIFE

Drumoig Hotel & Golf Resort
Drumoig, by Leuchars, Fife
Tel: 01382 541800
Fax: 01382 542211
House sales 01382 541189
E-mail: drumoig@sol.co.uk

Type of Accomodation Hotel, AA 3 stars
Number of Rooms 24 lodge style rooms,
5 superior rooms
Room Facilities All en-suite
Packed Lunch? Ask
Season Dates All year
Prices On application

Special Features
Situated on A914 between
St Andrews and Dundee.
An 18 hole Championship
golf course is on our
doorstep. New Scottish
National Golf Centre on site.

Yorkston House
Mr Finlay MacKenzie
68 & 70 Argyle Street, St Andrews,
Fife KY16 9BU
Tel: 01334 472019

Type of Accomodation Guest House,
STB 3 stars
Number of Rooms 10
Room Facilities En-suite, Tea/Coffee,
Guest lounge
Packed Lunch? No
Season Dates January to November
Prices B&B from £22pppn

Special Features
Breakfast from 7.30am by
arrangement. Late key
provided.

STRATHCLYDE

Glenhaven
Straiton Road, Kirkmichael
KA19 7PR
Tel: 01655 750510
E-mail: ann-foreman@glenhaven.com
www.glenhaven.com

Type of Accomodation Country House
Number of Rooms Sleeping 6-8 or 2-4
Room Facilities n/a
Packed Lunch? n/a
Season Dates March to October
Prices £500-£700 depending on number
of people

Special Features
Luxury accomodation in
wing of listed coach house.
Tranquil sheltered location
close to all golf courses.

**Prestwick Old Course
Hotel & Restaurant**
13 Links Road, Prestwick
KA9 1QC 9BU
Tel: 01292 477446
Fax: 01292 477671
E-mail: paul@prestwickhotel.co.uk
www.prestwickhotel.co.uk

Type of Accomodation Hotel
Number of Rooms 7
Room Facilities All en-suite
Packed Lunch? Ask
Season Dates All year
Prices £32.50 B&B

Special Features
Ideal base for a golfing
break in West of Scotland.
Overlooking the 14th &
18th greens of Prestwick
Golf Club. Additional 20
courses within 20 minutes
drive. Bar/restaurant

Savoy Park Hotel
16 Racecourse Road,
Ayr KA7 2UT
Tel: 01292 266112
Fax: 01292 611488
E-mail: mail@savoypark.com
www.savoypark.com

Type of Accomodation Hotel
Number of Rooms 15
Room Facilities En-suite, TV, Sky TV,
Tea/Coffee, hairdryer
Packed Lunch? Yes
Season Dates All year
Prices single £55-£65pn, double £37-£47.50 pppn

Special Features
Traditional red sandstone
building, Lounge bar and
restaurant. Central to
many golf courses.

South Beach Hotel
Troon
Tel: 01292 312033
E-mail: info@southbeach.co.uk
www.southbeach.co.uk

Type of Accomodation Hotel, STB 3 stars
Number of Rooms 34
Room Facilities All en-suite
Packed Lunch? Yes
Season Dates All year
Prices single £35-£65 B&B, twin/double £60-£87,
superior twin/double £75-£95

Special Features
Restaurant, 2 bars, drying
rooms, secure club storage.

Accommodation Guide

GRAMPIAN

Aberdeen Patio Hotel
Beach Boulevard,
Aberdeen AB24 SEF
Tel: 01224 633339
Fax: 01224 638833
E-mail: patiosales@globalnet.co.uk
www.patiohotels.com

Type of Accomodation Hotel, STB 4 stars, highly commended, AA 4 stars
Number of Rooms 124
Room Facilities All en-suite, leisure club
Packed Lunch? Ask
Season Dates All year
Prices Single (Mon-Thurs) £88 B&B (Fri, Sat, Sun £42), Double (Mon-Thurs) £98 B&B (Fri, Sat, Sun £55),

Special Features
5 minutes from Royal Aberdeen Course, 20 others within 30 minutes drive. Driving range and golf superstore 2 minutes drive away.

The Banff Links Hotel
Swordanes, Banff AB45 2JJ
Tel: 01261 812414
Fax: 01261 812463
E-mail: swordanes@btinternet.com

Type of Accomodation Hotel
Number of Rooms 8
Room Facilities All en-suite
Packed Lunch? Ask
Season Dates All year
Prices Special golfing breaks and group discounts

Special Features
Great choice of courses

Banff Springs Hotel
Golden Knowes Road,
Banff AB45 2JE
Tel: 01261 812881
Fax: 01261 815546
E-mail: info@banffspringshotel.co.uk

Type of Accomodation Hotel, STB 3 star
Number of Rooms 31
Room Facilities All en-suite. Gymnasium
Packed Lunch? Ask
Season Dates All year
Prices B&B from £36 pp

Special Features
Plenty of golf courses within a short drive. 'Taste of Scotland' Restaurant.

The Burnett Arms Hotel
25 High Street, Banchory
AB31 5TD
Tel: 01330 824944
Fax: 01330 825553
E-mail: theburnett@totalise.co.uk
www.burnettarms.co.uk

Type of Accomodation Hotel, AA 2 stars, RAC 2 stars, STB 2 stars
Number of Rooms 16 (6 twin, 6 dbl, 4 sgl)
Room Facilities All en-suite, Remote TV + Sky, Phone, Tea/Coffee. H/dryer
Packed Lunch? Yes
Season Dates All year
Prices Single £40-£55, Twin/Dbl £56-76, Discounts for parties of 10 golfers or more

Special Features
Situated only 3 minutes from 2 18-hole courses with 20 others within 30 minutes.

The County Hotel Banff
Banff, Aberdeenshire AB45 1AE
Tel: 01261 815353
Fax: 01261 818335
E-mail:
enquiries@thecountyhotel.com
www.thecountyhotel.com

Type of Accomodation Hotel
Number of Rooms 5, 1 Family room, 1 4-poster double, 1 twin, 1 single, 1 double
Room Facilities 4 en-suite, 1 private b/room
Packed Lunch? On request
Season Dates All year
Prices £38-£75 per room

Special Features
Walking distance to Duff House and the Royal Golf Course. Beautiful views over coast. French cuisine.

Kilmarnock Arms Hotel
Cruden Bay,
Aberdeenshire AB42 OHD
Tel: 01779 812213
Fax: 01779 812153

Type of Accomodation Hotel
Number of Rooms 14
Room Facilities All en-suite
Packed Lunch? Ask
Season Dates All year
Prices On application

Special Features
New Falcon Restauarant, public & lounge bar. 5 mins walk from Cruden Bay golf course. 30 minutes from Aberdeen and central for local courses.

The Marcliffe at Pitfodels
North Deeside Road, Pitfodels,
Aberdeen AB15 9YA
Tel: 01244 861000
Fax: 01244 868860
E-mail: enquiries@marcliffe.com
www.marcliffe.com

Type of Accomodation Hotel STB 5 star
Number of Rooms 42
Room Facilities En-suite
Packed Lunch? Ask
Season Dates All year
Prices On application

Special Features
Close to Royal Aberdeen
and many other golf
courses in area. Excellent
restaurant.

The Seafield Hotel
19 Seafield Street,
Cullen, Moray AB56 4SG
Tel: 01542 840791
Fax: 01542 840736
E-mail: info@theseafieldarms.co.uk
www.theseafieldarms.co.uk

Type of Accomodation 3 star Hotel
Number of Rooms 21
Room Facilities All en-suite (most with bath &
shower), hospitality tray, TV and CH
Packed Lunch? On request
Season Dates All year
Prices From £32.50pp B&B

Special Features
Close to beach and Cullen
Golf Course. 15 courses
within 30 minutes drive.
Outdoor activities can be
arranged.

**The Spires Executive
Apartments**
531 Great Western Road, Aberdeen
Tel: 01224 209991
www.thespires.co.uk

Type of Accomodation Apartments
Number of Rooms 2 bedroomed apartments
Room Facilities Well-serviced
Packed Lunch? No
Season Dates All year
Prices On application

Special Features
Ideal for your golf break.
One night stay upwards.

TAYSIDE

Dalhousie Lodge
Edzell, by Brechin,
Angus DD9 6SG
Tel: 01356 624566
Fax: 01356 623725
E-mail:
dalhousieestate@btinternet.com

Type of Accomodation Lodge, full-board,
short-stay and self-catering
Number of Rooms 7, sleeping up to 12
Room Facilities Well equipped
Packed Lunch? Ask
Season Dates All year
Prices On application

Special Features
Comfortable, secluded
country house. Many
championship golf courses
within easy reach.

Grey Harlings House
Mrs Janet Scrimgeour
East Links, Montrose,
Angus DD10 8SW
Tel: 01674 673980

Type of Accomodation Guest House
Number of Rooms 5
Room Facilities En-suite available, Colour TV,
Tea/Coffee facilities, CH
Packed Lunch? No
Season Dates All year
Prices B&B £20pp

Special Features
Situated on 2 golf courses.
25 minutes to Carnoustie.
Numerous other links and
inland courses nearby.

Letham Grange
Colliston, by Arbroath DD11 4RL
Tel: 01241 890373
Fax: 01241 890725

Type of Accomodation Hotel
Number of Rooms 42
Room Facilities All en-suite, Sky TV, hairdryers
Packed Lunch? Yes
Season Dates All year
Prices single from £65, twin from £42.50 pppn

Special Features
Historic country mansion.
Central to many courses
and 6 miles from
Carnoustie. 2 courses
attached to hotel.

Accommodation Guide

Ascot House
7 Cawdor Street, Nairn IV12 4QD
Tel: 01667 455855
Fax: 01667 451900
E-mail: ascot7nairn@aol.com

Type of Accomodation Guest House, STB 3 star
Number of Rooms 11
Room Facilities 1 S, 2 D, 1 T, 5 ES
Packed Lunch? Ask
Season Dates All year
Prices B&B £20-£35ppn

Special Features
2 minutes walk to town centre and ideally located for Nairn's 2 Championship golf courses.

Gigha Hotel
Isle of Gigha
Argyll PA41 7AA
Tel: 01583 505254
Fax: 01583 505244
www.isle-of-gigha.co.uk

Type of Accomodation Hotel, STB 3 stars
Number of Rooms 13
Room Facilities All en-suite
Packed Lunch? Ask
Season Dates March to October
Prices BBEM £60pp

Special Features
Nearby Achmore Gardens and our 9 hole golf course with beautiful views.

Glenaveron
Golf Road, Brora,
Sutherland KW9 6QS
Tel: 01408 621601
E-mail: glenaveron@hotmail.com
www.glenaveron.co.uk

Type of Accomodation Guest House, STB 4 stars
Number of Rooms 3 (1D, 1T, 1F)
Room Facilities All en-suite, non-smoking
Packed Lunch? Ask
Season Dates All year
Prices BB single from £28-£33,
D/T from £25-£28

Special Features
3 minutes walk to Brora Golf Course and only 25 minutes drive to Royal Dornoch Golf Course.

Kinloch House Hotel
By Blairgowrie, PH10 6SG
Tel: 01250 884237
Fax: 01250 884333

Type of Accomodation Hotel
Number of Rooms 20
Room Facilities En-suite, phone, TV, trouser press
Packed Lunch? Yes
Season Dates All year
Prices DB&B single £90, double/twin from £195, suite from £230

Special Features
3 rosette restaurant, health and fitness centre. Teetime booking facility.

Glen Mhor Hotel
9-12 Ness Bank,
Inverness, IV2 4SG
Tel: 01463 234308
Fax: 01463 713170
www.glen-mhor.com

Type of Accomodation Hotel
Number of Rooms 45, Singles, Doubles, Twins, Executive Rooms and Junior suites
Room Facilities All en-suite, TV, Tel/Modem,
Packed Lunch? Yes
Season Dates All year
Prices B&B from £41 pppn, sharing to £60ppn

Special Features
2 restaurants, riverside location, parking available. 28 courses within 1 hour drive, including Royal Dornoch and Nairn. 3 local courses (Tee times can be reserved).

The Mansion House Hotel
The Haugh, Elgin,
Moray IV30 1AW
Tel: 01343 548811
Fax: 01343 547916
E-mail: reception@mhelgin.co.uk

Type of Accomodation Hotel, STB 4 star, highly commended, AA 3 star
Number of Rooms 23
Room Facilities All en-suite. Leisure facilities
Packed Lunch? Ask
Season Dates All year
Prices Single £80 B&B, Double £120 B&B

Special Features
Elegent, welcoming hotel set within private woodland. 10 golf courses within 10 miles.

Navidale House Hotel
Helmsdale, Sutherland KW8 6JS
Tel: 01431 821258
Fax: 01431 821531
www.contact-my-idea.com/
navidale/navidalehouse.htm.

Type of Accomodation Hotel and 2 Lodges
Number of Rooms 10
Room Facilities All en-suite
Packed Lunch? Ask
Season Dates All year
Prices DB&B £60pp

Special Features
Recently refurbished to a
high standard and ideally
located for golfing.

Pitgrudy Caravan Park
Poles Road, Dornoch,
Sutherland IV25 3HY
Tel: 01862 821253
Fax: 01862 821382
www.host.co.uk

Type of Accomodation Caravan Park, STB 5 star
Season Dates May to September
Prices 40 touring pitches, 10 holiday caravans
Number sleeping 2 to 5
Shops near Yes
Season dates May to September
Prices £7.50 per pitch per night,
Caravans £95 - £295 per week

Special Features
Golfers' paradise with
several golf courses within
a short drive

Silver Sands Leisure Park
Mr G Kerr
Covesea, West Beach, Lossiemouth
Morayshire IV31 6SP
Tel: 01343 813262
Fax: 01343 815205
E-mail:
holidays@silversands.freeserve.co.uk
www.silversands.freeserve.co.uk

Type of Accomodation Caravan Park,
Thistle, STB 4 stars
Number of Units 45
Number sleeping 6/8
Shop near? Yes
Season Dates March to October
Prices From £175. Touring from £7.50

Special Features
Next to Moray Golf Club.
Ideal base for many
courses throughout
Morayshire

Some useful numbers

Rail	**National Rail Enquiries**	0845 7484 950
Flights	**British Airways**	0845 773 3377
	British Midland	0870 607 0555
	Easyjet	0870 600 0000
	Go	0870 607 6543
Car hire	**Avis**	0870 606 0100
	Europcar	0845 722 2525
	Hertz	0870 599 6699
Travel news	**AA**	0870 550 0600
	RAC	0906 470 1740
Weather	**Glasgow Met. Office**	0845 300 0300

Need help planning your holiday?

Alyth Golf Desk Ltd
Leroch, Alyth, Blairgowrie PH11 8NZ
Tel: 01828 633323
Fax: 01828 633888

E-mail: strathmoregolf@sol.co.uk
www.alythgolfdesk.co.uk

Golf packages to suit every taste and budget. Over 60 courses. One call takes the hassle out of your holiday.

Golf Connections
9 Hopeward Mews, Dalgety Bay, Fife KY11 9TB
Tel: 01383 820211
Fax: 01383 820211

E-mail: enquiry@golfconnections.co.uk
www.golfconnections.co.uk

Tailor made golf tours for Scotland. On and off course activities to meet individual requirements of male and female golfers.

Golf Roots Scotland
29 Haldane Avenue, Haddington, East Lothian EH41 3PG
Tel: 01620 829604
Fax: 01620 829604

E-mail: enquiries@golfroots.co.uk
www.golfroots.co.uk

Personalised tours for discerning golfers. We will organise all golf, accommodation and transport – you can relax and enjoy the golf.

Ian McIntosh Travel
22 Braehead Grove, Edinburgh, EH4 6BG
Tel: 0131 339 2995
Fax: 0131 339 3284

E-mail: ritamcintosh@ianmcintoshtravel.freeserve.co.uk

Tailor-made itineraries including accommodation, tee-times, transport for all of Scotland except the Old Course. Lead name, handicaps required.

Qualitee Golf Tours
18 Inchmurrin Cresent, Balloch, Dunbartonshire G83 8JJ
Tel: 01389 750830
Fax: 01389 755968

E-mail: dphipps@btconnect.com

Our sole aim is to provide you, our valued client, with the best value for money golf package you'll find.

Scot World Travel
5 South Charlotte Street, Edinburgh EH2 4AN
Tel: 0131 226 3246
Fax: 0131 220 1271

E-mail: douglas@scotworldtravel.uk.com
www.scotworldtravel.co.uk

Tayleur Mayde Golf Tours
21 Castle Street, Edinburgh, EH2 3DN
Tel: 1 800 847 8064 (USA)
Fax: 0131 225 9113

E-mail: info@tayleurmayde.com
www.tayleurmayde.com

The Scotland Tours Company Ltd
30 Canmore Street, Dunfermline, Fife KY12 7NT
Tel: 01383 727999
Fax: 01383 727927

E-mail: enquiries@scotland-tours.com
www.scotlandgolftours.com

*Prompt service, quality locations, great golf, ideal vehicles, detailed itineraries
– for high quality well-organised golf tours, contact Scotland Tours.*

Thistle Golf (Scotland) Ltd
Suite 427, The Pentagon Centre, 36 Washington Street, Glasgow G3 8AZ
Tel: 0141 248 4554
Fax: 0141 248 4554

E-mail: info@thistlegolf.co.uk
www.thistlegolf.co.uk

*High quality tailor made golf tours throughout Scotland including tee-times, accommodation, vehicle
hire and sightseeing. Corporate days also arranged.*

Wilkinson Golf
The Boathouse, Hawkcraig Road, Aberdour, Fife KY3 OTZ
Tel: 01383 861000
Fax: 01383 861010

E-mail: gary@wilkinsongolf.com
www.wilkinsongolf.com

Tailor made golf vacations around Scotland and Ireland. Itineraries to suit all budgets and size of group.

If calling from outwith the UK, replace the initial '0' with '+44'

Tell them you saw them in Scotland Home of Golf

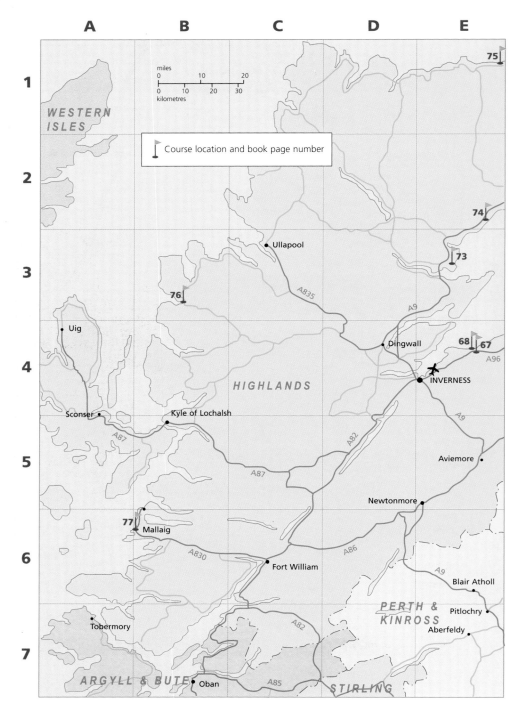

A B C D E

1

**WESTERN
ISLES**

75

miles
0   10   20
0   10   20   30
kilometres

2

![Course location and book page number]
Course location and book page number

74

• Ullapool

73

76

A835

A9

3

• Uig

• Dingwall

68 67

★ INVERNESS

A96

4

HIGHLANDS

A9

• Sconser

• Kyle of Lochalsh

A87

A82

• Aviemore

5

A87

• Newtonmore

A830

77
Mallaig

A86

A9

6

• Fort William

• Blair Atholl

A82

**PERTH &
KINROSS**

• Pitlochry

• Tobermory

• Aberfeldy

7

ARGYLL & BUTE • Oban

A85

STIRLING

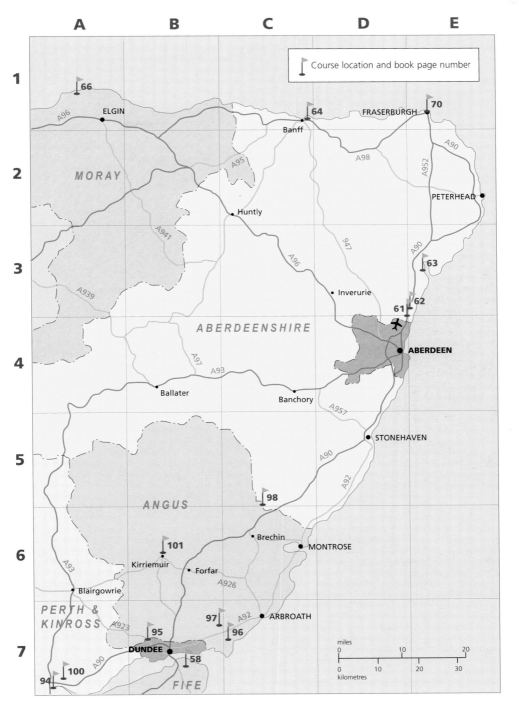

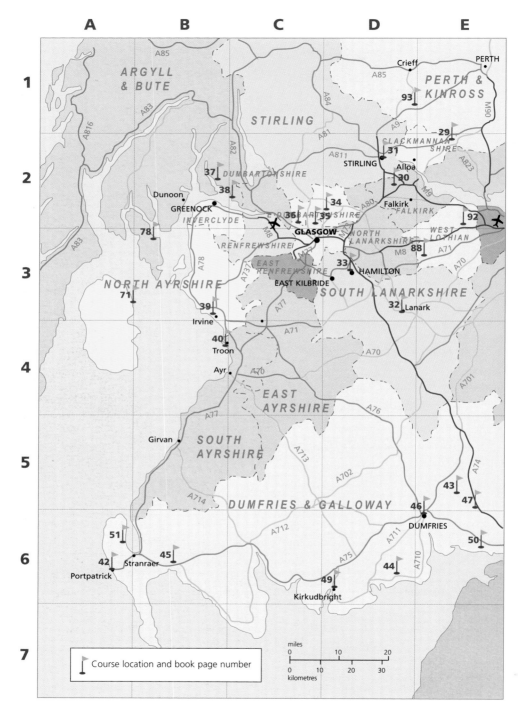

miles
0   10   20
0   10   20   30
kilometres

▌ Course location and book page number

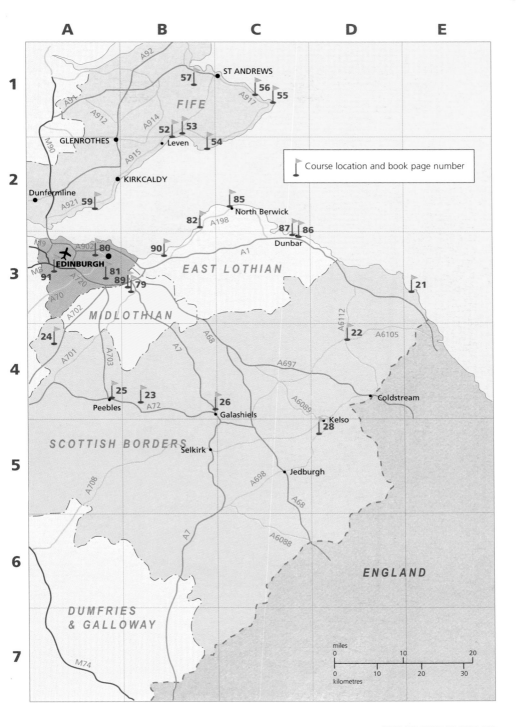

A   B   C   D   E

1

A92

57 ST ANDREWS

FIFE   A917   **56**   **55**

A94

A912

A914

A915   **52**   **53**

GLENROTHES   Leven   **54**

M90

2

KIRKCALDY

Dunfermline

A921 **59**

| Course location and book page number

85

North Berwick

82   A198

87   **86**

Dunbar

M9   A902   **80**

EDINBURGH   **90**

A1

EAST LOTHIAN

3

M8   A720   **81**

91   **89**   **79**

A70

MIDLOTHIAN

A702

21

A6112

24

A701   A703

A7

A68

22   A6105

4

A697

25   **23**

Peebles   A72

26

Galashiels

A6089

Coldstream

Kelso

28

SCOTTISH BORDERS

Selkirk

5

A708

A698   Jedburgh

A68

ENGLAND

6

DUMFRIES
& GALLOWAY

A6088

7

M74

miles
0   10   20
0   10   20   30
kilometres

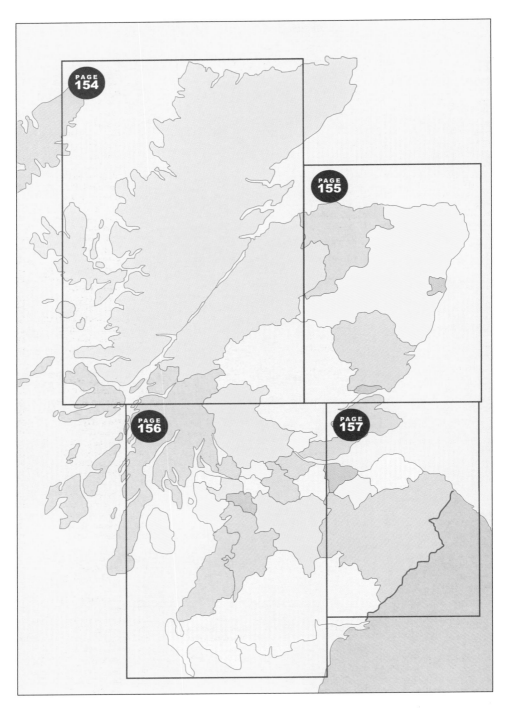

PAGE
154

PAGE
155

PAGE
156

PAGE
157

INDEX